MURDEROUS ACTS

KEVEN McQUEEN

MURDEROUS ACTS

100 YEARS OF CRIME IN THE MIDWEST

QUARRY BOOKS

AN IMPRINT OF
INDIANA UNIVERSITY PRESS

This book is a publication of

Quarry Books
an imprint of
INDIANA UNIVERSITY PRESS
Office of Scholarly Publishing
Herman B Wells Library 350
1320 East 10th Street
Bloomington, Indiana 47405 USA

iupress.org

Manufactured in the United States of America
First printing 2021

Cataloging information is available from the Library of Congress.
ISBN 978-0-253-05844-7 (paperback)
ISBN 978-0-253-05845-4 (ebook)

I have run out of people to dedicate books to,
so this one is for you.
Friend me on Facebook and check out my website,
Kevenmcqueenstories.com!

CONTENTS

ACKNOWLEDGMENTS

EASTERN KENTUCKY UNIVERSITY DEPARTMENT OF ENGLISH; EASTERN Kentucky University Interlibrary Loan Department (Stefanie Brooks and Heather Frith); Chris Flook, President of the Delaware County [IN] Historical Society; Daniel Allen Hearn; Jeffrey, Denise, and Amber Hughes; Dave Hulsey, Lesley Bolton, Rachel Erin Rosolina, Carol McGillivray, Anna C. Francis, and everyone at the Indiana University Press; Amy Hawkins McQueen and Quentin Hawkins; Darrell and Swecia McQueen; Darren, Alison, and Elizabeth McQueen; Kyle McQueen; Michael, Lori, and Blaine McQueen and Evan Holbrook; Craig and Debbie Smith; and Mia Temple.

MURDEROUS ACTS

1

MURDEROUS MISSOURI

The Maxwell Trunk Murder

There is no guarantee of lasting fame for poets, novelists, artists—or murderers. Some infamous slayings remain in the public consciousness decades after their commission, and some don't. Everyone is familiar with Jack the Ripper's dark deeds, yet probably not one person in a hundred thousand has ever heard of the contemporaneous Maxwell Trunk Murder even though it was the subject of much excited talk from our great-great-grandfathers. Jack the Ripper, whoever he was, made the cut (so to speak) and attained criminal immortality; Maxwell did not. This is his story.

On March 30, 1885, a twenty-five-year-old "girlish-looking, blonde young man" checked into the Southern Hotel in St. Louis, Missouri. Claiming to be from London, as well as a doctor and a nobleman, he signed the guest register with the imposing name Walter Henry Lennox Maxwell, and the duly impressed staff gave him room 144. A few days later, the hotel received a telegram from another Englishman, wealthy merchant Charles Arthur Preller, asking if Maxwell was registered there. The staff replied that he was. On April 3, twenty-nine-year-old Preller showed up and checked into room 184.

The hotel staff noted that Maxwell's manner was "very effeminate, which he even carried so far as to walk with short, mincing steps like a woman." A witness later described Preller as being "of a retiring, almost effeminate nature." The staff also observed that both Maxwell and Preller seemed "dude-ish" and "dandified," not unlike Oscar Wilde, and spent a lot of time together in Preller's room. The staff jumped to the (then) obvious conclusion: Maxwell and Preller must be "good friends and old acquaintances."

On April 6, Maxwell disappeared from the hotel. He had paid a week's rent in advance, so it was several days before the staff realized he was not returning. Meanwhile, an unappetizing reek was coming from Maxwell's room, which gained strength and pungency with each day. Upon inspecting room 144, the staff found that the source of the smell was a zinc trunk Maxwell had left behind. Porters, bellhops, and the like had learned through hard experience to be wary of foul-smelling trunks. On April 14, the hotel staff forced open the small trunk and found the ripe corpse of a man folded inside, clad only in pants, tongue protruding, and skin black with decomposition. He had a cross cut into his chest, and his head had been severed to make for easier packaging. The killer had written a mysterious message and pasted it on an inside wall of the trunk, right behind the victim's head: "So perish all traitors to the great cause." An artist for the *St. Louis Post-Dispatch* held his nose with one hand and, with the other, sketched the open trunk and its contents. The drawing was widely reprinted in the nation's papers and undoubtedly caused many readers to gag on their breakfast of oatmeal and marmalade. The trunk was hustled off to the morgue, but the smell lingered in the hotel corridor long after it was gone.

A second trunk of Maxwell's contained only papers, likely to the relief of the *Post-Dispatch*'s artist. Seven trunks belonging to Preller were found in Preller's room, containing passports for Russia, Spain, and Mexico and hundreds of dollars' worth of clothes, tapestries, and rugs, which suggested that Preller had been much wealthier than Maxwell.

It was the coroner's solemn duty to determine whether the less-than-spruce man in the trunk was Preller. The corpse had dark hair and eyes, revealing it to be Preller rather than the blue-eyed, blond Maxwell. The killer had shaved Preller's handsome moustache, perhaps to make identification of the body slightly (*very* slightly) more difficult. A chemist detected chloroform in the body. It appeared that Maxwell had waited until Preller was asleep and then held a cloth saturated with the powerful anesthetic under his victim's nose until death overtook him.

The wounds on Preller's body were postmortem, made during his killer's spirited attempt to cram the corpse into the tiny trunk. Maxwell likely intended to smuggle the chest out of the hotel but panicked and fled, leaving behind not only the body but also his own personal items and bushel baskets of incriminating evidence, including prescription forms showing that a few days before he disappeared, he had visited a St. Louis druggist, J. A. Fernow, who told detectives he had sold Maxwell six ounces of chloroform. A partly filled bottle of the drug was found among the fugitive's abandoned possessions. At the inquest held on April 18, a salesperson positively identified Maxwell as the customer who, on April 6, had purchased the trunk that housed Preller's body.

As the investigation unfolded, little pieces of the false identity Maxwell had created for himself were stripped away. He turned out to be neither a doctor nor a baronet, but rather a struggling solicitor and the son of a schoolmaster in Hyde, England. On June 10, it was ascertained that his real name was Hugh Mottram Brooks, so from this point he shall be called that rather than Maxwell in the narrative. Brooks had a girlfriend named Whitaker back in Hyde, whom the locals considered "much too good for him," as they felt Brooks was a fool and a ne'er-do-well. A couple of months before the murder, Brooks had turned up in Chicago so "dead broke," as he put it, that he offered to write for a newspaper to make money to pay his hotel bill. But a witness who saw Brooks on a train heading west the day after he fled St. Louis noticed that the formerly indigent Englishman somehow had attained plenty of cash.

As is true of so many murderers, Brooks's crime consisted of one-third devilish cunning and two-thirds incompetence. Despite his head start of over a week, only the day after the body was found he was traced to San Francisco, California, where he had purchased a memorably foppish hat. He called himself Theodore Cecil Dauguier and claimed to be a French army officer, but whenever he was spoken to in French, he always replied in English. From San Francisco, he sailed to Auckland, New Zealand, on the Australian steamer *City of Sydney*. Technology was on the side of the law; cablegrams could travel faster than steamers, and Brooks was arrested in Auckland as he minced down the gangplank on May 6. He hired a couple of attorneys right away, presumably using money stolen from his victim. He needed these professionals very badly, as Preller's clothes were found in his possession, including a bloodstained shirt and two handkerchiefs embroidered with the initials C.A.P.

New Zealand authorities turned Brooks over to United States officers on June 18, and on August 10, the steamer *Zealandi* arrived in San Francisco with the officers and the extradited prisoner. He was jailed for safekeeping, still feebly claiming to be French. He would admit only to having known Preller, something he could not credibly deny since he had some of the victim's clothing.

Bizarre theories surfaced, purporting to explain the crime. The *Boston Herald* published an interview with a local physician, transplanted Englishman Dr. E. H. Graham-Dewey, who claimed that Brooks had visited Boston before his ill-fated trip to St. Louis and had expressed more than ordinary interest in procuring a cadaver. The doctor told Brooks that the law restricted the sale of bodies to medical schools. Three days later, according to the doctor, Brooks confided that he had successfully stolen a corpse. Graham-Dewey thought that for some reason Brooks had taken the body with him to St. Louis. Graham-Dewey further suggested that perhaps Brooks and Preller were playing a gruesome practical joke and that Preller would come out of hiding if Brooks were arrested. That Brooks fled to New Zealand suggests that if it were a prank, it was an unusually elaborate one.

A second possibility suggested by the *St. Louis Republican* was that Brooks had brought the corpse to their fair city as a subject for medical experiments, but once it commenced decomposing, he realized he would have a hard time getting rid of it. (This theory requires us to suppose that Brooks had no idea an unembalmed corpse would go bad after a few days.) The newspaper conjectured that Brooks and Preller fled the city, as it would be easier to leave the body behind than to explain how they got it in the first place: "A corpse in one's trunk at a leading hotel would obviously be enough to frighten any man who had come by it without murder when he considered the certainty that, being found with it, he would be arrested as a murderer, with a case of circumstantial evidence against him." This speculation made little sense but was rich with entertainment value.

Others thought Brooks and Preller were trying to pull off an insurance fraud. The gaping, asteroid-sized hole in this theory was that there was no insurance policy favoring Brooks in the event of Preller's death. Brooks himself capitalized on this lame theory, boldly stating from his San Francisco jail cell on August 13 that the whole thing was a clever swindle and that, given time, he would produce the living, breathing C. Arthur Preller!

He never made good on his promise. Two days later, the St. Louis police exhumed the body of Preller and found that "the remains, which were embalmed before burial, were found to be in an excellent state of preservation and looking even better than when interred," according to a news account. This meant that his acquaintances might positively identify his body in court. Brooks arrived in St. Louis on August 16, as a crowd estimated at three thousand waited to catch a glimpse of him at the train depot. He had refused to speak a single word about his case on the long ride from California.

Any doubts that "Maxwell" was actually Brooks disappeared on October 24, when Brooks's father, Samuel, arrived at the St. Louis jail and identified the prisoner. The old man admonished him, "It would have been better for you to be dead than here, and I did not believe the report until now. Your poor mother is nearly dead, and the family is all but ruined." Brooks the younger seemed more annoyed than comforted by his father's visit, and Brooks the elder convinced himself that his son must be innocent and, if not that, then insane.

Brooks's arraignment came on November 14. He pled not guilty. He did not go on trial until May 1886. Before then, he had presented a brand-new defense to the *St. Louis Post-Dispatch* with his attorneys' approval. He could hardly deny having killed his friend, so he took the only open route by claiming it was an accident. Preller suffered from "a private disease," Brooks said, dropping heavy hints that a venereal disease had caused a stricture in Preller's urethra. The treatment required the insertion of a catheter. Brooks said he had prescribed chloroform to help Preller sleep through the uncomfortable procedure, despite the fact that prescribing chloroform for mild pain is akin to killing head lice with napalm. But, alas, Brooks did not realize that Preller had a heart condition, and the dose proved fatal. Then Brooks took the perfectly reasonable actions of beheading the corpse, cramming it in a trunk, and spending the night in the room with the remains. Making the best of a bad situation, the next morning he packed the deceased's clothing and escaped to New Zealand. Who wouldn't have done the same under the circumstances? (Brooks claimed not to have taken the dead man's money, as he had plenty of his own, a lie effortlessly exposed by prosecutors.) Shaving Preller's moustache and pasting the arcane message inside the trunk—"So perish all traitors to the great cause"—were not evidence of premeditation, claimed Brooks, but the fruits of drunkenness and fear.

Needless to say, this feeble yarn did not survive scrutiny when Brooks went to trial on May 21. The first witness for the prosecution, J. A. Frazer of Toronto, was a professional artist who well remembered the face of Preller. When Frazer visited St. Louis at the request of the police, the body was again exhumed for his inspection. He recognized the well-preserved corpse immediately, noting that the body bore a scar over the left eyebrow that was identical to Preller's. Cross-examination failed to shake Frazer. But the prosecution's real bombshell was exploded on May 24, when it revealed that detective John McCullough, who had been arrested for forgery, had spent forty-seven days in the cell adjoining Brooks's. Even though McCullough had a less-than-sterling character, the prosecution considered him a good enough witness to put on the stand, for the talkative Brooks had voluntarily made many damning admissions to his new friend.

For example, Brooks had wished aloud that he could hire someone to falsely testify in court as to his financial solvency before he left Boston for St. Louis. He had wanted to accompany Preller on a trip to New Zealand, but the wealthier man told Brooks that he could only afford a ticket for himself. This angered Brooks, and "he made up his mind on account of [Preller's] meanness to fix him," as Detective McCullough put it. Brooks confessed to McCullough that he had intentionally killed his friend with chloroform and the motive was robbery. He took $700 from Preller and then went on a wild spending spree, buying everything from a pair of binoculars to a spot of fun at a house of ill fame with a girl named Grace, to whom he boasted that he "had just killed a man." (To add further insight into Brooks's character, although he had agreed to pay Grace twenty dollars for her services, he gave her only five, "telling her that was enough.") After all these adventures, he sailed to Auckland, confident that his cleverness had won the day.

Brooks's attorney, P. W. Fauntleroy, cross-examined the detective with vigor. He succeeded in making McCullough look like a sleazy character, but even a sleazy character can tell the truth sometimes. As a reporter wrote, "The direct testimony was not materially shaken, and the opinion prevails that the chances of the defendant for acquittal have nearly vanished." After McCullough's damaging testimony, the defense had little choice but to put Hugh Brooks on the stand on May 26 and May 27, which resulted in removing whatever doubt might have remained concerning his guilt. Under oath, Brooks swore to the absurd story he had released earlier to the press: that he had attempted to perform minor surgery on Preller to relieve the latter of his embarrassing "private disease." (His attorney Fauntleroy blamed the victim by asserting that Preller had *insisted* on the gassing and the operation.) Brooks testified that the death was accidental and that, horror-stricken, he had run away with Preller's money and left the body behind. He admitted he had bought some luxuries with the money and, at last, explained the meaning behind the strange message he left with the body: "My idea was that the authorities would find it, and that it would puzzle them until an autopsy should be held." He had wanted to make the murder look like a political assassination.

The prosecution, anticipating that Brooks would tell this fairy tale on the witness stand, mercilessly tore it asunder. Physicians had exhumed Preller's well-preserved corpse yet again and performed an examination to see if he had a venereal disease—meaning they amputated a very personal portion of Preller's anatomy. They found no trace of the "private disease" or the stricture alluded to by Brooks. (The defense demanded the opportunity to have this piece of Preller examined by its own medical experts.)

The prosecution provided additional evidence that Brooks was a pathological liar. A couple of examples: When shown a medical school diploma, Brooks stated that he had forged it merely as "an exercise in penmanship." When it was pointed out that no catheters were found among his medical equipment, he claimed that he threw them overboard in a fit of disgust en route to Auckland. During cross-examination, the prisoner's vocabulary consisted mostly of "I don't know" and "I don't remember." It was by now so patently obvious that Brooks had committed the cold, premeditated murder of his companion for gain that even his fellow prisoners ostracized him. "He seems to feel that everybody has abandoned him to his fate," remarked a reporter in an article datelined May 30. "His vanity has been sorely wounded, and, as that was what chiefly sustained him, he has nothing left to buoy him up."

The case went to the jury on June 1. Judge Van Wagoner instructed them that if they believed the state's case, they should return a verdict of murder in the first degree; but if they believed that the death was caused by Brooks's unintentional bungling with the chloroform, they should find him guilty of manslaughter in the fourth degree. As a third option, if they believed the chloroform had been administered with care and that the death resulted from Preller's alleged heart condition, the prisoner should be acquitted. The judge added that a verdict of guilty could be returned on circumstantial evidence—a wise thing for him to say, since most people, then and now, erroneously believe that "circumstantial evidence" is synonymous with "inadequate evidence." On June 5, the verdict was announced: Hugh M. Brooks was guilty and must hang for the murder of Preller. The *Louisville Courier-Journal* remarked, "He will receive on the scaffold the punishment he has so richly earned, and which in his own country—England—would long since have been meted out to him."

But Brooks's neck was safe for the time being. The verdict was followed by two years' worth of appeals and legal wrangling. It is an object lesson for anyone who believes American justice was swifter in the good old days than it is now. Brooks was to have been executed on August 17, 1886; then the date was moved to September. In September, he received a postponement of two months to allow attorney Fauntleroy's appeal to the Supreme Court of Missouri, which, on January 31, 1887, granted a stay until April 1. This was extended still further, and, on June 20, the court affirmed the decision of the lower court. The reconvicted Brooks was to be hanged on August 12. The date was pushed back to August 26 so that the defense could appeal to the United States Supreme Court, but, in July, Fauntleroy decided that his client's execution was inevitable and said he would make no further efforts to rescue Brooks from the beckoning hangman.

August 26 came and went; no hanging. On October 12, the United States Supreme Court declared that it would hear Brooks's appeal after all. Nothing more was heard of the case until January 10, 1888, when the press announced that "the Attorney General of Missouri yesterday . . . moved to dismiss the appeal of Hugh Brooks." Thirteen days later, the case came bouncing back to Missouri because the US Supreme Court rejected the appeal. Defense attorney Fauntleroy, who must have reentered the case after all, stated that his client's only hope now was executive clemency—that is, a pardon from Governor Albert Morehouse. When Brooks received the bad news, the jailers put him on a suicide watch. They might rightly have been more worried about his smoking habit. A physician expressed concern because the prisoner smoked up to fifty cigarettes per day of a brand laced with morphine. (During the same era, the soft drink Coca-Cola contained a smattering of cocaine; opium, morphine, and laudanum were readily available over the counter in any drugstore or in patent medicines. It must have been glory days for drug fiends.) Perhaps Brooks found his spiked cigarettes a way of coping with his impending death sentence, but the doctor was afraid he might literally smoke himself to death.

The prisoner's father, Samuel Brooks, tried to get the sentence commuted. He won much sympathy, but pressing business forced him to return to England in March, pleased with how nicely he had been treated in the United States. He wrote an appeal to the public via the newspapers, started petitions in America and England, and met personally with Governor Morehouse. He left St. Louis convinced that he had done all he could.

On April 2, the US Supreme Court refused to rehear the case. The date of the hanging was set for July 13. On June 28, the governor stated that he would not grant Brooks's lawyers a sixty-day respite but would listen to appeals for commutation of the sentence. He heard many, including appeals from clergymen, Brooks's attorneys, and the condemned man's mother and sister.

The July 13 deadline came and went; still no hanging. On August 3, Governor Morehouse received an application from the British government for a postponement of Brooks's execution on the grounds that both murderer and victim were English subjects. Perhaps the appeal that affected the governor most came from his own daughter, a dedicated humanitarian who urged that the sentence be commuted to life in prison. It should be noted that she met Brooks's pitiable father but not the calculating, egotistical prisoner.

In the end, Governor Morehouse did not take his daughter's well-intended advice. An ugly incident had taken place in Missouri a few years previously under Governor Thomas Crittenden, who had pardoned Nodaway County murderer Charles Stevenson. Stevenson was a master carpenter and made toys for the governor's small daughter in the penitentiary's workshop. The girl had taken ill in 1884 and, on her deathbed, asked her father to promise he would pardon Stevenson, "who had been so good to her." After all, how bad could a guy be who made charming playthings for a little girl? Of course, Crittenden could not refuse, and, on his last day in office in 1885, he paroled Stevenson, who had served seven years of a twelve-year sentence. It seems like a heartwarming story straight out of *McGuffey's Eclectic Reader*, and no doubt Crittenden, his daughter, and anti–death penalty advocates thought they had done the humane thing. And so, they had—but it was humane only for Stevenson. Upon his release, he returned to Nodaway County, and, less than a month later, he shot a young German, who suffered miserably for two days before he passed unto his fathers. A lynch mob broke into the jail at Maryville and hanged Stevenson from a bridge only a few hundred yards from the residence of present Governor Morehouse.

Perhaps Morehouse remembered that wrongly paroled corpse swinging within sight of his house when his own daughter attempted to talk him into commuting Brooks's sentence. Despite the pleadings, petitions, and requests from the British government, he finally decided he would not interfere with the law. Brooks received word on August 9 that he would be hanged the next day. He whiled away his limited time chain-smoking those narcotic cigarettes.

Justice, far too long delayed, finally came on August 10, 1888, three weeks before Jack the Ripper committed his first acknowledged murder in Brooks's home country. The former Walter Henry Lennox Maxwell walked to the gallows with fellow prisoner Henry Landgraf, who had shot his girlfriend in March 1885. An Englishman to the end, Brooks wore a Prince Albert coat. Right up to the last moment, Brooks nervously hoped for the arrival of a telegraphed reprieve. Landgraf had no such false expectations. Bystanders noted that Brooks was ashen-faced and trembling as the noose was adjusted. After the trap was sprung, the executed men were taken to the morgue, photographed, and autopsied.

Notorious murderers often fascinate women of less-than-discriminating tastes, and Hugh Brooks was no exception. Scores of beauties attended his trial and visited him while he was imprisoned. Until the police forbade her to do so, "a notorious courtesan of St. Louis" supplied Brooks with dinner and champagne in his cell daily. Perhaps she had not heard about Brooks's shortchanging of poor Grace, her sister of the street. Women's interest in the Little Chloroformer, as the press dubbed him, did not cease with his death. An "unknown but beautiful lady" paid a man named John Shevlin generously to guard Brooks's grave in Calvary Cemetery every night. The precaution paid off when Shevlin foiled an attempt to steal Brooks's body on the morning of September 7. He fired a pistol, and the resurrectionists fled, leaving in their wake only a shovel, rope, and a cloud of graveyard dust.

In two other respects, Brooks generated interest from beyond the grave. In June 1897, his executioner, Michael Fortin, was sent to the mental institution. He had spent nearly a decade brooding over his role in ridding the world of the famous murderer.

In addition, within a few years of the murder, the Southern Hotel was having trouble with room 144, where Brooks had killed Preller. The chamber had achieved great notoriety. Some people insisted on staying in the "murder room" just so they would have a thrilling story to tell friends. Meeker travelers refused to rent it. The hotel's proprietors changed the room number from 144 to 133 in hopes of fooling the unwary, and "every employee of the hotel, from bellboy and porter to clerk, was sternly cautioned not to give any information whatever about the room," said one account.

Curiosity seekers were bad enough, but then rumors emerged that the room was haunted—that Preller's spirit was indulging in what F. Scott Fitzgerald called the "whimsical perambulations of the buried." Guests who did not know about the room's history would go to the hotel office "at all hours of the day and night, and without vouchsafing an explanation would demand a change of room. They would always be accommodated without question of any kind." The *New York Times* noted that hotel employees would spend the night in the room, but their slumber, if any, would be disturbed by "groans and frightful noises alternating with the opening and shutting of wardrobe doors."

In January 1889, a reporter for the *St. Louis Republic* (not the more famous *Republican*) caught wind of a recent incident. The credible witness was a "prominent businessman of well-balanced mind, sound intellect, and good, broad common-sense, unclouded by any of the 'isms' that occasionally cloud the perception or incline one to belief in the supernatural." The man, described elsewhere as "one of the best-known men in the city," claimed to be unaware of the hotel room's infamy. He noticed that bellhops would leave the room as fast as possible, not even waiting for their tips. At around ten o'clock every night, the lights were turned off in the outside corridor, and the employees could not be persuaded to go through the darkened hallway.

On the first night of his stay, the businessman was awakened repeatedly by tapping on the bed's headboard. It always came in a pattern: one tap, a brief pause, then two taps in quick succession. The next evening, he noticed that the dresser drawers refused to stay shut. On the third night, he was awakened by an explosion in the fireplace, even though the housekeeper had cleaned the hearth of all debris. He thought it sounded like a firecracker. It was followed by a second, louder detonation, and then by a third that was the loudest of all. "I arose, dressed, lighted the gas and looked at the hearth. It was completely filled with a slaty substance that looked like ore of some kind, and one of the large cubes that made up the hearth was torn from the brickwork or tiling. Pieces of slate were thrown across the room."

That was too much for the businessman, who went downstairs and asked the night clerk to come to see the odd debris. He refused "with a sickly smile." The customer returned to the room and encountered no more phenomena, though he got no sleep. The next day, he demanded and received a room change.

The reporter ended his article: "The manager of the hotel, Mr. Lewis, had nothing to say when the story was told him by a *Republic* representative, nor could he suggest any explanation."

Two Frenchmen Walk into a Hotel . . .

It sounds like the start of a ribald joke, but what happened was the reverse of funny.

Genuine French counts seldom visited St. Louis in pioneer times. Theron Barnum, the proprietor of the City Hotel, must have been delighted when two titled young brothers—Count Gonsalve de Montesquie and Count Raymond de Montesquie (pronounced mon-TESS-kew)—patronized his establishment at the corner of Third and Vine on October 28, 1849, not long after the mysterious death of Edgar Allan Poe in Baltimore.

(The exact spelling of the brothers' last name is difficult to ascertain, since the press rendered it at least eight different ways. The most common spellings were Montesquie and Montesquiou. Were they related, one wonders, to Baron de Montesquieu, the Enlightenment-era French philosopher with a slightly different name spelling?)

Barnum's opinion of the Frenchmen's regality must have been shattered on the night of October 30, when his minor-aged nephew and employee, Thomas Kirby Barnum, heard a tapping on his window. Thomas pushed aside the curtain to peer outside when someone fired through the window, fatally wounding him. Two buckshot lodged in the arm of his servant and roommate, J.J. McComber. The man in the adjoining room, Albert Jones, came to the door to see what was going on. A bullet and six buckshot in his head killed him instantly. The assassin (or assassins) also peppered with shot William Hubbell and H. M. Henderson, who came to investigate.

Several hotel patrons followed the attacker to his room. They identified him immediately as Raymond, the younger of the French guests, though later testimony, particularly that of Flannegan the night guard, claimed that Gonsalve was the sole shooter. Both brothers were arrested, jailed, and guarded against a large crowd in the street that didn't exactly want to ask for escargot recipes. On November 1, authorities took the de Montesquies to Jefferson Barracks for safekeeping.

An inspection of their trunks revealed letters "proving them to be Parisians of great wealth and family" and $1,500 in German gold to boot. At least they were genuine nobility, not imposters.

The de Montesquies' guards thought Gonsalve was insane. He insisted that God had ordered him to go on the shooting spree and said that he and his brother would defend themselves in court. Police discovered that Gonsalve had tried to kill a landlord in Alton, Illinois, a few days before the counts graced St. Louis with their presence—a fact that strengthened the general conviction of his insanity.

Raymond de Montesquie stated that he had long feared his older brother was insane and said that his intervention was the only reason Gonsalve had not murdered the man in Alton. Raymond said a feeling had washed over Gonsalve at Barnum's Hotel, an irresistible feeling that he *must* kill two men—any two random men would do; the urge was not particular. Raymond insisted that he had pursued Gonsalve to prevent carnage, but by the time he had caught up with his brother, the damage was done. Gonsalve was conscious of his guilt, said a contemporary account; he "exculpate[d] his brother from all blame, and claim[ed] that he alone should be made to suffer for the consequences of his act."

Thomas Kirby Barnum died on November 7, a week after the shooting. A few days later, his uncle filed a lawsuit to gain the Frenchmen's property to cover the loss of services to his business caused by the untimely death. Barnum estimated Thomas's value at $3,000, so he probably ended up possessing that trunkful of German gold.

In January 1850, reporters observed that Gonsalve de Montesquie's fragile health was sinking, while Raymond seemed resigned to his own fate of being jailed or hanged. On February 1, the court indicted Gonsalve for first-degree murder. Raymond was held as a witness. However, the next day, the court indicted Raymond as well. The two witnesses with the best view of the shooter, McComber and the late Barnum, had said it was Raymond.

Their joint trial began on March 25 in a courtroom crowded with female spectators. The state's strategy was to try the Frenchmen only for Thomas Barnum's murder. If, somehow, the brothers squeaked by with an acquittal, they could then be tried for killing Albert Jones. The defense argued that Gonsalve was guilty but unaccountable due to insanity.

In early April, several witnesses, including Dr. William Carr Lane, testified to Gonsalve's insanity. The defense provided evidence that the brothers' father, the late Count Alfred de Montesquie, had also been mentally ill. A dispatch published on April 8 read, "The depositions of John Carrigan and J. M. Jackson, the landlord and a boarder at a hotel in Springfield, Illinois, and that of a landlady of a small tavern about twenty miles south of that place, were read, which furnished additional evidence in proof of [Gonsalve's lunacy]." Then there was the man Gonsalve had tried to exterminate in Alton. Whatever Gonsalve's problem was, it appears he had a violent grudge against landlords and hotelkeepers.

Raymond's attorneys maintained that their client had shot no one; indeed, he had tried to stop the mayhem. What about the statements from McComber and the dying Barnum then? The defense offered a rich harvest of explanations: the two shooting victims could not see their assailant clearly, since they were in a lit room, and he was standing outside in the darkness; plus, Barnum and McComber were agitated; plus, they had only a glance at the shooter before they tried to run away; plus, the two de Montesquie brothers resembled one another; plus, Gonsalve admitted to the crime but said Raymond was guiltless.

The state made closing arguments on April 18. The jury could not agree and were discharged two days later. They voted seven for acquitting and five for convicting Gonsalve, and eight for acquitting and four for convicting Raymond.

The de Montesquies faced trial again at the next term of criminal court. The defense made a motion that the brothers be released on bail in the meantime. No doubt these members of the French peerage would have loved to get out, since they shared the St. Louis jail with fifteen other persons charged with or suspected of murder, including two Pawnee Indians and a member of the Sauc tribe. In early May, the aristocrats did get bail—$20,000 to secure Raymond's liberty and an astonishing $40,000 for Gonsalve, the greatly differing sums indicating that the latter was considered the greater risk to St. Louis society. (The modern equivalent of Gonsalve's bail would be $963,000.)

Once sprung, the brothers took rooms in Sisters Charity Hospital. Raymond seemed to regain his enjoyment of life, his "excellent health and buoyant spirts," as a *St. Louis Reveille* reporter wrote—or, in his native tongue, his joie de vivre! But for Gonsalve, the sweet air of freedom had no salubrious effect. He was "reserved and melancholy . . . apparently sick, both in body and in mind." At times, he was catatonic.

The second trial began on June 4. Exactly two weeks later, Gonsalve drank laudanum in his hospital room. He kept the drug in his trunk upon leaving France for the United States, which suggests that the authorities did not carefully inspect the brothers' trunks and that the vial was over-looked when Mr. Barnum had attached the counts' valuables to assuage the loss of his nephew/factotum. Gonsalve had written a note reading, "I have sought my death voluntarily by poison." Seeking is not finding, however, and an alarmed Raymond sent for a doctor, who gave the sui-cidal man a dose of emetics—drugs that triggered prodigious, world-class vomiting and a favorite tool of the era's medical profession. Gonsalve survived to face a jury after all.

At the end of June, the jurors announced that they were hopelessly deadlocked after deliberating for forty hours. The final tally was nine votes for convicting the brothers, three for acquittal. The prosecutors decided to try the Montesquies for killing Albert Jones instead. The defense insisted that the brothers be tried separately the third time around.

Again, the major question seemed to be Gonsalve's state of mind. By the end of August, he was so violent that Raymond had to take quarters in a separate room in the hospital. Gonsalve threatened to kill one of his frequent visitors—his brother-in-law, another French count, and became increasingly withdrawn, depressed, and paranoid. His frame was emaciated and his face gaunt. He stared out his window wordlessly for days. He refused to see anyone, not even hospital person-nel, servants, or his brother. Either he was insane or doing a masterful imitation.

There was no third trial. In mid-October, the governor of Missouri gave Gonsalve—a man who was either a lunatic, a murderer, or both—an unconditional pardon. On October 23, the elder count boarded the steamship *Europa* to return to France. So the judicial system decided the easiest way to deal with Gonsalve de Montesquie was to shuck him off on someone else, perhaps to murder more hotel owners or landlords in the future. If Gonsalve was not a murderer, he was still insane and seemingly dangerous. As de Montesquieu (the philosopher, not the killer) said concerning the legal system, "The severity of the laws prevents their execution." Raymond was considered sane and some thought him the actual killer, so he remained in St. Louis.

At the end of the month, the governor discharged Raymond as well. Within days, he too was on his way to Paris. It appears that Raymond got into no further trouble, but a news story from May 1852 tells us: "Young [Gonsalve] Montesquion [sic], the insane Frenchman . . . has been committing further violence since his return to France and has been lodged in an insane asylum." Legend has it that he died there.

However, at least one person benefited from the sordid episode. In November 1851, the Countess de Montesquie gave a jewel-studded missal (a Catholic liturgical book including a year's worth of masses) to the Chouteau family of St. Louis, who had been kind to her sons while they were lodged in the frontier Bastille.

The Murdered Parsons Family

Aficionados of the macabre must not overlook *Sleeping Beauty*, a book by Dr. Stanley Burns featuring memorial photographs of the dead dating from the nineteenth to early twentieth centuries, when it was not thought unseemly or bizarre to take photos of deceased friends and relatives. Sometimes people took pictures of dead outlaws or their victims. One unforgettable photo in the collection shows the five murdered members of the Parsons family of Licking, Missouri, lying fully clothed and side by side on a bed. They look tolerably presentable, considering that they were variously shot, bludgeoned, slashed, and immersed in a river. This is their story—a story of murder, revenge, and a trivial motive.

Carney Parsons, age thirty-one, farmed with his wife, Minnie. They had three young sons: Jesse, age six; Frank, age three; and baby Edward, age one. Parsons wanted to resettle in the northern part of the state. In October 1906, he sold crops and land to twenty-year-old neighboring farmer Joda (or Jodie) Hamilton as a sort of clearance sale.

Hamilton fancied himself slighted (see below) and thirsted to take revenge before Parsons moved away and out of easy reach. On the afternoon of October 12, he grabbed a shotgun and lay in wait in a forest by the highway, two miles east of Success. Gradually, the Parsons family came into sight riding in a pioneer-like covered wagon drawn by two mules. When they got close enough, Hamilton leaped out of the brush. He fired both barrels at Carney Parsons, killing him instantly. Though it was unnecessary, he hit Parsons over the head with the butt of the gun.

However, Hamilton could not leave so many witnesses. According to his confession, he "beat the head of the mother almost to a pulp" (an exaggeration, as the death photo shows). After that, he clubbed the three boys and cut their throats. He loaded the five bodies into their covered wagon and carted them to Big Piney River, about a mile away. He hid the wagon in the bushes and unhitched the mules, riding one home and leading the other. The first thing he did when he got to town was attend a church service. Certainly, he needed to.

After church, he waited until nightfall and returned to the wagon. He dumped the bodies in the river and hurried away, likely admiring his own cleverness.

The next day, fishermen found two of the children. Further search turned up the other bodies. Hamilton drew attention to himself by riding a mule known to have been Carney Parsons's property. He was arrested immediately, and it took the law considerable ingenuity to save him from falling prey to a mob of gentlemen who wanted to take him to a so-called necktie party. He was hurried to a jail in a town near the Arkansas border. Police were so solicitous of his well-being that they refused to even name the town.

Hamilton wasted no time trying to save the mob the trouble of killing him. In his cell, he ineffectually stabbed himself in the chest and neck with a knitting needle and beat his head against the wall. His efforts to court death came to nothing, so he gave up and confessed. He said he had killed Mr. Parsons in self-defense but offered no such excuse for killing Mrs. Parsons, two small children, and a baby. Why had Hamilton undertaken the inconceivably savage overkill of an entire family? Because he *thought* Mr. Parsons had stolen his saddle. Perhaps it was a really good saddle.

If Joda Hamilton had not regretted murdering the Parsons family beforehand, he surely lamented it on December 21, the day he made a necessarily brief acquaintanceship with the hangman in Houston, Missouri. On his first trip through the trapdoor, the rope broke, and Hamilton hit the ground with a splat that was the subject of much disapproving comment from spectators. Officials picked up the partially conscious prisoner and carried him back up the scaffold stairs. He was launched properly on the next attempt, but the doctor in attendance believed that Hamilton was fatally injured by the fall and was likely dead before the trap was sprung the second time.

Hamilton's body was turned over to his father to do with as he pleased.

2

MICHIGAN MAYHEM

Too Clever for His Own Good

America has a long-standing love affair with doltish criminals, as a Google search of terms such as "dumbest crooks," "stupid criminals," and "funny crimes" will prove. YouTube is a font of surveillance videos of foolish robbers. At one time there was a television show called *America's Dumbest Criminals*. Perhaps the old-school king of incompetent criminals should be Robert Irving Latimer—that's Irving to you!

To be fair about it, Irving Latimer really wasn't a dummy. His murder scheme was replete with clever details and diabolical planning. Somehow, despite his best efforts, it fell asunder at every joint and seam. The ignominious destruction of every part of his plan graces it with an evergreen fascination.

Irving's father was Robert F. Latimer, a leading pharmacist in Jackson, Michigan. Irving worked as his clerk. On October 21, 1887, the seemingly healthy family patriarch complained that he felt ill and walked home from his office. After a brief spate of coughing, vomiting, chills, and numbness, he died of "paralysis of the heart," which appears to be 1887-ese for either a heart attack or a stroke.

Irving Latimer followed in his father's career footsteps. Using his inheritance and borrowing $3,000 from his mother, Marietta, he purchased his own Jackson drugstore. Twenty-three-year-old Irving lived with well-to-do Marietta in her First Street mansion after she was widowed, ostensibly to comfort her. He taught Sunday school. He was well-dressed, soft-spoken, and courteous. In other words, a perfect son.

Or so he seemed. In fact, there was a barely hidden dark side to Irving. It was whispered in town that whenever he went to Detroit twice a month, presumably to buy stock for his drugstore, he patronized brothels. These rumors later proved to be only too true; even at the time, he created a scandal by bringing a known prostitute to a dance. Neighborhood gossip held that he murdered his father for his inheritance. This was never proved, but considering what happened later, it seems plausible.

Also on the downside, despite managing his own pharmacy, he was bad with money; he was a spendthrift who lived well beyond his means. His business should have prospered, but he spent the profits on high living and "sporting women." It was said that he strategically placed a mirror in his store so that if debt collectors entered, he could see them coming and flee out the back door. After he became celebrated coast-to-coast in a manner not to his liking, it came out that he was behind in paying taxes and owed money to sixty creditors. The average amount he owed was $35, which does not sound like an insurmountable sum until we calculate that $35 was equal to over $890 in modern currency. He couldn't even pay the interest on his many loans. By autumn 1888, his financial crisis was at its zenith. A desperate Irving gingerly approached his wealthy mother and asked if he could borrow enough to get out of debt. Her disheartening answer was something along these lines, "Absolutely not, Irving! You already owe me $3,000, which is due to be paid on January 31, 1889. No more loans, and I expect full payment on that day."

The modern equivalent of $3,000 is nearly $76,500. Plus, Irving owed a bare minimum of $2,100 (in 1888 money; $53,500 in ours) to his creditors. There was the ticklish matter of those delinquent taxes and the fact that he also owed an overdue loan to a Detroit bank. The reader can appreciate his seemingly insoluble predicament.

But *was* it insoluble? We shall never know exactly when the dark thought first crossed his mind, but at least six months before the January 31 deadline, Irving started thinking that he could renege on the $3,000 he owed his mother and inherit $12,000 to boot. Not only that but she also possessed her own house and the one next door, and if Irving acquired them, he could sell them at a great profit. The allegedly doting son started seeing his mother as a cash cow—or, to be more precise, a sacrificial cow. If it was a choice between her continued existence and Irving Latimer's happiness, well, she just had to go. It would be done on the night of Thursday, January 24, 1889, and it would be a perfect murder because if there was anything Irving was certain about, it was that he was smarter than everyone else. He spent days carefully planning every detail of his foolproof plan.

The way the murder was *supposed* to happen:

In October 1888, Irving started sleeping some nights in a spare back room in his pharmacy on the pretense of working late. That way, it wouldn't look suspicious when his mother was left alone at home on the chosen night.

Irving would tell neighbors and customers that he intended to spend the night of January 24 in Detroit since he had to be a pallbearer at a funeral. He would make sure witnesses saw him boarding the train. Once there, he would check into the seedy Griswold Hotel rather than the upper-class Cadillac Hotel where he customarily stayed, because no one at the Griswold would recognize him.

In the middle of the night, he would slip out of the hotel and take a train to Ypsilanti, then another back to Jackson. His mother would be alone except for her dog, Gyp. Getting past the watchdog would be no problem since it knew him. He would enter the side door with a key. Once inside, he would tiptoe to her second-floor bedroom and shoot her in the head with his .32-caliber revolver, killing her instantly and painlessly. He would break the lock on the cellar door and hide valuables to make it seem she was a victim of a burglary gone sour. Then it would be a simple matter to take a late train back to Detroit, sneak into the Griswold, get in bed, and feign shock and horror like a tragedian the next day when he received the inevitable news about his poor mother.

That was the plan, anyway. This is what *actually* happened:

On Wednesday, January 23, as Irving was secretly making his final schemes, a boy who worked at his drugstore asked if he could have the day off on January 24. Irving said, "Sorry, no, you will have to come in that day, as I will be at a funeral in Detroit." Irving left the pharmacy, walked a few doors down to the sheriff's department, and requested permission to use the telephone. He called a friend in Detroit and said that he would be coming to the funeral the next day. Irving made sure he was overheard, for what better witness to his conversation than an unimpeachable source, the sheriff?

That evening, after closing the pharmacy, Latimer boarded the train for Detroit as planned, with a suitcase containing dark clothes for a disguise and his .32.

He checked into the Griswold Hotel and then passed some time, likely at a house of ill fame. He returned to the hotel at 9:00 p.m. and made certain that witnesses saw him take his key and go to room 42. A bit later, he sneaked out through the side door, went to the depot, and took the 10:10 train to Ypsilanti. From there, he stealthily boarded another train to Jackson. He arrived a little after 1:00 a.m. and trudged the dark side streets. The plot was unfolding perfectly! Then he got to his mother's house . . .

He entered the side door with a key, as planned. Irving assumed that he had good enough aim to end his mother's life quickly with a shot to the head. Instead, he shot her in the jaw. She sprang from her bed and ran to the window to open it and cry for help.

Terrified, Irving shot her in the neck, which still did not cause instantaneous death. She was getting too noisy for Irving's liking. What if she recognized him and called out his name? When he placed a handkerchief over her mouth to stifle her cries, she bit his thumb to the bone. Somehow murder in real life wasn't quite as easy as simplistic novels and stage melodramas made it seem!

When she was finally and mercifully dead, Irving dumped dresser drawer contents on the floor to make it seem like a burglary. He also broke the cellar door lock, in accordance with his elaborate scheme, to make it look like burglars entered there. But in his haste, he didn't realize that the vandalism was unnecessary, and in fact incited suspicion, since neighbors knew that Mrs. Latimer never locked the cellar door. In addition, Irving's wounded thumb dripped blood everywhere he went in the house, so detectives were able later to trace his every move.

Irving missed the late train back to Detroit, where he intended to establish his alibi at the hotel, so he had to settle for one leaving Jackson at 6:20 a.m. on January 25, which was cutting his preplanned schedule too closely for comfort. With every minute he had to wait, he ran the risk of acquaintances seeing him. He also had no ticket. He paid the porter his fare and a fee for a sleeping car and then, perhaps out of sheer nervousness, went to his berth. The porter and the conductor wondered why anyone would want a sleeping car that late in the morning, and such bizarre behavior made Irving memorable to them. Both watched curiously when he got off the train. They later recognized him from a photo of Irving Latimer.

Meanwhile, back in Jackson, a neighbor noticed that Mrs. Latimer didn't let her dog, Gyp, out in the morning, as was her habit. She called the police, who found the body of Mrs. Latimer on her bedroom floor. (An autopsy indicated that neither shot was fatal, and she probably drowned in her blood.) The murder was discovered much sooner than Irving anticipated. The staging of the crime scene suggested burglary—except a search indicated no missing valuables. In his mounting panic, Irving had forgotten to hide them.

Irving had been sublimely confident that Gyp would recognize him and not bark. He was correct, but it worked *against* him. Because neighbors did not hear barking, police naturally concluded that the animal was familiar with Mrs. Latimer's attacker.

It was the sad duty of Chief of Police John Boyle to locate Irving Latimer and break the news. But Irving wasn't in the spare room in his drugstore. The assistant boy who had to work that day told the police that the boss said he was going to a funeral in Detroit, which persons in the sheriff's office confirmed.

It was well known in Jackson that when Latimer went to the big city, he always registered at the Cadillac. Captain Boyle was surprised when he called and found the pharmacist was not there. He contacted every hotel in Detroit until he found that someone signing his name "R. H. Latimer of Jaxon" (rather than, correctly, R. I. Latimer from Jackson) was registered in room 42 at the Griswold. When Boyle called with the news, Latimer pretended to be horrified and hurried to the train yard to get a ride to Jackson, playing the role of grief-stricken and bereft orphan to the hilt.

While waiting at the depot, Latimer got an unpleasant surprise. After undergoing so many complicated subterfuges *not* to run into anyone he knew, whom should he meet but an old acquaintance, Detroit newspaper editor Lou Burch? Even worse, Burch had already heard the news about Marietta Latimer's murder. "Where have you been?" asked Burch. "I've been looking all over town for you!"

"Uh, at the Griswold Hotel."

Burch replied that he had already checked there and was told Latimer wasn't in. Latimer had no answer except to comment that he had a headache.

If he expected sympathy at his homecoming in Jackson, he was greatly taken aback when he was greeted instead with cynicism and suspicion. Captain Boyle asked the name of the person whose funeral he attended.

Caught up short, Irving confessed with a show of embarrassment that there *had* been no funeral; he simply had wanted to impress his young assistant by seeming important. Boyle hardly was satisfied by this nonanswer.

"Anything missing from the house?" the police officer asked.

"No, nothing seems to be," answered Irving in a moment of honesty.

"Any theories as to why the watchdog didn't bark?" asked Boyle.

Irving lamely theorized that perhaps the burglar had spent days in the vicinity making pals with the dog.

It did not escape Boyle's notice that Mrs. Latimer's murder occurred exactly a week before Irving was due to pay her that much-begrudged $3,000. This, plus his proven lies and feeble answers to inquiries, rocketed Irving right to the top of the suspects list.

Boyle went to Detroit. Witnesses remembered seeing Irving there on the night of January 24. Things went from bad to worse for him: he had checked into the Griswold, thinking no one there would recognize or remember him, but the porter had seen a man with a hat pulled down over his eyes sneaking out the side entrance on the night of the murder. This was especially memorable because the side entrance was for women only. Because Irving had arrived back in Detroit later than he anticipated, he was unable to rumple his bedsheets as planned to make it look as though he had spent the night in room 42, and the chambermaid had noticed the bed's pristine condition. Fifteen minutes after she checked on the room, she witnessed a man sneaking into it. The two hotel employees saw a photo of Irving and agreed that he was the man.

A barber whose shop was on the same street as the Griswold Hotel remembered a visibly nervous young man asking for a shave on the morning of January 25. The tonsorial artiste saw that the man had no cuffs, a noticeable fashion blunder by the standards of the time, and also had bloodstains on his coat. "I had a nosebleed" was the customer's explanation. The barber recognized his strange patron when shown a photo of Irving Latimer.

Irving had also had his bitten thumb treated at a drugstore. The clerk remembered him.

Then Boyle discovered not one but two witnesses who actually saw Latimer away from his hotel room on the night of January 24. Train employees said he took the 10:10 from Detroit to Ypsilanti, and from there, he took a second train to Jackson an hour later. No doubt Irving had fancied that by making a roundabout journey to his hometown, he was cleverly leaving a trail that would be impossible for investigators to untangle, but, as writer Anna Mary Wells noted, "The amount of ingenuity wasted on this elaborate and useless alibi is perhaps the most astonishing feature of the case. If Irving Latimer had chosen to sleep on the cot at the drugstore and creep home in the middle of the night to murder his mother, he could have done so without exposing himself to a single witness. The trip to Detroit had provided eight excellent ones."

When police arrested Irving, they, like the barber, noticed that his detachable cuffs were missing, yet his cuff links were in his pocket. The cuffs had been spattered with blood, so he had removed them, yet he didn't have sufficient sense to change into a different shirt before leaving the house. He was still wearing his bloodstained coat and shoes when questioned, having violated Rules for Murderers No. 1 by not destroying them immediately. However, he couldn't have done so in any case since he had neglected to bring an extra suit to his hotel. Nor had he disposed of his .32-caliber revolver, found in a drawer at his pharmacy.

When Irving went to trial, he hired two high-priced lawyers with his inheritance money, in essence forcing his mother to pay for the defense of the son who murdered her. First, he had to cook up some legitimate reason for being in Detroit on the night of January 24, since it was obvious that he had not attended a funeral as claimed. He couldn't devise one, so he invented an *illegitimate* reason, perhaps thinking it harder to disprove: Irving said he ventured to the city to meet a floozy named Trixie. She stood him up, so he went to the Gratiot Avenue brothel where she worked. According to Latimer, one of her coworkers said Trixie had boarded the 10:10 train. He looked for her at the station, thought he saw her in the last car, paid the porter his fare, and climbed on. He rode all the way to Ypsilanti before realizing Trixie wasn't aboard, so he got off at the station and chose to return to Detroit. But then he thought, hey, why not just go home on the next train to Jackson? He arrived there at 1:08 a.m. and slept in the spare room in his store so as not to wake his dear mother. But, dash it, he remembered that he had left his suitcase back at the Griswold. So he had to take an early morning train back to Detroit to retrieve his items, rather than have someone there simply ship them by express.

The reader will note that this masterpiece of storytelling was calculated carefully to explain away his reason for going to Detroit, the witnesses who saw him at various places, his renting a room at the Griswold and then being absent from it, his well-documented train travels, and why he didn't sleep at his mother's mansion when he returned to Jackson in the middle of the night. The jury didn't believe a syllable of it.

The prosecutors, on the other hand, listed all the aforementioned clumsy errors Irving made in his crime, all of which pointed to him, and mentioned a few extra ones besides. The reader will recall that he thought it smart to make an ostentatious call to a friend in Detroit from the sheriff's office so he would have a witness to the call. Instead, he had to explain why he went somewhere else to perform this task when he had a phone in his pharmacy. He had no reasonable excuse for his bitten thumb. He couldn't account for why he had cuff links but no cuffs when he was arrested. The Trixie he allegedly went to Detroit to meet was never found.

It took the jury all of twenty minutes to find Irving Latimer guilty. Michigan had no death penalty and thus had not stretched a neck since 1830, seven years before it officially became a state, so Irving was sentenced to serve a life sentence in the state prison—right there in his hometown of Jackson, on Mechanic Street.

Irving seemed a model prisoner, just as he formerly seemed a model son. Because he had been a pharmacist, he became head of the prison dispensary. However, despite all evidence to the contrary, he still fancied himself the master criminal. On the night of March 26, 1893, he took advantage of his captors' trust by planning another crime—jail breaking—which he carried out with his customary level of competence. He was allowed out of his cell to get his two guards, who considered him a friend, a nauseating snack of sardines and lemonade. Irving made a bad meal worse by adding prussic acid (hydrogen cyanide) and opium (or perhaps nitroglycerine). He swore later that he merely intended to make his guards unconscious, not kill them, but one died. It could be argued that Michigan's failure to hang this man for the cruel, premeditated murder of his mother resulted in the death of another human.

Irving fled, but, fortunately for society, he was as inept at hiding as he was at murder and pharmacology. He was recaptured at Jerome three days later and returned to prison. He was so thoroughly chilled in his thin prison uniform that he seemed relieved to be caught.

As years melted into decades, he became something of a prison celebrity, giving occasional interviews and corresponding with reformers and politicians. He sounded downright snobbish about what he deemed the low quality of modern prisoners: "We used to have train bandits, bank robbers, safe blowers—all fairly intelligent men . . . Now what do we have? A mob of ignorant, half-educated boys . . . who think they know it all."

His cell was decorated with plants, books, and a typewriter that he kept warm by writing ceaseless appeals for a pardon. Penal authorities regained their trust in the elderly Irving despite his having killed a guard, and he was again allowed to be a prison trusty. He gadded about town with the warden and went to the movies. In 1929, he noted that he had spent forty years behind bars.

A new prison was constructed on Cooper Street in 1934, and all the prisoners were sent there except Irving, who said he couldn't bear to leave his old home. He was permitted to remain as a watchman, making him the only prisoner there. Not long afterward, the governor pardoned Irving. As of May 11, 1935, he was a free man again after forty-six years. He was sixty-nine years old and, of course, completely unequipped to deal with a world he had not been part of since 1889, a nineteenth-century man thrust abruptly into the twentieth to fend for himself. He might have been better off without that pardon he had so badly wanted.

He made a precarious living doing odd jobs and getting handouts in bread lines—quite a step down, even from prison life. In 1940, he was arrested for vagrancy and sent to Eloise State Hospital for the poor, where he died on August 29, 1945, surrounded by health-care professionals, protected from murderers, and proclaiming his innocence right to the very end to anyone who would listen.

Perfect murders are common in fiction; in real life, not quite so much.

The Right to a Speedy Trial

The Sixth Amendment to the Constitution promises: "In all criminal prosecutions, the accused shall enjoy the right to a speedy and public trial." Perhaps *enjoy* isn't quite the correct word, but, depending on many factors, such as jurisdiction, the heinousness of the crime, the social prominence of the defendant, the amount of evidence, and whether or not the proceedings become a media circus, a murder trial might last anywhere from a few days to several months.

In the case of an especially loathsome murder, defense attorneys find it advantageous to delay the start of a trial and, once it begins, to drag the proceedings out as long as possible. With the passing of time, the initial excitement cools down, and witnesses' memories fade. Thus, their clients are more likely to get a generous verdict. A possible danger of this strategy is that criminals don't take punishment seriously, and it encourages further depredations, as observed by Solomon long ago: "When the sentence for a crime is not quickly carried out, people's hearts are filled with schemes to do wrong" (Ecclesiastes 8:11). In the Michigan of yesteryear, however, they took the Founding Fathers' word about *speedy* trials seriously, as illustrated by several examples from the state's history.

Every parent's worst nightmare came true for Mabel S. of Mount Morris, near Flint, Michigan, on January 12, 1928. She stood on the porch awaiting her five-year-old daughter, Dorothy, who was walking home from kindergarten. When Dorothy was only a block away, an old sedan pulled up alongside her. A stranger got out, threw the child in the car, and sped away, as Mabel watched. Mabel ran to the nearest police station. Despite an immediate all-points bulletin, the kidnapper was not caught.

The police broadcast Mabel's descriptions of the man and his car. Before evening, Archie Bacon informed authorities that a matching car got stuck in the mud near his farm, three miles from Dorothy's home. The driver got out, carried a bundle to a creek, and returned to his car two hours later without it. Bacon unwittingly helped the stranger extricate his car from the mud. The stranger was middle-aged, light complexioned, and wore a light suit and dark overcoat. Bacon's description of both man and auto matched the distraught mother's in every detail.

Detectives found Dorothy's dissected body in the creek near Bacon's farm. The torso was trapped under the frozen water, but part of the body was missing. The child's clothing was scattered through the forest.

The Michigan State Police established a cordon around the territory, hoping to catch that old Dodge sedan, but without luck. Luck was exactly what they needed: a check with a nearby mental institution revealed that no one had escaped in three weeks, and none of the inmates resembled the kidnapper. They also found that more than five hundred psychopathic offenders were registered in Detroit alone, all wandering free as the afternoon breeze while awaiting admittance to the state's overcrowded insane asylums. Some were staying with relatives or guardians, at least, but it was anyone's guess where others were. A number of promising suspects were arrested, interrogated, and freed due to confirmed alibis or lack of evidence.

Suspicious men were arrested or surveilled in Detroit, Flint, Bay City, and Lapeer—even a doctor in Waverly, New York, merely because someone thought he resembled the abductor and had visited Detroit recently. Citizens formed vigilance groups and so abused their power that authorities decided it was wiser not to reveal further clues. For example, men who worked at an auto factory with Dorothy's father were so incensed by a remark made by a coworker as he discussed the case that they gave him a world-class thumping. Amateur detectives, well intended or not, mostly got in the professionals' way and made their job harder. Curiosity seekers blocked the muddy road at Bacon's farm with their cars and scoured the creek where Dorothy's body was found, creating innumerable distracting shoeprints.

On January 15, three army airplanes soared over the region in search of the Dodge sedan. So many persons came to the funeral parlor to see Dorothy's body—fifteen thousand by one estimate—that they had to be trooped through the establishment in double columns.

The mystery ended on January 16. The abductor and killer wasn't a free-range lunatic or a professional kidnapper. He was Adolph Hotelling, a carpenter who lived at Owosso in Shiawassee County, thirty miles from Mount Morris. (Some later sources refer to him as Reverend Hotelling, probably because it makes a more shocking and, therefore, better story, but it appears he was simply a church deacon who had just been named an elder.) He seemed compelled to draw suspicion to himself. He had boasted to carpenters building a schoolhouse in Flushing that once the reward for Dorothy S.'s killer got large enough, boy, could *he* tell the authorities a story! He also abruptly painted his old sedan and kept it in his garage as though wary of taking it on the road.

Hotelling was arrested in Owosso. He tried to cut his throat with a pocketknife on the way to police HQ. Nothing suspicious about that! Archie Bacon was brought in and, without hesitation, identified him as the man he had aided, after which Hotelling confessed. He had been driving through Mount Morris looking for work when he saw Dorothy and instantaneously got the urge to abduct her. "I don't know what came over me," he said repeatedly.

When he got stuck in the mud a few minutes after the kidnapping, he put Dorothy in a sack and carried her to the creek. There he stabbed her twice. He mutilated the body postmortem and had been troubled by horrifying nightmares ever since.

Police took the prisoner to Flint, thinking the change of location might protect him from lynch mobs. It didn't help a bit. The state of Michigan had never had a death penalty, but ten thousand persons gathered outside the prison, determined to enact the roughest of rough justice if they could only get their hands on Hotelling. Police fought the crowd in hand-to-hand combat and threw canisters of tear gas. Someone tossed a bomb into the police station, and clouds of the gas drifted inside. A rioter fired a shot at Hotelling's guards; idlers threw rocks at the jail and smashed four civilians' cars. The National Guard arrived and convinced the mob to disperse. Hotelling was hustled off to Lansing, and there was no more trouble—except for newsboys, who were trying to make a living selling papers. The issues declaring that the killer had been taken from the city were seized from their hands and shredded by angry persons who felt they had to destroy *something*.

That's when Hotelling's constitutional right to a speedy trial kicked in. He agreed to plead guilty; his conscience would not permit him to do otherwise. His trial began on January 18 and ended a half hour later. Only three witnesses were called, as only three were necessary. Hotelling pled guilty as promised. There was nothing for attorneys to debate.

The judge remarked, "The details as shown by this confession and the proof almost convince me we should have capital punishment in this state," and sentenced Hotelling to the maximum penalty: life imprisonment in solitary confinement, with hard labor, at the prison at Marquette. The prisoner got additional punishment of an extralegal, unexpected sort: as he was brought into the courtroom, Dorothy S.'s father sprang out of an anteroom and landed a blow in Hotelling's face with a satisfying splat.

Only a week after he murdered a child, Adolph Hotelling was in his cell in the cold, cold Upper Peninsula. There he died in 1955.

A neighbor saw Evelyn S., described as "a pretty 17-year-old farm girl," walking on the road from Free Soil through a swamp at about 10:30 p.m. on July 30, 1932. Evelyn was heading for home a half mile away. Another neighbor heard a scream issuing from the swamp thirty minutes later. The only clues to her disappearance were tire tracks, prints from a woman's shoe, a few blond hairs caught on a twig, and signs of a struggle. On August 3, reclusive farmer Francis Nash, who sported fresh scratches on his face and neck, rushed to the police station at Manistee and admitted to murdering Evelyn—as well he might, since a few hours before, her body had been found buried in the basement of a vacant summer cottage near his home. He was in mortal terror of encountering a lynch mob.

Nash confessed that he had propositioned Evelyn—who was half his age and at least six inches taller than he—that night, for what location could be more romantic than a lonely road leading through a spooky swamp in the dead of night? She slapped him. In a fury, he struck her in the head with his fist and knocked her out or killed her instantly, he wasn't sure which. He hurried home, got a rope, and tied her hands behind her back. He also secured a line around her throat as a precaution in case she revived. He "borrowed" some nearby farm equipment and used it to drag Evelyn away to the cottage. In the cellar, he listened for her breathing— she didn't seem to be. Any pulse? Nope, don't think so! He got a shovel and buried her. The coroner later determined that she had been strangled.

Nash sure was nervous when he got home, though. He was so upset, he said, that he actually lost a half hour's sleep over it. A few days later, the body was found, and he thought he should "clear my conscience and have it all over with," as he put it. The feisty mob that was gathering in Manistee also influenced his decision.

He was rushed to Traverse City under police protection to have his day in court, which was *literally* a day in court. On August 4, he was examined, arraigned, and sentenced to life in Marquette at hard labor. Snappy justice was done in less than twelve hours.

On April 4, 1933, Carl B. had a quarrel with his wife, Mattie Sue, in their Grand Rapids home and left in a huff. He returned two days later, hoping for a reconciliation. Instead, he found Mattie Sue strangled in her bed and their two children dead; Carl Jr. had been strangled and placed in a car, and little Thalbert asphyxiated when someone left the gas jet on in the kitchen. Carl suspected that "someone" was boarder Henry Bedford, a school principal, who was stretched out across two chairs in the kitchen and unconscious. It appeared that he murdered the family and then tried to commit suicide via gas. Bedford was taken to the hospital, where he said he had *no idea* what happened but thought perhaps some fiend had drugged him and placed him in the gas-filled kitchen to frame him. Carl had long suspected Bedford of having an affair with his wife, which detectives found a more intellectually satisfying explanation for the massacre than Bedford's.

Before the day was over, Henry Bedford admitted the painfully obvious. He received a life sentence of hard labor on April 7, less than twenty-four hours after murdering Mattie Sue and the children.

William Mahler of Kalamazoo used a hatchet to express his disagreement with Charles G., who died on January 10, 1935. Within eight hours, Mahler was arrested, charged with murder, and sentenced to life in solitary at Jackson Prison.

William Hanson's girlfriend, Marguerite K., had a job in a Ludington hospital. She said she wanted to break up, so he visited her at work with a shotgun hidden under his coat. He killed her in the X-ray room and destroyed a machine with a stray shot. He pled guilty at a special nighttime court session and got a life sentence. The entire drama—murder, arrest, sentencing, and destruction of hospital property—occurred in one eventful day, November 14, 1935.

George Blank of Ithaca tried to be *subtle*. On January 5, 1936, he killed his pregnant wife with chloroform and then set the house on fire. He thought everyone would believe she died in the blaze, and he could collect the insurance. Medical examiners found no soot in her lungs, proving she had ceased breathing before the fire started. Three hours after Blank confessed on February 26, he was sentenced to life in prison.

Perhaps these guys played "What a Difference a Day Makes" on their harmonicas while serving time.

Crazy Jealous

Elizabeth G., twenty-five years old, was the daughter of a dean at Michigan State College in East Lansing. She planned to be married on December 12, 1936. On December 8, she and her lifelong friend Hope M. were addressing wedding invitations. The bridal shower was scheduled for that night, and Hope had been chosen to host it.

Without warning, Hope produced a pistol and shot her friend five times near the heart. "I did it on an impulse and don't know why." Hope shrugged. "For about a year, I've frequently had an impulse to kill." She added that she had wanted to see a psychiatrist, but "nobody took me seriously."

Everybody certainly took her seriously now. A state police medical adviser examined Hope and said she had dementia praecox, a now obsolete term (replaced by *schizophrenia*) that referred to a psychological disturbance that began in young adulthood and grew steadily worse with age.

Not all the experts agreed with his diagnosis. The circuit court named another psychiatrist to head a sanity commission, and, after examining Hope for two days, he opined that she was "putting on an act in some ways." In any case, she had deep-seated problems; a week before she killed her best friend, Hope had attempted suicide via sleeping pills, and an inspection of her cell revealed a sharpened nail file.

It may well be that the second psychiatrist was right. Hope hanged herself in her jail cell, using her pajamas as a noose, on December 15, leaving a note asking "the world [to] forgive me for what I did in a jealous mood."

She left other messages hinting strongly that her motive wasn't insanity but rather jealousy because her friend was about to be married. Her cell contained a magazine in which Hope had written despondent thoughts beside an advertisement depicting a married couple: "I merely thought Bess was going to have something I never would have. I couldn't stand the fact of being the only one left." Elizabeth's pending marriage meant that Hope would have been the only bachelorette remaining in their social circle.

One of the two psychiatrists who examined Hope said that she suffered from an inferiority complex. It seems an inadequate explanation, but it's probably the only one we will ever have. Hope's body was cremated and the ashes thrown to the winds at her favorite vacation spot, Sleeping Bear Point in Leelanau County.

Blood Bank, or: The Seldom-Used "I Soiled My Trousers" Defense

Herbert Field, who hailed from Lewiston, Maine, came to Manistee first. Later, George Vanderpool of New York and his wife settled in the town. Vanderpool had some capital saved and was interested in starting a business. He founded the town's first bank in December 1868, in time to profit from a post–Civil War boom in the lumber industry.

Vanderpool invested $2,500 in the bank with contributions from friends in Muskegon who were impressed by his business skills and solid reputation. Field became a copartner in February 1869 after investing $7,000 from a Manistee "acquaintance," fifty-five-year-old Rachel Hill. But let us eschew limp euphemisms; it appears that Field and Hill, who lived in the same house and called themselves aunt and nephew, were neither related nor mere acquaintances. All indications are that Field was a kept man—the live-in lover of a much older, much wealthier woman. At a certain future trial concerning an unpleasant upcoming event, she testified that she "adopted" Field in 1868.

Altogether, Vanderpool and Field had $9,500. In modern currency, that would amount to at least $154,000, so the firm was off to a solid start. Their bank was in a two-story building on a riverbank, sharing space with a dentist, a lawyer, and a shoemaker. Their financial institution was cozy and unpretentious: an oblong room twelve by fifty feet with a teller's counter. There was an office behind a curtain on a wire. A spittoon humbly awaited customers' expectorations. The only guard to speak of was Field's dog.

Within a year, the establishment had turned a profit of $3,000—in modern currency, over $50,000. Field offered to buy out Vanderpool's share in the bank. Vanderpool turned down his offer, and the partnership continued.

On the surface, the two young men remained best friends. Nevertheless, did Vanderpool secretly resent Field's attempt to become sole proprietor? Subsequent events lead one to wonder.

When Vanderpool went on vacation in Wisconsin in July and August 1869, Field began drawing out his $7,000 investment—one should properly say Rachel Hill's investment—a little at a time in small sums. He didn't take all of it, but when Vanderpool returned, he found that the books were not balanced, and the bank was missing at least $1,700. Field reassured his partner that the money was around there *somewhere*. In fact, he had been stashing it in a vault at the local drugstore.

The bankers still seemed on friendly terms. Vanderpool said he had changed his mind, and if Field wanted to run the business by himself, that was fine with him. On September 4, they signed papers officially dissolving their partnership.

The next day, Vanderpool asked Field if he would mind coming to the bank to discuss business. It was Sunday, so the bank was closed, and there would be no customers to disrupt their discussion—and, perhaps, something sinister that Vanderpool had planned. Field disappeared from town after this meeting.

Rachel Hill was concerned when Field did not come home on Sunday night. On Monday morning, she sent a message to Vanderpool, who was cleaning the bank with great vim and industry. He responded that Field had probably just gone off on a little jaunt and would return soon. But when he had not returned by Tuesday, the authorities asked his erstwhile partner to describe their last meeting.

To paraphrase Vanderpool's story:

Well, we met at the bank a little after 10:00 a.m. on Sunday. Field and I realized we had forgotten to finalize some business from the day before. We wrote final receipts for each other, but we needed witnesses. We went to the shoe store in our building and had A. A. Smith and William Ramsdell sign the papers. Then we went back to the bank. I realized the place needed cleaning, and what better time than when no customers were around? As I cleaned the spittoon, Field played roughly with my dog, tossing it in the air. I remonstrated gently, but he persisted. Suddenly there was a knock at the door—it was Mr. Ramsdell from the shoe shop, ordering us to stop being so noisy on a Sunday. We didn't dare open the door. Ramsdell rattled the knob, found the door locked, and went away. We were quiet for a while, and then Field indulged in more dog flinging. But he dropped the canine. It ran all around the room and knocked over the furniture as we chased it. And then—well, it's embarrassing to admit it, sirs, but after all of this activity, I came down with an abrupt attack of the summer complaint! [The genteel, old-fashioned term for diarrhea, that is.] I made a perfect ruination of my vest and pants. But fortune, which had frowned on me in the form of soiled breeches, smiled again. My friend Field just happened to have a spare pair of trousers and a vest in an office trunk. I put my own feculent clothes in the furnace but didn't burn them quite yet. Then, wearing Herbert Field's spare garments, I left with my dog. Last time I saw my dear friend Herb, he was stretched out on a couch in the bank, reading and saying that he had letters to write.

The bank must have been untidy indeed, since Vanderpool returned first thing on Monday morning to finish cleaning. His tasks included prying up the secured carpet, scrubbing the floor—but how could it have gotten dirty if the carpet had covered it?—and sloshing pails of water around. Fortunately for Vanderpool, the floor was not level, and the water ran out the back door and into the river below. Vanderpool cut the carpet that lay under heavy objects such as the desk, stove, and safe, and also sliced off a piece that he said his watchdog had stained. He burned the sullied carpet and his befouled pants and vest in the stove.

Bookkeepers audited the bank's books on September 8. They found two entries documenting payments from Vanderpool to Field for $1,400 and $1,700. Upon closer inspection, they found that the sums were originally $400 and $700. As the auditors did their stuff, officers discovered the remains of the carpet and clothing in the stove and also proof that Vanderpool had not cleaned the bank as well as he thought: blood spots were on the pieces of carpet he had not burned, and more had leaked through the floorboards.

In short order, the suspect was escorted to a cell. With Herbert Field missing and Vanderpool in jail, Manistee was utterly bereft of bankers.

On September 17, a weighted body in the Manistee River washed ashore at Frankfort. A letter addressed to "Herbert F." was found on the corpse. In addition, Field's dentist identified him. Fingerprint identification was unknown in 1869, but even then, a positive match was possible by inspecting teeth. An autopsy revealed two fearsome wounds, one on the back of the head and one on top, the angles suggesting that the attacker struck him from behind. The weapon was possibly a hatchet known to have been kept in the bank.

As though there were not enough suspicious circumstances against the dapper young banker, the sheriff found gold coins Vanderpool hid in his woodshed in the interval between Field's disappearance and Vanderpool's arrest. Then he forged a letter by two sailors confessing to the murder. Jailhouse personnel found it before he could smuggle it out. These events did little to burnish Vanderpool's standing in the community. He explained that he was innocent but had written the phony letter in a desperate bid at freedom. Whatever his financial acumen might have been, he wasn't exactly a criminal mastermind.

After a brief delay, Vanderpool's trial began in Manistee on February 1, 1870. He was fortunate not to have been lynched before the proceedings commenced, such was his newfound unpopularity. He retold the improbable yarn about his last meeting with Field; investigators and the prosecution noticed—you probably did too—that the banker's story seemed carefully contrived to explain away a number of fishy circumstances: the racket issuing from the bank when it was closed, the establishment's freshly scrubbed appearance, Vanderpool's missing clothes, the newly missing carpet pieces, and the equally missing Field.

A scientist, Dr. Duffield, testified that the blood spots found in the bank were human. The defense's expert witness, Dr. Douglass, conceded that the stains were blood, all right, but declared that they might be from an animal. (Nevertheless, was it not suspicious timing that Vanderpool waited until the same day his partner went missing to cut holes in the carpet and try to scrub the stains away?)

Asked to explain this sanguinary evidence, Vanderpool offered criminology's oldest, lamest excuse for blood's presence where it should not be: "I have nosebleeds," he said. At least he showed creativity when he said that his business partner Field *also* was plagued with the same affliction—and the watchdog, too!

Three defense witnesses claimed they had seen Field alive hours after he was allegedly killed in the bank, but under cross-examination, all admitted they might be mistaken.

The defense also pointed out that Vanderpool had gone door-to-door through Manistee on the day of the murder, seeking medicine he could not buy since the drugstore was closed on Sunday. However, he had made these ostentatious appearances on Sunday *afternoon*, not in the morning. It is evident that he was trying, in his usual ham-fisted fashion, to establish an alibi. The defense contended that it would have been foolish for Vanderpool to have walked around town on that fateful Sunday wearing his victim's pants; clearly, they took his "summer complaint" story seriously.

Vanderpool's attorneys additionally claimed that it would have been impossible for Field's weighted body to have drifted the twenty-eight miles from Manistee to Frankfort. However, the annals of crime are full of examples of weighted bodies that became unmoored and floated considerable distances, usually due to increased buoyancy caused by decomposition's gases. They argued, too, that not enough blood had been found at the bank to warrant an assumption of murder. They overlooked that Vanderpool had cleaned up *some* of it.

After deliberating only six hours, the jury decided that the defense arguments were—well, a big load of summer complaint. They found Vanderpool guilty of first-degree murder. Several months later, the *New York Times* questioned the verdict in an editorial that included the old, seemingly indestructible logical error of assuming that "purely circumstantial evidence" is synonymous with faulty or weak evidence. Vanderpool got a life sentence in Jackson Prison—the same jail that would later be home to Robert Irving Latimer, bungling matricide.

According to the *Times*, many Michiganders agitated for a retrial, claiming that Vanderpool did not get an impartial jury in Manistee, an assertion that may well have been true considering that there had been talk of lynching him there. Citizens in Muskegon and Pontiac contributed to a fund on the prisoner's behalf. Vanderpool's attorneys at his second trial successfully requested a change of venue.

The new trial, which began in Kalamazoo on October 23, 1870, concluded with a hung jury on November 21. "There was great rejoicing among the ladies" in Kalamazoo, said a local paper, "some of whom, on meeting the jurors in favor of acquittal on the sidewalks, manifested their decided satisfaction and approbation by giving them a hearty kiss." *That* was a good day to be a Vanderpool juror! Nevertheless, the *Times* threw a bucket of historically accurate, typhoid–germ laden, ice-cold well water on the supporters' joy by pointing out that Vanderpool had not been found legally innocent and, by necessity, would have to be tried again.

Thus far, Vanderpool's two trials had cost Michigan taxpayers $25,000 in 1870 dollars, which translates to nearly a half-million dollars in modern currency. The *Detroit Tribune* remarked, "The policy of the defense seems to have been to utterly confuse the case by such a mass of testimony, involving details innumerable, and so many contradictions, that the agreement of any twelve men in regard to it would be impossible. If this was the design, it has succeeded completely."

The third trial began in Hastings, Barry County, on August 8, 1871. The third time was the charm. The jury found him not guilty, and Vanderpool was free as an American robin (Michigan's state bird, whose scientific name is richly comic in the context of Vanderpool's defense: *Turdus migratorius*). In three steps, he had gone from life in prison to a hung jury to an acquittal. According to author Larry Wakefield, "It is said that the verdict so angered the people of Manistee that they refused to reimburse Barry County for court costs, and the matter was unsettled for years."

As Vanderpool's defense attorneys prepared to leave Hastings, Herbert Field's mother stepped forth and cursed them for all she was worth: "The blood of my son is in Michigan, and will yet be avenged upon Vanderpool and his defenders! You will have your share of the punishment, and I shall meet you at the judgment!"

Field's so-called "aunt," Rachel Hill, remained in Manistee. The brokenhearted recluse committed suicide by morphine overdose in the winter of 1873.

Vanderpool was free. However, "free" does not necessarily mean "happy." He spent the rest of his life as an impoverished itinerant shoe salesman, which some might contend is a fate worse than hanging.

Bonus for readers who might be troubled by the summer complaint—a home remedy I gleaned from an 1848 newspaper! Just mix one part sulfuric acid (*not* diluted) with seven parts acidic essence of lemon (not lemon oil), and then drink it as you would lemonade. The Boston physician who recommended this cure called it, without irony, a "pleasant remedy" and assured that if taken daily with only gruel as food, it would cure not only diarrhea but also flatulence, nausea, and vomiting and would work miracles for the bowels—at the cost, one surmises, of only the esophagus, the stomach lining, and a few teeth.

Mrs. Tabor's Many Contradictions

The story began when Maud Tabor, daughter of the late Lester Tabor and his widow, Sarah, disappeared in 1916. She left Lawton without a word and without even sending postcards to her friends. Mrs. Tabor told some people that Maud had gone to Salt Lake City, Utah, to follow a teaching career; she told others that Maud was in Colorado looking after mining property. It wouldn't be the only time Mrs. Tabor displayed a talent for inconsistency. Finally, when gossip reached an intolerable crescendo, Mrs. Tabor told inquirers that Maud died out west. The first half of her statement was true.

Rumormongers, temporarily content, found a new reason to go on living near the end of 1919. Mrs. Tabor and her son Walter left the house, which, by then, was occupied by her other daughter, Florence Critchlow, a graduate of Northwestern and author of mostly unpublished magazine articles, poems, plays, and mystery novels. Little did she know that she was about to launch a genuine mystery that no fictioneer would dare invent.

On November 30, Florence wanted firewood to take the edge off the mansion's chill. She remembered a convenient pile of shingles in the basement. Rummaging around in the stack, she felt something fleshy. It was a stockinged human foot poking through a hole in a trunk—ironically, a hope chest. She excavated the box, steeled her nerves, opened it, and found the real-life counterpart of Mrs. Bates in the movie *Psycho*.

The remains were shriveled, mummified, unnaturally twisted to fit in the chest, and resembled the missing Maud Tabor. She wore silk stockings and a bridal gown, complete with veil and orange blossoms. Perhaps significantly, at the time of death she had been pregnant—at the point of childbirth, in fact.

Dr. Warthin, the dean of the University of Michigan's pathology department, believed that the thirty-five-year-old had died during an abortion. Florence had long been suspicious of one of Maud's suitors, Joseph Virgo, who was previously married to women named Lena, Sadie, and Blanche, and advised police to look into him. They found Virgo in South Bend, Indiana. As a witness at the coroner's inquest on December 2, he positively identified the corpse as Maud. Virgo knew what he was talking about when it came to scrutinizing the dead, as he was a former undertaker.

Adding to the strangeness, Maud's body had been embalmed. The question of who preserved it was never answered, but ex-mortician Virgo thought perhaps the Tabors had done it to incriminate him. He muttered, "They did it to throw suspicion on me. That certainly puts me in a bad light."

The case was bizarre *enough*; however, as the late, great professional shill Billy Mays used to say, "But wait, there's more!" When sister Florence Critchlow took the stand, she refused to admit to finding the body, refused to admit the corpse was Maud, and would not say how long she had known of the body's presence in the cellar. In fact, she refused to say anything at all.

Notable by their absence at the inquest were the dead woman's mother, Sarah Tabor, and brother, Walter. The coroner wanted to ask them questions, though gingerly and with great solicitude, since Mrs. Tabor was reportedly eighty years old. (She was actually around seventy-three, but she did not correct the press or police as to her true age, perhaps thinking that the older she seemed, the more sympathetic she would be.)

However, he didn't get to ask. Walter was allegedly in South Bend—in fact, he had recently traveled to Chicago with Virgo, so they must have remained on good terms—and no one knew the whereabouts of the mother.

A few days later, elderly Mrs. Tabor and Walter were traced to Yreka, California. She told police there that the cadaverous-looking Virgo wasn't merely a boyfriend of Maud's—he was once Mrs. Tabor's employee and married Maud on September 18, 1915. They separated soon afterward, asserted Mrs. Tabor, because he demanded money from the wealthy family he had joined. She said the couple parted ways after only two days, but they did not officially divorce. For his part, Virgo denied having been both Maud's husband and the father of her child. He was fibbing about the first part, at least, since a prosecutor later presented the marriage license. Virgo also claimed that he had had no contact with Maud after they separated, and her death came as news to him, since Mrs. Tabor had told him—as she had told everyone else—that Maud was alive and out west.

After Mrs. Tabor and Walter were extradited to Michigan, Lawton police asked about the strange artifact in her cellar. Her attitude was something along the lines of "What body in the basement? Oh, *that* body in the basement!" Her explanation, or rather her first one, was that there had been no abortion. Instead, Maud took chloroform for an ear ailment (or asthma—the story changed later, as did so many of Mrs. Tabor's stories). On May 1, 1916, she overdosed accidentally and died at home. Mrs. Tabor further explained that she and her daughter made a solemn pact to share the same grave, so, of course, she had to keep Maud above ground until her own time came—see? It was all just a silly misunderstanding! She confessed that she *may* have misled people into thinking Maud was still alive and out west. Why, she had even waited five months to tell Walter that his sister was dead! Later, perhaps realizing how peculiar this sounded to normals, she reduced the time to two days.

For some reason, officials found her story neither intellectually satisfying nor plausible. The coroner determined that Maud died from either a botched abortion or an overdose of chloroform, so on December 11, Mrs. Tabor, Walter Tabor, and Maud's estranged husband, Joseph Virgo, were charged with murder. However, so much confusion surrounded Maud's demise that on December 20, prosecuting attorney R. H. Adams said he was unsure whether to hold a trial.

Mrs. Tabor—who, at first, insisted there had been no abortion—now insisted there *had* been one, after all, and Joseph Virgo had performed it in a deserted farmhouse, where he kept Maud for three days, and then brought her home to die. Mrs. Tabor even signed an official statement accusing him. It was "in direct contradiction to the story told by the aged woman at the inquest," observed the *New York Times*. "It is not true, not a word of it," snorted Virgo. He was arraigned for murder on December 23.

However, on January 15, 1920, Walter told a deputy sheriff, in confidence, that Maud had been murdered, and his mother alone was guilty. He retracted his statement the next day. Later, Walter charged that the deputy tricked him into thinking he was one of his mother's attorneys.

The prosecution tacitly admitted their case against Joseph Virgo was weak when they reduced the charge from murder to manslaughter. On

January 16, he was set free. In the end, only Sarah Tabor went on trial for Maud's death. She was released on her own recognizance on April 3, which suggests that no one considered her much of a threat to society.

As the months passed, the state reduced charges against Mrs. Tabor from murder to manslaughter and delayed the trial until October. When that time came, a reporter noted that the proceedings were a national sensation due to the defendant's high standing in her community and "the unusual features of the case." The prosecution, probably feeling it had a losing hand, asked that charges be dismissed. The judge denied the request.

The trial was a public embarrassment for the proud Mrs. Tabor. As the *New York Times* remarked years later, in Lawton she "in other days . . . had been leader in the social life and lady bountiful to the village poor." When she saw the crowd at her trial, she remarked, "They have come to my funeral."

On February 4, 1921, the matriarch sat before a packed court and again told the story of Maud's untimely death and overdue burial. Many crucial details were embellished or notably different. In previous testimony, Mrs. Tabor said that her daughter's death by overdose was an accident; this time it seemed that Maud knew her end was near: "Maud had a premonition of her fate. The day before she died, she felt that the end would come soon. She had a horror of being buried out in the cemetery with Virgo's other wives, and taking my hand she cried over and over again, while tears streamed down her cheeks, 'You won't let them take me out there, will you, mother? You won't ever let them take me away from you?' I spent the greater part of the last night with Maud in her room holding her hand and assuring her I would obey her request."

Evidently, Mrs. Tabor quaintly interpreted the phrase "You won't ever let them take me away from you" to mean "Keep my body in the cellar." Maud's "having a premonition of her impending death" does not quite square with an overdose of chloroform, somehow, unless Mrs. Tabor was implying that Maud had committed suicide. Previously, Mrs. Tabor denied that Maud had an abortion; later, she said Maud died when Virgo forced her to have one; now, she maintained that an overdose killed Maud while she gave birth: "Parturition [childbirth, that is] had only begun and Maud was suffering terribly from asthma. At times, the suffering became so great she would scream out, and she kept inhaling more and more of the chloroform. One time when I left the room for a few minutes she must have taken more of the fluid than she knew, for when I returned there was only a little left and a great deal was scattered over the bed clothing and the floor. The fumes, together with what she had taken, overcame her and her body soon became rigid."

So Maud overdosed on chloroform—but to relieve an earache? Or asthma? Or birth pains? Or to commit suicide? At various times, Mrs. Tabor suggested all of these explanations.

Although Maud was married when she died, Mrs. Tabor really didn't want the fact that she had died in childbirth to become known:

> I left her body lying on the bed for about a day. I don't remember just how long. I was numb with terror and grief. Had Maud's baby been born, I would have welcomed it as the happiest event in my life. I did what I believed was best for her. She had had a great deal of trouble with her husband and we dreaded the publicity if the facts became known. The more I reflected on it, the more I became convinced I ought to bury the body in the basement. Maud always had a perfect horror of the conventional funeral, the fuss, the ostentation, the hollow mockery, and all that. So I placed the body in the hope chest, and lowered it into the basement myself by means of ropes held around the door posts.

Mrs. Tabor explained further that it had been her idea to deck out the corpse in a bridal outfit and that she had waited a *whole week* before putting Maud in the cellar. Had she also performed an amateur embalming? She didn't say, but she did contradict herself yet again: at the inquest she claimed that Joseph Virgo performed an abortion on Maud just before she died, but now she said he was not present at the death scene.

The prosecutor asked, "Why did you bury her there? Why so secretly?"

Mrs. Tabor offered four reasons that made sense to her, if to no one else: "First, I was afraid to stay home alone if it were known Maud was dead. Second, if that were known, certain persons might have harmed me. Third, if Virgo knew about her death he might have taken her body from me. Fourth, because of the agreement we had made between us that both were to be buried in the same grave."

She did not explain whom she thought might have "harmed her" if word of Maud's death got out. Perhaps these conflicting details confused jurors—or perhaps they sympathized with Mrs. Tabor in her old age—but, in any case, they could not agree. The judge dismissed the manslaughter charge on May 23. The simplest explanation is possibly the best one: Maud, separated from her husband, died in childbirth, and the grieving mother stashed her body in the cellar to spare the family public embarrassment. If so, it really didn't work out the way she planned.

Mrs. Tabor did not return home in triumph. The cost of going to trial wiped out her fortune. She left Lawton and moved to Lake County. Less than a year later, in March 1922, the press reported that the once-wealthy woman was penniless and living on public charity. Lake County authorities did not want to keep her as a charge and demanded that Van Buren County pay for her upkeep. Officials there voted to keep her in the Van Buren County Infirmary, also known as the county poorhouse, in perpetuity.

Daughter Florence, the largely unsuccessful writer who so many years before opened the trunk and came face-to-face with her three-years-dead sister, swallowed poison on the back porch of her cottage at Pine Lake in Olivet, Michigan, in March 1931. She had been dead three weeks before the discovery of her remains. Six months later, Mrs. Tabor died on September 14, 1931, at the Gourdneck Lake home of her son, Walter. This time the press gave her actual age, eighty-five.

If every story must have a moral, perhaps this one is: to avoid suspicion and a trial, give your dead a conventional burial.

3

ILL-TEMPERED ILLINOIS

Brockelhurst, the Proto-Starkweather

Twenty-year-old juvenile delinquent Charles Starkweather of Lincoln, Nebraska, became one of America's all-time most infamous killers when he went on a murder spree that took the lives of eleven people between the end of 1957 and the beginning of 1958, including the family of his fourteen-year-old girlfriend, Caril Ann Fugate. Starkweather terrorized the residents of Nebraska and Wyoming by keeping on the move, stealing cars to confuse law enforcement, and killing seemingly at random. Whether Fugate, who accompanied him, was a willing participant or a terrorized hostage has been hotly debated ever since. Starkweather and Fugate were captured on January 29, 1958. He went to the electric chair on June 25, 1959, placing part of the blame on Caril and allegedly wishing she could sit in his lap when the chair was turned on.

Perhaps Starkweather thought that his evil deeds were original. They weren't. Twenty years before, another killer's career resembled his in many details, only with a much lower body count.

While "Starkweather" is a perfect, ironically apt name for a mass murderer, the subject of our story had the less threatening name of Lester Brockelhurst. Like Starkweather, Brockelhurst had the itch to travel and kill. In 1937, the twenty-three-year-old Rockford native traveled through Illinois, Texas, and Arkansas, committing one murder in each state.

Like Starkweather, Brockelhurst brought his girlfriend along. She was eighteen-year-old Bernice F., also from Rockford. The term "serial killer" would not be coined for forty years, so newspapers had no idea what to call Brockelhurst. They settled on the droll phrase "crime tourist." As with Caril Ann Fugate, investigators could never decide Bernice's level of guilt.

Brockelhurst robbed and killed Rockford tailor Albin T. and a Fort Worth tavern owner, Jack G. The crime that brought his downfall occurred in Arkansas. On May 6, rich Lonoke County planter Victor G. picked up the hitchhiking lovers. Brockelhurst (and, for all we know, Bernice) rewarded his kindness by shooting him, throwing his body in a ditch, and stealing his car. The couple fled to Brewster, New York. When arrested there, Brockelhurst was wearing his victim's shirt and carrying a gun that was positively identified as the murder weapon.

The states of Illinois, Texas, and Arkansas petitioned Governor Lehman of New York to extradite Brockelhurst and Bernice. On May 17, 1937, Lehman announced that he would send the criminal couple to Arkansas, since it had a more solid case against them than either Texas or Illinois. Brockelhurst realized that Arkansas didn't fool around when it came to capital punishment and that his days were numbered—and not a very high number at that. Before leaving New York with the Lonoke County prosecutor, he asked, "How long will it be before I get the electric chair?"

"Six days at the least after your trial starts. Thirty days at the most, you'll get the chair," was this official's less-than-reassuring answer.

On May 19, a cooperative Brockelhurst was back in Arkansas. He showed the Lonoke County sheriff the spot where he shot Victor G.: "You'll find his spectacles in the weeds in that ditch. I threw them there after I shot him."

Like Starkweather, Brockelhurst went on a multistate killing jag and stole cars with his girlfriend. Like Starkweather, Brockelhurst was cold-bloodedly proud of his crimes. One marked difference between the two was that while Starkweather kept up a sneering, James Dean–like mask of studied arrogance, Brockelhurst fainted at inopportune moments. "He fainted several times on the train from New York," noted a press account, and he toppled over near the steps of the Lonoke County courthouse. A large but orderly crowd of curiosity seekers had congregated to look at him and Bernice; perhaps he mistook them for a lynch mob.

Let it be understood that the Arkansans weren't so eager to fry Lester's hide at the soonest opportunity. On June 10, a circuit judge had him committed to a mental hospital at Little Rock for observation. He must have had no skill in the fine art of faking insanity, since he was back in jail by June 21, where he tried to hang himself in his cell. He said he was "tired of waiting for the chair." Perhaps he was really annoyed by the summer heat; in those days before universal air conditioning, the temperature in his all-steel cell was 112 degrees.

Brockelhurst and Bernice asked permission to have a jailhouse wedding, but the sheriff refused. Bernice looked at her prospects for the future, found them bleak, and decided the wisest course was to testify against her former boyfriend. The day after his botched suicide attempt, the deputy prosecutor told reporters, "They are not friendly any more. He's got the idea that she is trying to make it hard for him." Considering that Brockelhurst was caught driving his victim's car, wearing his shirt, and carrying a gun conclusively tied to the murder, it's hard to understand how he expected Bernice to make his path easier.

On June 24, a Lonoke jury took twenty-two minutes to find Brockelhurst guilty of first-degree murder and recommend the electric chair. He fainted. So did his father. Officers carried an unconscious Brockelhurst to his cell.

Bernice went on trial next. Just as Caril Ann Fugate would do, she claimed none too convincingly that she participated in the crimes only because she was mortally afraid of her boyfriend. The jury, not wishing to execute an attractive teenage girl, acquitted her on June 25. She responded in a fashion not recommended to the reader. Instead of gratefully slinking out of town as quietly as possible, "The [family], who have been staying in a tourist camp here, were parading up and down the street tonight, apparently gloating over their victory," in the words of Lonoke's mayor. He pointed out to Bernice and her family that a crowd was gathering and that its members were unhappy with the verdict and disgusted with Bernice's refusal to comport herself with dignity. The family took his friendly advice and scooted out of town "at a high rate of speed."

On August 12, Brockelhurst's father visited him at the prison farm in Tucker, Arkansas, bearing glad tidings: the death sentence was to be appealed. Brockelhurst keeled over in a dead faint, perhaps unconscious from joy this time. Nevertheless, the sentence was upheld, and the court ruled that he was destined to sit in the most unwelcome of chairs on March 4, 1938. Brockelhurst boasted, "I will never be electrocuted." To make sure he didn't cheat justice, the warden at Tucker had him chained to the floor of his death row cell.

On March 3, Brockelhurst got a last-minute stay of execution. He was so close to death that his head was already shaved, no doubt inspiring many sobering thoughts.

Any hopes Brockelhurst might have cherished were snuffed on March 17. His attorney admitted defeat after his petition for a writ of habeas corpus was refused. Brockelhurst was on his own.

The next day, Brockelhurst made that last too-short stroll; no word as to whether he fainted on the way, but it would be understandable if he did. In a final prefiguring of Charles Starkweather, at the end, Brockelhurst shifted the blame onto his girlfriend, Bernice. During a twelve-minute oration before the main event, he complained that he murdered and robbed to please Bernice who, as the Three Stooges would have put it, wanted to go places and eat things. He whined, "I am guilty and am paying for my crime, but Bernice is as guilty as I am."

In 1958, Caril Ann Fugate received a life sentence but was paroled in 1976 and went into hiding. Here the parallel with Bernice F. falls apart: Caril stayed out of trouble for the rest of her life, but Bernice was still in hot water for the federal crime of transporting a stolen car across state lines from Arkansas to Tennessee and from there to New York. After fleeing Lonoke with her family, she returned home to Rockford under a $1,500 bond. Two years later, on May 19, 1939, she went back to Little Rock, Arkansas, to take her lumps. She was given a five-year sentence for crossing state lines with the triple purpose of transporting a stolen car, evading prosecution, and avoiding giving testimony. The judge who passed the sentence excoriated the jury that had let her off so easily in 1937.

Soft-Hearted Chicago

Chicago is violent now, but it always was. At the end of 1921, the coroner estimated that the city had averaged a murder per day during the year. Specifically, there were 352 murders within 365 days.

The press made a big fuss when gangster "Big Dave" Earsman expired from appendicitis on March 10, 1930. Why? Because he was the first Chicago gangster to die of natural causes in over two years, which means, of course, that Earsman died of *un*natural causes—for a Chicago mob figure. Less than a month later, on April 1, came news that Martin "Babe" Mullaney was the twentieth gang-related murder victim since the dawn of the New Year.

Chicago found more dubious cause for celebration on December 3, 1933, when the city went *an entire month* without a gangland slaying. The state's attorney crowed prematurely, "Chicago is now freer from crime than any large city."

Most of this carnage was the work of men, but murders committed by women in Chicago's criminal heyday are of even greater interest.

That women were seldom severely punished for murder in times past is a historical fact, but it is politically incorrect to mention it. Before the Nineteenth Amendment to the Constitution was ratified in 1920, women could not vote or serve on juries. On the plus side, all-male juries were leery about punishing women to the fullest extent of the law. If jurors could find a reason—*any* reason, however irrational—to let a female defendant off easy, they generally would, no matter what the charge. If she claimed self-defense or the "unwritten law," that was sufficient. If she was young, even better. If young *and* pretty, the odds were overwhelmingly in her favor that she would walk free as the April breeze. It was a nationwide phenomenon, as shown in Laura James's book *The Beauty Defense*, as well as in several volumes by this author, but nowhere was it better illustrated than in Chicago—allegedly rough, tough, brawling, unsentimental Chicago. With all due respect to Carl Sandberg, he might better have dubbed the city Husband Butcher for the World.

In a 2002 article in the *Journal of Criminal Law and Criminology*, Professor Jeffrey S. Adler notes that between 1875 and 1920, 102 Chicago wives murdered their husbands. Only sixteen were convicted. Juries found only seven out of eighty white women guilty. One had her sentence remitted by a judge. Only two were sentenced to more than a year in prison. Possibly as a result of cause and effect—that is, women realizing they could literally get away with murder if they put on sad faces before a jury of male softies—between 1875 and 1920, the rate of husband-murder in Chicago tripled, while other forms of homicide *merely* doubled.

Judging from a *Chicago Tribune* article circa September 1900, the city's women were creatively violent. The newspaper tabulated a list of weapons the so-called gentle sex had employed over the course of a year, as gleaned from police records. Thirty-one women had used firearms, but the most common instruments of mayhem were broom handles (186 cases) and table knives (102). Other missiles included stove-lid lifters, rolling pins (as depicted in oh so many cartoons!), plates, hatpins, hairbrushes, hand mirrors, mops, flatirons, curling irons, umbrellas, shoes and slippers, forks, books, potato mashers, riding whips, and lamps. One woman beaned some other human with a nursing bottle.

But never mind the exotic weaponry. The topic under discussion is the ease with which Chicago women using these objects—and deadlier ones—escaped the clutches of justice. In April 1914, the *Louisville Courier-Journal* remarked, "In two years fourteen women have been acquitted in Chicago of charges of murder. In some of these cases the defense offered was of the flimsiest character." The city's district attorney called it "a public scandal," explaining, "The blame must fall on the jurors who bring in a verdict of acquittal whenever a woman charged with murder is fairly good looking and is able to turn on a floodgate of tears or exhibit a capacity for fainting." Mrs. Virginia Troupe was one of few women to face actual punishment; she received a sentence of fourteen years for killing her husband in 1905. It was statistically proven that Chicago women had a 75 percent better chance of being convicted for stealing or gambling than for murder. The Associated Press noted that at least twenty additional women suffered no consequences for committing assault with a deadly weapon.

Even when a woman was manifestly guilty and there was no room whatsoever for doubt, Windy City juries were still squeamish about recommending the death penalty. Let us move on to a cavalcade of specific examples.

Louisa Lindloff was a fortune-teller who had a side business insuring and poisoning relatives, from which she made an estimated $13,000 in pre–World War One dollars. She murdered at least six people, possibly more; yet, rather than give her the death penalty in 1912, a wimpish jury fixed her punishment at twenty-five years in prison, having somehow determined that an individual human life was worth slightly more than four years. (For further details on the murders and trial, see my book *Horror in the Heartland*.)

On May 3, 1918, cabaret singer Ruby Dean was acquitted of killing Dr. Leon Quitman. After her trial, state's attorney Maclay Hoyne complained that it was impossible to secure a murder verdict against a woman in Cook County: "Jurymen seem to be influenced by sentiment, sympathy, or the personality of the defendant. The average jury apparently believes every story told by a pretty defendant and will not accept facts as shown by the evidence." Dean was estimated to be the twenty-seventh woman tried for murder and acquitted in Chicago within the last twelve years. Fourteen were accused of killing their husbands, and most pled that they were victims of domestic abuse.

Dr. Anton Jindra would not marry pretty twenty-five-year-old Pauline Plotka, so, on February 15, 1918, she shot him. She was allowed bail and gave interviews, in which she came across as a petulant teenager. She was acquitted on June 27.

On July 7, 1919, Margaret Seithamier, a child of sixteen, shot attorney Benjamin Burr because he refused to enter the bonds of holy matrimony. The next day, she told her story to a coroner's jury "cheerfully," complete with giggle fits. She was acquitted on October 13.

In times past, the "unwritten law" was a concept holding that women should not be punished for murdering seducing cads, nor should women (or men) be held liable for killing despoilers of their homes. Nervous juries sometimes used it as a handy excuse to acquit women they really had no desire to convict. For instance, fifteen-year-old Lucy Rossati claimed the unwritten law after shooting Guy Depeso, and, on June 22, 1921, a coroner's jury deliberated for a few minutes and said, in effect, "Good enough for us!"

On June 24, 1921, Cora Isabelle Orthwein became the latest in a long parade of attractive Chicago woman to walk after committing murder, specifically that of her longtime lover, Herbert Ziegler. The fascinating tale is recounted in Michael Lesy's book *Murder City*.

Mrs. Emilio Panico was unhappy because her husband was neglecting his family due to an infatuation with the widow of mobster Gaetano Esposito. Mrs. Panico removed her competition with a knife, pled the unwritten law, and was acquitted by a sympathetic coroner's jury on July 27, 1921.

Sabella Nitti Crudelle was hardly a subtle criminal. She and her second husband, Peter Crudelle, walloped her first husband, Frank Nitti, in the head with a hammer and then dropped him down a manhole. When an all-male jury found Sabella guilty of first-degree murder in July 1923, they fixed her punishment as death by hanging. The national press reacted with unbridled astonishment, calling them "one of the most famous juries in the legal history of the country" for daring to find a Chicago murderess guilty. It looked like she was going to be hanged for sure. Her last day was set for October 12; a retrial was refused. However, as cynics noted, Mrs. Crudelle was neither young nor pretty. Some journalists were downright mean. A magazine called her "no longer young," "gaunt, unlettered, peasant-like," and "old and ugly." (And the author was on her side!) The article included photos of some of the red-hot babes whom Chicago juries recently had acquitted of the most serious of crimes. No one need have worried about Mrs. Nitti Crudelle for a moment. Both she and her husband got commuted sentences.

Redheaded Mrs. Beulah Annan of Owensboro, Kentucky, got into slight trouble on April 3, 1924. She shot Harry Kalstedt, who happened not to be her husband, in her apartment, and then spent hours playing jazz records before deciding it *might* be a good idea to call up Mr. Annan and the police. So good-looking was Mrs. Annan that the police called her "Chicago's prettiest slayer," which means the verdict was a foregone conclusion. She posed for newsreel cameramen on May 23 and then faced a jury that called itself "beauty-proof." Her claim of self-defense did not explain her long delay before calling the cops. (One of the items brought in as evidence was a bloodstained phonograph record.) Her story also did not clarify why Kalstedt had been shot in the back. The very next day, the proud "beauty-proof jury" acquitted Mrs. Annan after deliberating for an hour and a half. The murder was partially the basis for the hit play, and later the Broadway musical, *Chicago*.

Okay, so Beulah was young, pretty, and sympathetic. What about Eliza Nusbaum, fifty-eight years old and nicknamed Grandma? On December 29, 1925, she hired four persons—including her younger lover, John Walton Winn—to clobber her husband, Albert, with a hammer so she could marry Winn. On March 6, 1926, Winn was sentenced to death. He made the hangman's acquaintance on April 15, 1927. But "Grandma" was given life imprisonment, although equally guilty.

Catherine Cassler, a thirty-five-year-old matron—and decidedly unattractive, judging from her picture in the papers—helped two other women beat cabinetmaker William Lindstrom to death in December 1926 as part of an insurance scam. Cassler's coconspirators were given life sentences, but, on May 19, 1927, a Chicago jury recommended she be hanged, upon which the gentle dove wittily replied that she hoped all the jurors' wives would die. As months passed, she decided that she preferred the noose to life in prison. She was scheduled to swing on October 21, 1927, but "true to Illinois precedent," as one paper put it, the execution was stayed. She joked that she was so fat she'd probably have broken the slab at the morgue anyway. She also remarked, "If it is finally decided I must hang, I will trip to the gallows as lightly as though I were the best-dressed woman in town on my way to church." Her braggadocio was never put to the ultimate test; although it looked for a while as though she might actually be executed, the charges were dropped, and Cassler was set free in May 1929. The *very next month*, she was held on suspicion of shooting a woman named Cameola Sater and dumping the body in a swamp near Hebron, Indiana. Cassler suspected Sater, who was to have been married a few days later, of having an affair with her husband.

Beautiful twenty-six-year-old Dorothy Pollak admitted that she shot her philandering husband, Joe. Nevertheless, she was considered such a dreamboat that a crowd of ten thousand fought to see her when she attended Joe's funeral at Bohemian National Cemetery on August 1, 1932. As the crowd pushed forward, two children and a woman were shoved into Joe's open grave, and the preacher nearly met the same indignity. The press dubbed her "Chicago's most beautiful killer." (She had usurped this particular crown from Beulah Annan, the former "Chicago's prettiest slayer.") Cagily, Pollak allowed photographers to plaster her likeness all over the city's papers; in one widely reprinted photo she sits on a desk, displaying a shapely gam. Pollak was so darn gorgeous that when she went on trial at the end of the month, the prosecution demanded the case be tried by a sole judge rather than a jury or perhaps a jury made up of only women. Pollak said she'd rather take her chances with a lone (and male) judge than twelve women. Perhaps she feared a death penalty born of jealousy. She chose wisely: the judge acquitted her on September 1, saying the killing was self-defense. Strange to say, as she left the courthouse, she no longer allowed her photo to be taken. She said something about opening a beauty shop.

Pretty nurse Bernadine Dunning shot her lover, Detective Sergeant Louis Kolb, with his own service revolver. She said she did it "to defend her honor"—that is, she invoked the unwritten law. Investigators found that she had been intimate with the married Kolb for over a year. No matter; she was freed by a jury the day after she went on trial in April 1935. "Throughout the trial she seemingly entertained no doubts as to how the Chicago jury would view her situation," wrote a reporter, and if Dunning had been paying attention to newspaper headlines from the past several years, she had no cause for alarm. She committed a serious breach of court etiquette by not thanking the jury after they let her off the hook. She gave "not even a farewell glance or smile at the chivalrous citizens who had upheld her wounded honor," said that reporter. Dunning left the jailhouse winsomely playing with a pet kitten, so the press was happy anyway. It was revealed later that one hard-nosed juror thought she should serve "a year or two," but the others argued him out of it.

Mildred Mary Bolton, described as a forty-six-year-old "plump matron," shot her husband, Joseph, twice in the back on June 15, 1936, for calling her "a vile name." Referring to a woman who had been acquitted recently for shooting her husband in a bar, she asked, "Betty Martin got away with it, so why can't I?" Why not, indeed? Going on trial didn't worry Mildred in the least; she openly boasted, "They just don't convict women of murder in Cook County." She was so unemotional in court that the press nicknamed her Marble Mildred. She even retained her calmness when the prosecutor said to the all-male jury, "If you want to protect American manhood, if you want to protect the lives of husbands and businessmen from nagging, contemptible, vicious creatures to whom they might be married—I implore you gentlemen to consider this case calmly and deliberately and give her what she deserves—the electric chair."

She, and everyone else, got a big surprise on July 16, when a jury consisting of eleven married men and one widower found her guilty after less than an hour's deliberation and recommended the chair. She was the first woman in Chicago's history to be sentenced to this particular punishment. The date was set for February 26, 1937, but three hours before she was to have struck a blow for gender equality, her sentence was commuted to life imprisonment. Marble Mildred said she didn't really care one way or the other. The press observed that Illinois had not executed a woman since Elizabeth Reed was hanged for murder in 1845. Mrs. Bolton's *other* punishment came when a judge ruled that she was not entitled to collect the $10,000 life insurance on the man she murdered.

Stella Maddox was heartbroken when she discovered that her husband, Daniel, was romantically interested in a blonde. On March 18, 1937, she intended to shoot herself in the head, but Daniel tried to wrestle the gun away from her. It went off, fatally nailing him instead. That was the story she told the jury, anyway, which deliberated for every second of twelve minutes on May 12 and set her free. In his closing argument, assistant state's attorney J. S. Boyle, knowing well what he was up against, pleaded with the jury, for all the good it did: "Is this community going to pin medals on women who murder their husbands? Must we be that chivalrous? Because a slayer is a woman doesn't lessen her guilt."

It wasn't until 1938 that the state of Illinois finally executed a second woman, Marie Porter (see elsewhere in this book for her story). But even so, she wasn't tried in Chicago, where, very likely, she'd have been acquitted at best or sent to prison a few years at worst.

Mr. Merry Finds an Unorthodox Use for Potatoes

Christopher Merry may have been just a humble Chicago potato peddler, but evidently he was very good at his trade. Though only twenty-five, he had saved enough to purchase several houses. He had his choice of homes but resided at 50 Hope Street.

Merry also had a wife, twenty-two-year-old Paulina, and a three-year-old son. There were some things he did *not* have: a peaceable outlook on life, an abiding love for his wife, and the ability to keep his sulfurous temper in check. His mother, whom he often struck and bullied, claimed that his personality had changed after a head injury in his youth.

Merry drank heavily and physically abused his wife, who disappeared on Friday, November 19, 1897. She had had her husband arrested recently for beating her with a club. He paid a fifty-dollar fine in court the day before her disappearance and was *livid* about it. She had moved in with her brother and made the grave mistake of returning home the day after Merry got out of jail. No one could find her, and her husband didn't seem concerned.

Someone sent the police an anonymous note, urging them to look into this neighborhood mystery. Investigators queried Merry's young son, who said he saw Daddy hit Mommy and then lower her through a trapdoor into the cellar.

Neighbors said Merry loaded something into a covered wagon on the morning of Saturday, November 20, and drove away. After police learned this, Chris Merry and his low-life brother-in-law, James Smith, became missing persons.

Nine days passed since Paulina's vanishing. At last, on November 28, guilty feelings (and some unsubtle police threats) overcame Thomas Hickey, an employee of the stable where Merry kept his horses. He spilled a hogshead's worth of beans.

Hickey said that he and James Smith had been visiting the Merry residence on November 19. Instead of the whiskey and poker game they were probably hoping for, they saw Mr. Merry choke his helpmate into insensibility and then beat her to death with a poker "to put her out of her misery."

Hickey knew what he was talking about. He led authorities to a largely uninhabited part of the city near Eighty-Seventh and Western Avenues, presumably one of Chris Merry's many properties. The otherwise industrious spud salesman had a lazy streak when it came to body disposal. Paulina Merry was found under mere inches of dirt by the roadside; her discovery was inevitable.

Well, Paulina was found—but where were her cruel husband and his sidekick Smith? There was a nationwide manhunt. They were thought to be in Omaha on November 30, but it was a false alarm. A couple of hobos were arrested at Braidwood, Illinois, on December 15; not them either. According to one news account, dozens of innocent men were picked up on suspicion of being either Merry or Smith.

The genuine articles were arrested at Eddyville, Kentucky, on December 16. Three days later, they were back in Chicago. A reporter who witnessed their less-than-triumphant homecoming said, "Merry's crippled feet, incased in a pair of old overshoes, shuffled painfully across the tiled floor of the railroad station in sorry comparison with the lighter tread of his partner in crime."

As the reader probably guessed, Merry had transported his dead wife to her burial site in that covered wagon under a load of potatoes, anticipating by many decades a scene in Alfred Hitchcock's *Frenzy*.

Chris Merry was found guilty and sentenced to be hanged; Smith got off with a lighter sentence, since he had only conspired to hide the body.

Doctors announced plans to X-ray Merry's condemned head before his execution to see if that brick he had taken upside the head so many years ago somehow altered his alleged formerly winning personality. His attorneys expressed a forlorn hope that maybe, just maybe, the examination could lead to a commutation of their client's sentence.

It was not to be. On April 22, 1898, Merry met the very last in a long line of legal officials, a fellow wearing a black hood.

Chicago's *Other* Homicidal Sausage Baron

One of America's most infamous murders occurred in the Chicago of long ago. Because it was extensively covered by both the respectable press and yellow journalists, as few trials ever had before, it lingers in the public imagination.

Adolph Luetgert was a wealthy sausage manufacturer whose physical size and bank account were matched only by his sexual appetite and his gusto for breaking the seventh commandment—"Thou shalt not commit adultery," that is. When his long-suffering wife, Louisa, disappeared on May 1, 1897, the police instinctively felt he murdered her—but they could not find her body. Adolph claimed that Louisa—a frail, bedridden invalid!—had run off with another man. It speaks volumes about the contempt he held for law enforcement, to say nothing of his high opinion of himself, that he didn't come up with a more believable story.

Probing the background of the so-called "sausage king" showed that he had suffered recent financial setbacks and was interested in making a wealthy young widow his new sausage queen.

Witnesses said they saw Louisa and Adolph entering his factory, the Luetgert Sausage and Packing Company, on the night she disappeared. A watchman confirmed it and said that the boss had told him he could take the night off. Nothing suspicious about that!

When detectives inspected the building, they were repelled by a weird stink coming from a vat. When drained, its bottom was coated with a strange sludge, bone fragments, and a gold wedding ring that was quickly identified as Louisa's. Thinking fast, Adolph said something along the lines of, "When my beloved Louisa abandoned me, she left her ring behind. I have been keeping it in my vest pocket out of sentimentality. It must have fallen out while I was repairing the vat."

There was other suspicious evidence, such as Luetgert's curious purchase of a large amount of potash, a substance perfect for disintegrating a human body, for which he could cough up no satisfactory explanation. He had bought the potash and more arsenic than one would think absolutely necessary the day before Louisa vanished.

A smirking Adolph went on trial in August. He told his tear-jerking tale about how the wedding ring got in the sausage vat. Readers of detective fiction expect a clever murderer to be foiled by a seemingly trivial, easily overlooked detail, and in the Luetgert case, life imitated art: Louisa's friends and physician pointed out that her finger joints were so swollen with arthritis that she couldn't have removed her wedding ring even if she had wanted to. That eradicated Adolph's smirk pretty effectively, as did an anthropologist's testimony that the bones found in the vat were human, not porcine.

It seems too horrible to be true—almost like an elaborate trap in an episode of *Batman*—but Luetgert actually dissolved Louisa's corpse in lye in a vat used for the manufacture of sausage. Unanswered question: Did he intend to use the vat to make food later for unsuspecting customers?

Luetgert's defense attorneys confused jurors with false reports that a living, breathing Louisa had been spotted at various locations in the country, sometimes thousands of miles apart on the same day. The result was a hung jury, but the jurors at Luetgert's retrial, held in January 1898, were not so easily bamboozled and found him guilty. He dodged the gallows and received a life sentence on February 9, 1898. The "life sentence" turned out to be little more than a year and a half. He died of heart disease on July 7, 1899.

The Luetgert Sausage and Packing Company building still stands on the south side of the 1700 block of West Diversey Parkway, but it has been converted into condominiums as effectively as Louisa Luetgert was converted into slurry. Or was she really converted into sausage and, uh, eaten by unwitting Chicagoans? People have wondered about that since 1897. Probably not, since after the human meat was dissolved in lye, there simply was nothing substantial left to consume, and Luetgert burned what little remained in the factory furnace. But citizens must have looked askance at their breakfasts for a while.

Now we come to the man who is the main focus of this chapter. Hard as it may be to believe, another Chicago sausage seller tried essentially the same trick as Luetgert, only with even *less* success.

South Side hog butcher Albert August Becker was tired of his wife, Theresa, and fancied a seventeen-year-old named Eda (or Ida; accounts vary). He asked her to marry him.

"Who's that woman living in your house?" asked the wary Eda.

"Oh, she's just the sister of my former wife. She's my housekeeper!" he replied lamely.

The situation was intolerable. He had to get rid of his wife somehow— and soon! Becker must have followed the sensational Luetgert business in the papers and thought, "Hey, it worked so well for *him!* Why don't *I* try it?"

So on January 27, 1899—only a year after Luetgert was sentenced to life in prison—Theresa Becker disappeared from human view. Like Luetgert, Albert said she ran away with another man. A few days later, he married Eda. Note that he felt perfectly free to get married a second time although insisting his first wife merely had absconded, which suggests that he knew better. A newspaper editorial remarked dryly, "Susceptible young ladies who receive the addresses of brand-new widowers would do well to demand of them death certificates of their former wives, and have them verified at the proper office."

Naturally, all of this got the neighbors' attention, and a month after the disappearance, they informed the police. Investigators couldn't find Theresa's body, but on February 25, they found human bloodstains on the walls and floor of a barn behind the Becker residence at 5017 Rockwell Street. A flustered Albert made many contradictory statements and was arrested.

Just as Luetgert was tripped up his wife's jewelry, so was Becker: earrings that he swore he had bought for Eda were proved to have belonged to the missing woman.

As in the Luetgert case, human remains were major evidence. Detectives found charred teeth, blackened human bones, and a kneecap in a kitchen stove in Becker's cottage and deduced that Theresa had been murdered, dissected, and cremated piece by piece. The same anthropologist, Dr. George A. Dorsey, identified the remains as human in both cases.

The similarities between the crimes were not lost on the national press. The *Louisville Courier-Journal* called it "Another Luetgert Case," and the *New York Times* referred to Becker as "Chicago's Second Luetgert" and the "new Luetgert."

There was, however, a major difference between Luetgert and Becker: the latter was not as stubborn as the former. While Luetgert denied all evidence against him until it was logically impossible to do so, on March 1, Becker broke down and confessed that he had drowned Theresa in Lake Michigan by the Randolph Street viaduct after a heated argument on January 27. He claimed he killed her in a fit of anger without premeditation. The police didn't believe him. His story did not explain the many bloodstains in his barn, nor did Theresa's drowned body turn up at the viaduct.

The theory that he was lying gained support on March 11, when the floor of Becker's barn was removed and searchers found a piece of Theresa's black calico dress and a disgusting lump that an anatomist identified as a chunk of human lung.

On March 14, Becker confessed again. This time, the story was more reasonable: he said that during a quarrel, he had hit Theresa in the head with a hatchet, killing her instantly. Then he cut her body into pieces and—note the shout-out to Adolph Luetgert!—he placed them in a kettle of boiling chemicals. Several hours later, after the fleshy parts were dissolved, he cremated the bones in the kitchen stove. He buried the parts that wouldn't burn on the prairie. How that piece of dress and the lung got under the barn, he could not explain. He insisted, as before, that the murder was not premeditated.

Becker's trial commenced on June 29 but ended almost as quickly as it began thanks to a most embarrassing clerical error: the indictment wrongly stated the victim's name was Elizabeth rather than Theresa! That got straightened out, and the trial began for real a few days later. Becker took the stand on his own behalf on July 5. He soon wished he hadn't, as he told a widely ridiculed, shiny new story under oath: he said Theresa's murderer was George S., the father of Becker's teenage bride, Eda. Becker would admit only to helping dispose of the body. The defendant, obviously unaware that it was essential to make a favorable impression on the jury, became so surly under cross-examination that the court brought in extra police protection for the prosecutor out of fear that Becker might leap from his seat and attack him.

The next day, the jury found Becker guilty. He was sentenced to hang, and that's precisely what he did on January 10, 1899. Unfortunately for Becker, the hangman was his equal in incompetence. The wife killer's neck did not break, and he swung for sixteen minutes before death overtook him. His role model, Luetgert, the once-proud sausage king, died in Joliet six months later on July 7. As that great philosopher Popeye the Sailor might have said: when it came to murder, Luetgert and Becker sure knew a lot about sausage.

Going Clubbing

On March 2, 1931, a man abducted Norma Newby and Frank James Murray and forced them to drive to Elmwood Park forest preserve outside Chicago. Once at their destination, the stranger kicked James out of the car and beat Norma to death with a heavy wrench. The abductor escaped.

Laborer Charles Pagel checked into a cheap hotel on January 9, 1932. He was found dead, with five hammer blows to the head.

Dr. James Shaffer, a fifty-six-year-old dentist, was attacked in his office on January 23, beaten so severely that his skull was caved in.

On January 31, garage night watchman Earl Gene Davis was killed with a hammer.

Except for the attack at the forest preserve, the bludgeonings took place on Chicago's North Side. The populace was understandably nervous about meeting the man the press dubbed "the Mad Clubber." None of the victims had been robbed, and the murders seemed as pointless and random as they could be. The few witnesses who glimpsed the maniac could hardly describe him, agreeing only that he was tall. Police theorized that the killer was insane or a drug addict.

Luckily, a solution was not long in coming. Davis's killer accidentally left a bottle of prescription sleeping pills at the scene. On February 2, police arrested twenty-seven-year-old Daniel Paul Harrison, a former automobile mechanic who confessed that the urge to kill overwhelmed him sometimes. When he had that itch, the only thing that could scratch it was killing people with a hammer. Harrison confessed happily to the murders listed above. He was believed to have also killed Charles Tyrell, recently hammered to death in a rooming house, but police could not tie him to the crime.

Investigators discovered some intriguing facts about Harrison. He was from North Carolina and had been something of a child prodigy not unlike Orson Welles, weaned on poetry, painting, music, and Shakespeare. He was aware of the mental illness that overtook him gradually and kept a secret diary in which he noted the progress of his strange thoughts. In one entry, he contemplated seeing a psychiatrist but was afraid he might be institutionalized if he sought professional help.

Harrison's first wife, Marie, also thought he might be mentally off-kilter. The major clue came when she awoke one night to see him standing by her bedside, holding a heavy clock and saying, "I'm going to kill you!" She survived the night by locking herself in the bathroom and survived the marriage by getting a hasty divorce.

Harrison wasted no time marrying his second wife, Margaret. Their marriage lasted less than a day. They were married in the afternoon, and, that evening, Margaret came home from the grocery store to find Harrison waving a hammer and saying, "I'm going to kill her! Kill, kill, kill!" Margaret filed for divorce soon after.

The event that pushed Paul Harrison over the edge occurred in December 1930. A car in a funeral procession broke down, and the garage sent him to repair it, after which he attended the wake. Gazing upon the face of the young woman in the casket brought him secret gratification, and, afterward, Harrison tried to recapture the feeling by crashing every funeral he could. But staring at corpses could satisfy Harrison only for so long, and he soon felt an intense desire to manufacture a few of his own, as melodramatically acknowledged in his secret journal: "Soon the satisfaction of looking at corpses probably will pass away and then I will kill! Oh, why was I born?"

Harrison lost his job at the garage and moved into a flophouse on West Van Buren Street. He sold his tools—all but the hammer, which he put to use as described. Charles Manson prosecutor Vincent Bugliosi observed that there is no such thing as a "motiveless murder"—that, while the motive may seem bizarre, inadequate, or inexplicable to us normals, it makes perfect sense in the killer's mind. Paul Harrison's reason for killing all those people was that he went into an instantaneous fury any time he heard the words *crazy* or *insane*. After Harrison abducted Norma Newby and Frank James Murray, Miss Newby made the fatal error of calling him crazy.

Harrison's hammer was hidden in his coat when he visited Dr. Shaffer's dental office. The dentist happened to be working a crossword puzzle. "What's a five-letter word for insane?" Shaffer asked himself rhetorically. Then he answered, "Crazy!" Out came Harrison's hammer.

The final victim, garage watchman Earl Gene Davis, was an unwitting acquaintance of the sought-after Mad Clubber. Harrison visited Davis's place of work and said, "Hey, loan me a car!"

Davis laughed, "You must be crazy!" He said the magic word, and that was good enough reason to kill him in Harrison's estimation.

Harrison was tried, found not guilty by reason of insanity, and sent to the Illinois Security Hospital for the criminally insane at Chester. His urge to kill was so great that he was kept in solitary confinement.

He reemerged in the public's consciousness on February 12, 1938, when he escaped from the hospital in the company of fellow homicidal maniac Peter Florek. Crazy though they were, the two were shrewd enough to make keys that unlocked their cell doors and two outside doors. They simply walked out of the asylum unnoticed. A hundred and fifty guards and officers searched high and low for them.

The panic that overtook the populace, which suddenly remembered very well why Paul had been put away, is worthy of a sociological study. Two Chicagoans in particular were veritable studies in terror: Paul's ex-wife Margaret and the psychiatrist whose testimony had put him away. Both were placed under round-the-clock police protection. The psychiatrist urged authorities and the press not to release his name. No doubt many newspaper readers decided that if they had the misfortune of making Paul's acquaintance, they would make a special point of avoiding the words *crazy* and *insane*.

Luckily for everyone, Peter and Paul were caught a few days after their escape, having somehow, one supposes, stifled their urge to murder each other. They spent the rest of their days in the asylum, as closely watched as a ripple in Loch Ness.

Try Harder, Hubert

Some murders are so craftily plotted that it takes detectives months or years to solve them. The Moor murder wasn't one of those; the puzzle wasn't so much the identity of the killer as his motive.

Marjorie Moor was found shot to death in a car parked six miles south of Marshall on the morning of August 15, 1932. No gun was present, so she hadn't committed suicide. On the contrary, she must have feared someone would take her life, since a note in her pocket urged that her parents be notified "in case anything happened" to her.

Marjorie's husband was Hubert C. Moor, a thirty-one-year-old high school teacher in Robinson. On the same day her body was found, the widower had staggered to a farmhouse and told a story that didn't exactly pass the smell test: he said the couple had been returning home from an Indianapolis visit to Mrs. Moor's parents, Reverend and Mrs. W., when a car pulled alongside theirs and forced them off the road. Hubert said thugs piled out and knocked him unconscious. When he came to, he found his wife dead in their car and no trace of the hijackers. After the police caught wind of this tale straight from a gangster B movie, they brought Moor in for questioning. In short order, they made telling discoveries:

- Mrs. Moor had been shot twice with a .25-caliber revolver. Mr. Moor owned one.
- Mrs. Moor was insured for $5,000. Mr. Moor was the sole beneficiary.
- Mr. Moor claimed the palookas had conked him on the noggin hard enough to render him unconscious, but doctors could find no injuries.
- He could offer no earthly or unearthly explanation why the would-be hijackers had merely knocked him out, yet murdered his wife, and then had abandoned the scene without their prize, the Moors' car.

After stringing the police along for a couple of weeks and fooling absolutely no one, on August 27, Moor threw in the towel and saved everyone a lot of bother by confessing. He explained his unenlightened motive the next day.

Like her husband, Mrs. Moor had been a teacher, and Mr. Moor had resented that she considered having a career more important than being a tidy housekeeper. The house had been so filthy, he said, that he was embarrassed to have company over. Above all else, he really hated dirty dishes, and the sink was always crammed full of them. Moor told the state's attorney, "Marjorie was not a home-loving girl. She was more interested in advancing her teaching and allied work than in making a home. She wanted a life apart from mine. Gradually we drifted apart. We had loved each other and I couldn't think of her leaving me for someone else. Death was the only way out. I had intended killing myself, also."

The night of August 14 was the last straw for Hubert Moor. He came home and beheld yet another sink teeming with dirty dishes. His mind snapped: "I brooded. I decided to kill her and I did just that. There was no quarrel." Ever since then Moor was haunted by visions of the face of his angelic, but messy, wife. He was put on suicide watch.

When Moor went on trial in January 1933, he honestly told the jury that his chief motive for murder was that their house "was always full of dirty dishes." Perhaps realizing that most people would not consider that sufficient reason to take a human life, he also hinted that he was insane: "God told me to shoot her. I heard Him." That wasn't good enough for the jury either. On January 14, they found Moor guilty of murder, with a sentence of death in the electric chair.

Moor's attorneys filed for a second trial on the grounds that their client was insane or at least had been when he had murdered his wife. The second trial was held in June 1934. A criminologist and a doctor testified that they thought Moor was sane; the defense presented the superintendent of the State Hospital at Alton, who thought Moor insane. The defense also presented letters written by Mrs. Moor in which she said she thought poor Hubert was losing his mind.

The evidence for Moor's insanity does not sound very convincing—several acquaintances testified that his "actions were peculiar" and that he had "hobbies, such as woodworking, which he would start and never finish." By those standards, it is safe to say, most of the human race is destined for the asylum. But the reasoning must have struck a chord with the jury. On June 4, Moor was spared the death penalty, but was not sent to an asylum. He was sentenced to life in the penitentiary at Menard. It would have served him right if he were given a job in the prison kitchen.

A Rash Act and a Rash

Thirty-eight-year-old electrician William Kappen of St. Louis, Missouri, was scheduled to marry Irene Traub on July 3, 1937. She waited for him to arrive at the church—and waited—and *waited*. Irene and the attendees finally concluded that he was not going to show up. Undoubtedly, their first suspicion was that Kappen had gotten cold feet and jilted Irene, but something far worse had happened.

Near the end of what was supposed to be her wedding day, the distraught bride-to-be read an evening newspaper account of a body that had been found shot in a roadside field that morning across the Mississippi River in Illinois. The description of the body sounded like Kappen, and the wedding party traveled to Belleville to see it. Their worst fears were realized.

Investigators searched the house Kappen had purchased for Irene. They found his wedding suit neatly laid out and a pack of cigarettes—interesting because he had not been a smoker.

An even better clue led directly to the murderers—a clue that sounds like something from a Hardy Boys mystery. Detectives had kept one detail about Kappen's body secret: it had been found in a field of poison ivy. They kept an eye out for suspects who had suddenly developed an itch, especially anyone acquainted with Kappen. They found one: Angelo Giancola, an employee of the dead man's embittered sister, Marie Porter. After his arrest, Giancola confessed that he and Mrs. Porter had killed Kappen for $3,300 in insurance money. He said that she had offered him $800 to help and also revealed that they were lovers. This fact seemed to titillate the national press as much as the murder itself, if not more, since Giancola was twenty-one and handsome, while Mrs. Porter was thirty-seven, weighed 250 pounds, and was the mother of four daughters.

When arrested, Mrs. Porter said, "If I go to the gallows or to the electric chair it will be with sealed lips," which wasn't exactly a denial. She had not been invited to her brother's wedding, which suggested animosity between them. Investigators found that Kappen had intended to name his wife as his insurance beneficiary after he married, and his sister would have been cut out of the policy. Mrs. Porter heartlessly chose the wedding day as the now-or-never moment.

At first Angelo Giancola claimed Mrs. Porter was the actual murderer; later he recanted and admitted that he had pulled the trigger, with assistance from his brother John. On July 12, Mrs. Porter confessed that she paid Giancola to get rid of her inconvenient brother.

On November 5, John Giancola was sentenced to ninety-nine years in prison, while Angelo Giancola and Marie Porter were sentenced to death in the electric chair. Now that the killers had been caught and the short-lived mystery solved, the newspapers were grateful to have another angle to flog: Would Illinois actually put Mrs. Porter in the chair, or would officials find some means of commuting her sentence? After all, it was so common in Illinois—and in America in general, in those days—for murderous men to be executed, while the female catalysts who had egged them on were given sometimes laughably lenient sentences.

To nearly everyone's surprise and to Mrs. Porter's discomfiture, Governor Horner refused to commute her sentence. This was particularly remarkable since Horner was openly opposed to capital punishment and previously had commuted three women's death sentences. In Mrs. Porter's case, the governor simply could not find any extenuating circumstances. Acting Governor Stelle gave her a week's stay of execution in January 1938 while Horner was in Washington—but that extra seven days of life was all she could hope for.

On January 28, Angelo Giancola and Marie Kappen Porter were taken one at a time to the chair that awaited them at Southern Illinois Penitentiary in Chester. Mrs. Porter was the first woman executed in Illinois since Elizabeth Reed was hanged for murder at Lawrenceville on May 23, 1845, and she was also the first woman in the Land of Lincoln to go to the electric chair. She probably felt as the Great Emancipator himself had when he told an anecdote about a man who had been tarred and feathered and ridden out of town on a rail: "If not for the honor of the thing, I'd rather walk."

4

NAUGHTY NEBRASKA

Mutual Terror of Omaha

Omaha doesn't seem like the kind of place where citizens quake in their boots because of random murders by unknown assassins. But it has happened twice, within only two years.

In February 1926, someone was shooting into houses at night. The adventure in mass panic began on the night of the fourteenth, when dairy employee William McDevitt was shot through a window. He was not robbed. No one heard the shot, so police thought the killer used a silencer. The killer left behind his "calling card": an empty .22-caliber automatic pistol shell.

For the next two nights, the sniper fired through the windows and doors of various houses. No one was killed or injured, but Omahans fairly expired from fright at every strange noise. Newspaper editorials recommended that people not turn on their lights at night and slink about as best they could in the darkness.

On the night of February 16, a drugstore window was shattered by a .22 pistol shell. The store was only a block from McDevitt's house.

The second murder occurred on the night of February 17–18, when Dr. A. D. Searles was shot in the back of his head in his office. The physician had recently refused to prescribe narcotics to a certain individual, whom officers considered the prime suspect until they found a .22 shell in the office.

The next attack took place across the Missouri River, in Council Bluffs, Iowa. On the night of February 19, railroad detective Ross Johnston was shot with a .22-caliber pistol in a train yard as he inspected a boxcar. Though hit four times, he survived to relate that the assassin shot him from behind a stack of ties. Johnston heard no shots. The sniper fled when Johnston fired his revolver.

As one might imagine, there was no nightlife in Omaha for a while. Businesses closed at dusk. People avoided windows, stayed out of doorways, and crawled through their homes like trench soldiers in the recent Great War.

Fortunately, the sniper's reign of terror lasted only slightly more than a week. On February 22, a railroad foreman, C. C. Bruce, spotted a man crawling out of a haystack near Bartlett, Iowa, thirty miles southeast of Omaha. Bruce gathered some friends and caught the stranger as he walked the tracks.

He was transient farmhand Frank Carter, age forty-six, armed and *very* dangerous. The railroad men overpowered him and took him to Bartlett on a handcar. Carter didn't deny his crimes for a moment and seemed only too proud of them. "I shot because I didn't want to get caught. I just get the inclination to shoot," he said. Next day he made this remarkable statement:

> It's not the killings that makes me feel bad. It's the shame of the thing. I should be ashamed of myself. When you get right down to the point of it, I had very little reason to shoot any of the men. I know what I've been doing. All I wanted was about $3 a day or so to live on. I was getting old and wasn't in condition to work much. As long as I could get a few dollars I was satisfied. I'll follow my lawyer's advice. If he tells me to plead guilty and throw myself upon the mercy of the court I'll do so. I know it will make no difference what I do. I'll get my just dues just the same.

That was as much of an explanation as he ever gave. One rather suspects his lawyer's advice did not include saying things like "I know what I've been doing," an admission of premeditation and sanity. Even in his formal statement to the authorities, Carter declared that he was not insane.

Carter's placidity was temporary. He announced on February 23 that he would escape before being brought to trial: "I'll kill any number of men that get in my way when I start." His threat resulted in an increase in armed guards watching his every move.

When Carter went on trial on March 18, he told the jury that he randomly shot his fellow men because he felt like such a failure and was having a midlife crisis: "I guess I didn't have a nose for money, like other robbers. I just didn't hold up the right people. I don't have any ability as I was too slow in changing to some permanent work. Anyhow, I just wanted enough to live on for a while. I do not like to be called a highwayman."

He also asserted for the third time that he was sane, though his attorneys were doing their best to use the temporary insanity defense. The jury declared him guilty of the murder of Dr. Searles. He was sent to the Nebraska State Penitentiary in Lincoln and scheduled to occupy a very special chair there on July 9. Carter's only comment was that he was really looking forward to the Fourth of July.

Almost a year passed before Carter sat in that chair on June 24, 1927. Allegedly, his last words were "Let the juice flow." Before he died, he boasted to reporters that he was guilty of forty-three murders, a number very few believed.

For some reason, it is ingrained in the popular imagination that there's no such thing as a black serial killer or at least that they are rare. That would come as surprising news to the multitude of victims of Wayne B. Williams, Derrick Todd Lee, Harrison Graham, Mark Goudeau, Lonnie Franklin (aka the Grim Sleeper), Carl "Coral" Watts (who some think might be one of the most prolific serial killers of all time), Shelly Andre Brooks, the Zebra killers who terrorized San Francisco in 1973–1974, Eugene Victor Britt, Matthew Emmanuel Macon, Vaughn Greenwood (perpetrator of the long-unsolved LA Skid Row Slasher murders), Henry Louis Wallace, Ivan Hill, Charles Lendelle Carter, Lorenzo Gilyard, Posteal Laskey (aka the Cincinnati Strangler), Carlton Gary, Ray Dandridge, Anthony McKnight, Chester Turner, Maury Travis, Paul Durosseau, Samuel Little, and Craig Price.

Earlier examples include the Servant Girl Annihilator, who preyed on Austin, Texas, in 1884–1885 and was almost certainly African American; Clementine Bernarbet, who claimed to have headed a murder cult in Louisiana and Texas in 1910–1912—whether she actually did is a matter of debate, but, if not, she likely axed a few people by herself—and Rufus Cantrell, an Indiana body snatcher who found murder easier than robbing graves (see my books *The Axman Came from Hell*, *Weird Wild West*, and *Forgotten Tales of Indiana*, respectively, for details on these cases).

Then there is the figure who kept Omaha in a lather of fear in autumn 1928. On the morning of November 18, he broke into the home of seventy-five-year-old Joseph Blackman and killed him in his sleep. The murderer had used an ax stolen from Blackman's neighbor across the street and impudently left the bloody weapon behind a woodpile.

On the morning of November 19, the assailant entered the home of milkman Waldo Resso, who was out making deliveries. When Resso returned, he found, to his horror, that his twenty-one-year-old wife and her eighteen-year-old sister, Gerta Brown, had both been hatcheted to death. Blackman's skull had been pulverized with the blunt end of an ax, but the two women were killed with the blade.

On November 20, the murderer invaded the home of Harold Stribling, just across the state line, in Carter Lake, Iowa; crushed his skull with five blows from a hatchet; and hit Mrs. Stribling in the face with the same. He forced her to walk three miles to a swamp and freed her three hours later. How he spent that time with her is not clear, but it appears that sexual assault was not involved. She made her way to town with a broken nose and a cut eye as her most serious injuries. She told police that the attacker was a black man in his early twenties.

Mr. Stribling survived, so, within three days, the killer's toll stood at three dead and two wounded. Omahans again spent their evenings in blind panic. On the night of the twentieth, sidewalks in a hundred city districts reverberated with the tread of five hundred policemen, not to mention hordes of civilian volunteers. A reward totaling $1,775 was offered. Bloodhounds were brought to the Stribling home—where the ax-wielder had left behind a good set of fingerprints—but could not follow the attacker's scent. Forty black men were held on suspicion, of which fifteen were arrested. Some policemen openly doubted that any were guilty. The activity seemed to have frightened the killer, who kept to himself on November 21.

Four arrested men were taken to Mrs. Stribling's hospital room on November 22. She identified none as the Hacker, as some reporters called him. The police admitted they were "baffled at every turn."

They weren't baffled long. The next day, they arrested Louisiana-born Jake Bird, aged twenty-seven, after he was identified by Mrs. Stribling, who, of the two surviving victims, had the longest, clearest view of her assailant. He was hurried to the state penitentiary for his own protection.

Bird went on trial in Council Bluffs in January 1929. The authorities had a problem: they couldn't tie him definitively to the three murders that had rocked their city, only to the nonfatal attacks on the Striblings. He was tried for assault and found guilty on February 2. The maximum penalty was thirty years.

Bird didn't even serve that much. He was set free in January 1933. This was an error, for Jake Bird may well have been one of the most industrious serial killers of that era. A hobo and occasional railroad worker, he was constantly on the move from state to state. Most of his victims were white women, and his weapon of choice was an ax or hatchet. He confessed to having murdered in Oklahoma; Michigan; Evanston, Illinois; Sioux Falls, South Dakota; Cleveland, Ohio; Orlando, Florida; Portage, Wisconsin; Louisville, Kentucky; Kansas City, Kansas; and, yes, Omaha.

He stayed out of the headlines until October 30, 1947, when he ax-murdered Bertha Kludt and her daughter Beverly in Tacoma, Washington. He was caught literally red-handed by police as he fled out the back door. After his arrest, authorities remembered his name and realized that he had been arrested for nearly identical crimes way back when in Omaha.

How many people did this man kill? He had enough insider knowledge to convince police that he murdered at least thirty-three across the country. Bird confessed to forty-four. He could have been guilty of as many as forty-six murders—or perhaps, as in the case of Henry Lee Lucas in the 1980s, authorities fed him details about unsolved homicides so that Bird could convincingly confess to them, and the cases could be declared officially solved. In any case, Bird certainly killed more than a few.

He was hanged at Washington State Penitentiary on July 15, 1949. Had there been enough evidence to convict him in the Omaha cases of 1928, his murderous career might have been shortened by twenty years.

With a Little Help from His Friends?

On September 4, 1908, Mrs. Grace H. Rustin sat in an Omaha room with a depressing piece of furniture: a coffin containing the body of her physician husband, Frederick. Late in the night of September 1, she had found him shot and barely alive on the front porch of their Farnam Street home. He died at the hospital an hour later. The question bedeviling Mrs. Rustin, and the proper authorities besides, was whether his death had been self-inflicted or murder. She, for one, did not believe it was suicide—not at all! She told a reporter, "I was awakened by a pistol shot. I waited some time and then something impelled me to go downstairs and see what was the matter. I went down, and opening the door slightly, looked through the crack. I saw my husband, Dr. Rustin, sitting in a chair and looking as though he was in trouble. . . . 'Oh, what is the matter, Fred? What has happened to you?' I exclaimed. 'A man has shot me,' he mumbled and then fainted."

Mrs. Rustin dragged him just inside the doorframe with no small difficulty. When her strength gave out, she had to leave him lying there. "That accounts for the reports which have gone out that the doctor was within the house when the fatal shot was fired," the widow explained to the reporter. Mrs. Rustin and her maid, Hannah (or Anna) Deneen, telephoned for two doctors, Langfeld and Lord, and also called Dr. Rustin's mother.

"Why were the police not notified earlier?" asked the reporter.

"I did not know of such matters," she responded. The doctors at the hospital told her they would inform the authorities, she said, but in the excitement of the emergency operation, they did not until after Rustin died.

Then there was the matter of domestic infelicity, which the reporter gingerly broached: "It has been said that Dr. Rustin and you did not live happily together, that there was trouble between you. What is the truth of that report?"

"There is not an iota of truth in that report," sniffed Mrs. Rustin. "We had been married more than ten years and during that time I never received a cross word from my husband. His conduct toward me was all that a husband's should be."

On the same day as Mrs. Rustin's stiff and formal newspaper interview, Omaha police arrested a young woman, Abbie B. Rice. It is doubtful they could do so on similar grounds today—there were no charges against her—but they wanted to hold her for safekeeping since she admitted being the last person to see Dr. Rustin alive before he went home and ended up with a bullet in his abdomen.

Mrs. Rustin stoutly denied her husband had been suicidal. As we shall see, she had a good financial motive to deny it. Not everyone was convinced. To hear the *Omaha World-Herald* of September 7 tell it, the physician had been not only enamored of self-destruction, he was downright eccentric on the topic. He had collected methods of committing suicide in much the same manner as other men might collect model trains and had experimented on himself with the same. Some of these techniques, said the paper, were unique and had "probably never been used by anyone" in the history of this sad world. Rustin's chief weapon against himself was his own medical knowledge. In May 1905, he had procured two cultures from the University of Chicago's bacteriological laboratory containing tetanus germs and typhoid. Shortly afterward, said the *World-Herald*, "Dr. Rustin inoculated himself with the bacilli of typhoid fever, and was so near dead that the attending physicians despaired of his life." It was thought that he had injected the tetanus germs into his body for good measure. Tetanus, aka lockjaw, is a bacterial infection that makes the sufferer literally unable to open his mouth, resulting in slow starvation for those who caught it back in the good old days. But the unlucky doctor survived, and in September 1907—a year before his death—he confided to friends that he tried to kill himself via disease to make it seem as though he had died of natural causes.

Weird stuff, but the jailed Abbie Rice finally broke down on September 6 and told an even stranger story. She said she had joined a suicide pact with Rustin. The plan was that he would go home and shoot himself; meanwhile she would drink laudanum and morphine at her place, but she chickened out. She said she called him four times that evening to inform him that she had changed her mind, but she thought he must not have heard the phone. Perhaps he was sitting out on the porch mustering courage to pull the trigger on himself? Investigators who searched Rice's home confirmed that they had found bottles of laudanum and morphine.

Did the doctor have a motive for suicide? In fact, he had. His widow admitted that the Rustins had been in such financial difficulty that they had seriously considered moving away from the wagging tongues of their Omaha neighbors and starting over elsewhere. The doctor had alienated his mother by borrowing a large sum from her and not repaying it, and he owed the bank $3,200, due for payment on the day of the shooting. *Maybe* that was a coincidence.

The inquest was held on September 8. Mrs. Rustin sat behind a screen for much of the proceedings to shield her from the gaze of the nosy. Dr. Langfeld testified that when he had arrived at the Rustin home on an emergency call that night, he found a watch and money on Rustin— but no gun. Langfeld said he thought the wound was not self-inflicted.

In fact, no gun was found at the scene or anywhere near it, which threw serious doubt on Mrs. Rice's suicide-pact story. Mrs. Rustin testified that her husband did not own a gun. On the other hand, Dr. Rustin had been conscious for a few minutes after Dr. Langfeld arrived but did not say someone else had shot him, though that is exactly what his wife said he told her.

Mrs. Rustin testified that her husband's life had once been insured to the tune of $75,000, though the amount was considerably less now due to the couple's financial troubles. At the time of his death, he had been insured for a total of $40,000 via five insurance companies.

The Rustins' maid, Hannah Deneen, told an interesting story. While Mrs. Rustin had been out of town visiting friends in Ellsworth a couple of weeks before the shooting, Abbie Rice had been a dinner guest at the house, accompanied by a bespectacled man whose name she did not catch.

The big question, of course, was, If Dr. Rustin and Mrs. Rice had entered a suicide pact, why? Mrs. Rice testified that the doctor wanted her to shoot him so that Mrs. Rustin would get the insurance money—which makes sense in a demented sort of way, since his friends said he had already tried to fake death via natural causes by injecting himself with virulent germs. The idea, she said, was that she would shoot him and then shoot herself afterward, but the plot was foiled when she lost her nerve.

One wonders what part of this alleged arrangement she felt was to her advantage, since the plan seemed entirely to favor the melancholy Dr. Rustin's interests. Mrs. Rice said, "I was to shoot him in his office. He wanted me to shoot him through the abdomen, so his family could get his insurance money. He thought he could trust me. He wanted me to give him two or three days to settle his business affairs before killing him. I hardly knew what to say when he said that. He wanted it done Sunday at his office. That was August 30. He thought the noise of the cars would drown the noise of any revolver shot."

Elaborating, Mrs. Rice said Dr. Rustin had then encouraged her to kill herself after shooting him through the abdomen (which, by the way, would likely result in a painful death; one would expect a doctor to have known that). According to Rice, Rustin instructed her to dispose of the empty cartridge after shooting and then go home and shoot herself with the same gun. "In that way, only one empty shell—not two—would be found when she died by her own hand and his death and hers could not be connected to bring shame and humiliation upon his family."

But what about the "shame and humiliation" that would be attached to Mrs. Rice's family? And did Rustin think no one would put two and two together when the duo committed suicide on the very same night and at roughly the same time, even though in different locations? When asked if she had accomplices, Abbie implicated one Charles Edward Davis.

The coroner's jury clearly didn't believe Mrs. Rice's story but was unsure whom to blame. On September 9 they brought in a verdict of gunshot "by a person unknown"—*not* suicide—and they recommended that this Charles E. Davis fellow be investigated. Davis was summarily arrested and released on bond. His brother Frederick stated that Charles had suffered from periodic spells of temporary madness for the past thirteen years and had spent three stints in an asylum for violent insanity. Not only that, stated Frederick, but also, Charles's insanity had seemed to be starting up again in the last two weeks—and Dr. Rustin had been his attending physician. Frederick Davis thought Rustin had committed suicide and that authorities were railroading his convenient scapegoat brother to distract from the true cause of death.

Davis's preliminary trial began September 24. Dr. Lord, one of the two physicians who had tended to the wounded Dr. Rustin, testified that when he was rushing to the Rustin house, he had met a man on the sidewalk who resembled Charles E. Davis, only two blocks from the residence and coming from its direction. Maid Hannah Deneen also swore that she had seen a man resembling Davis near the house. This evidence was considered convincing. Davis was bound over to the district court to answer to the charge of first-degree murder. Again, his wealthy brothers Frederick and Latham paid his bail.

The murder trial began on December 2. Mrs. Rustin held up well under cross-examination but Hannah, the maid, did not. Hannah had breezed through the earlier coroner's inquest and preliminary hearing, but under pointed, unfriendly direct questioning, she collapsed, and the trial was stalled for a ten-minute recess. Nevertheless, her testimony corroborated Mrs. Rustin's and added a new detail: on the night of the murder, Hannah had visited her sister, and, when she walked home, she had seen a man who resembled Charles Davis lurking about the Rustin residence.

In addition, a doctor bearing the aromatic name W. R. Lavender testified that he had performed the autopsy on Rustin's body and, in his opinion, the death wound was not self-inflicted. The person whom the jury, trial watchers, and journalists really wanted to see on the stand—the mysterious Mrs. Abbie Rice—was not called on the trial's first day. But perhaps they were satisfied by Hannah's well-timed fainting spell. It seems that the paramount question in the minds of spectators when women testified in those days was not so much "Is she telling the truth?" as "Will she give us a good show by fainting or at least pretending to?" The wise woman seeking sympathy while on trial did not let her public down.

One thing was certain: no one followed the proceedings more closely than the five life insurance companies that had policies on Dr. Rustin and stood to lose $40,000 between them if it were ruled that he had been murdered. Had he committed suicide, they would not have to fork over so much as a shiny new nickel. Naturally, they took the latter position.

The public's disappointment at not seeing Abbie Rice testify was assuaged when she took the stand on December 3. Her testimony took two days to unfold because the judge dismissed the jury twice so that attorneys could squabble over the admissibility of evidence. The prosecution won both times, and, at last, Mrs. Rice told the strangest version of her story to date. She testified now that Dr. Rustin had thirsted to commit suicide in an unobvious fashion and felt the best way was to hire someone else to do the dirty work and make his death appear to be murder. The hitman he chose, according to Rice, was none other than Charles Davis. Mrs. Rice said that Davis himself was suicidal and that he and the doctor had agreed to a weird quid pro quo: Davis would shoot Rustin on his porch as long as the doctor agreed to give Davis poison in advance so that he could make quick work of himself when the mood struck.

The case went to the jury on December 9. They acquitted Charles Davis, finding the idea that Dr. Rustin had hired the unstable fellow to murder him too extravagant to swallow. The verdict was good news for Davis but bad news for Mrs. Rustin. As noted, if her husband had been a suicide— or if he had hired someone to help him with this unpleasant chore—the insurance companies did not have to pay up. The $40,000 Mrs. Rustin thought they collectively owed her was not small potatoes; the equivalent in modern currency would be $795,000. So she sued them in separate suits filed on February 11, 1909.

The ensuing legal extravaganza lasted for months, and the full details would likely drive the reader to despair. Murder trials are interesting; insurance-related trials, as a general rule, are not. The trial began on November 7, 1910, in Louisville, Kentucky, of all places. The law held that such lawsuits could be filed in any place where the defendants or their representatives did business. A Louisville reporter noted that Mrs. Rustin wore widow's weeds, though her husband had been dead for over two years.

On November 15, the jury found in favor of Mrs. Rustin, by then living in Haverhill, Massachusetts. She ended up with a slightly reduced payout of $38,000. But, of course, that wasn't the end of it. The insurance companies appealed and lost their motion for a second trial in February 1911.

The companies appealed to a higher court, still arguing that Dr. Rustin had a mania for self-destruction and met his death through a suicide pact. On December 10, 1912, the Kentucky Court of Appeals declared that the insurance companies must pay Mrs. Rustin $33,000—not sure what became of that extra five grand, but, nevertheless, the widow enjoyed a financial triumph, as well as a moral victory. And the rest of us inherited a mystery. Was Dr. Rustin murdered or had he committed suicide, with or without help?

ſ

CRIMINAL KANSAS

Little Slaughterhouse on the Prairie:
The Benders and the Stafflebacks

The Bloody Benders of Labette County lived briefly, but very memorably, about seven miles from Cherryvale in Montgomery County. They have been the subject of Kansas legend—and sometimes fact—for over 140 years. They were a supposed family of German immigrants who rented the spare room in their cabin, which they optimistically referred to as an "inn," to wayfarers whose wandering days generally came to a permanent close soon after patronizing the Benders.

The family consisted of patriarch, John Sr.; matriarch, Elvira; and the adult siblings, John Jr. and the by-all-accounts attractive Kate. There is speculation that John the younger and Kate were actually a married couple rather than brother and sister. Creepy, if true, but nothing the family did would have been very surprising. For that matter, there is no solid proof that the Benders were a family at all. They may have been four unrelated, opportunistic weirdos drawn together by common interests, such as robbery and wholesale murder.

The Benders never seemed to be short of renters. Perhaps travelers were *really* attracted to the nondescript lodging by Kate's locally notorious advocating of what was then euphemistically termed "free love" (today, "promiscuity").

Based on the word of lodgers who became suspicious of their hosts and were wise enough to escape unscathed, the Benders' modus operandi was this: A bedsheet was stretched on a wire, bisecting the kitchen dining room. A lantern was placed in the room so that family members could see the silhouette of the latest customer as he sat in a chair. Kate entered and turned on the charm, sometimes discussing her ardent interest in spiritualism, which was only too appropriate since the Benders were in the ghost-manufacturing business. While the guest was thus beguiled, one of the Johns would whang him in the head with a sledgehammer. The Benders would then finish off the stunned victim with a cut throat. After rifling the body for money, jewelry, and other worldly goods, the Benders gave it an un-Christian burial in their vegetable garden and apple orchard.

The family kept this murderous business going for two years, from 1871 to 1873, until people got wise to the fact that journeyers checked in but seldom checked out in the usual sense of the term. The Benders took flight when they learned they were under suspicion. After they were gone, investigators disinterred between eight and eleven bodies on their property and possibly as many as twenty. The victims included a young girl.

The family's utter disappearance despite generous rewards for their capture increased their legendary status, as few things are more interesting than a mystery without an ending. Some hold that the Benders escaped justice and perhaps set up their industry elsewhere under assumed names; others maintain that each family member, including the women, was hunted down like curs and lynched by vigilantes without so much as a "Please, may I." One especially vicious legend states that Kate was burned alive like a medieval witch.

Not only did the Benders vanish, but so did their cabin. Souvenirs hunters dismantled everything on their farm and carried it all away, stone by stone, board by board, nail by nail, atom by atom. Three hammers that belonged to the Benders are now on display in the Cherryvale Museum. The sledgehammer is notably dented.

A final bizarre note on the Benders: Laura Ingalls Wilder, author of the *Little House on the Prairie* series, sometimes claimed that her family had stayed at chez Bender when she was a tot and were fortunate to escape with their lives. She even hinted broadly that her father, Pa Ingalls, had been among the vigilantes who grimly sought the Benders. Great story, but spoilsports have observed that the Ingalls family moved from the area in 1871, and the Benders' crimes didn't become public knowledge until 1873.

Life isn't fair, and death isn't either. The Benders—whether an authentic family or not—slaughtered up to twenty strangers for fun and profit and are legendary to this very day. However, a quarter-century later, another Kansas tribe did much the same as the Benders yet are largely forgotten outside the state.

The Stafflebacks of Galena in Cherokee County first came to national attention in September 1897. Like the Benders, they operated an inn and murdered travelers. Unlike their German counterparts, the Stafflebacks did not trouble to bury their victims but threw the remains down any of three abandoned, but very useful, mine shafts located near their home. A Galena correspondent for the *St. Louis Globe-Dispatch* described the clan: "A family of the lowest instincts and most brutal impulses, they seem to have been reared in crime and bred in infamy."

Their criminal career started, in Kansas anyway, in 1894. Sixty-five-year-old Nancy Wilson, aka Staffleback, was the materfamilias, and, if her newspaper portrait is accurate, she could easily pass for the paterfamilias. The rest of the brood consisted of her sons Edward, Mike, and George Staffleback; George's wife, Cora; and Charles Wilson, a lucky fellow who made his home in Ma Staffleback's heart. She took Wilson's surname, though it appears they were not legally wed since the papers euphemistically said he "*passed* as [her] husband." So let's just call her Ma Staffleback for convenience's sake and to be on the safe side.

The whole unsavory crew lived in a four-room frame and log house "in the western part of Galena, in the toughest part of town." The enterprising family realized that they could make money by renting out the women as prostitutes. News accounts use the plural, so the homespun hookers may have included the grim-looking, ultra-masculine Ma Staffleback as well as the younger Cora. Mrs. Staffleback's daughter Emma C. sometimes sold herself there, and the family also hired local talent named Rose B. and Annie M.

But prostitution was mainly a scheme for luring men into the house. Once unsuspecting customers were ensconced within the walls, their lot was not lovin' but violence, robbery, and murder. The family went too far when they killed salesman Frank Galbraith in mid-June 1897. He came to the house looking for Emma C. "She's busy now," Ma Staffleback answered. "Come back later."

Galbraith left and returned around three o'clock in the morning. Business is business, but the late arrival annoyed Mrs. Staffleback, who advised Galbraith to abandon the premises, if he pleased, or else she would decapitate him with a corn knife. Her alleged husband, Charles Wilson, feeling this was no job for a woman, said, "I'll get him," and rushed at Galbraith with a pistol. Galbraith fled, pursued by Mr. Wilson and George and Ed Staffleback. Ed fired at Galbraith, hitting him in the side. Working gal Annie M., who had followed the procession, saw Ed draw his knife. She begged, "Don't kill the man!" He administered a Bender-like coup de grace by slitting the wounded Galbraith's throat. Then Ed turned, glared at Annie, and told her to return to the house or she would get the same.

Annie slinked back in the direction of the house, but, instead of entering, she hid in the tall weeds and witnessed Charles Wilson and the two Staffleback brothers take Galbraith's valuables and toss his body down a nearby mine shaft. She heard the splash when the corpse hit the water at the bottom.

All returned to normal, or what passed for normal, at the Staffleback abode. A month later, a stranger to Galena, no doubt whistling and feeling as though all were right with the world, took a stroll among the abandoned mine shafts that dotted the area. Peeking down into one, he saw decomposing remains. When the police pulled the body out of the shaft, they found papers in its pockets identifying him as Frank Galbraith. The coroner held an inquest. Neighbors living near the shaft said they had heard shots coming from the vicinity of the Staffleback house around the time Galbraith was estimated to have died. The coroner ordered Ma, Ed, and Cora Staffleback to testify. Their testimony was so contradictory that the official had them arrested. When Cora took the stand, she lost her composure and described Galbraith's murder.

(The other family members were not called to testify. Mike and George Staffleback were both in jail, Mike for stealing from a freight car and George for committing a burglary at Baxter Springs. Elderly Charles Wilson was not subpoenaed since he had taken to his heels for parts unknown.)

George's burglary charge was set aside after the more serious charge emerged. He, Ed, and Ma Staffleback were put on trial for murder in Columbus and convicted—after which, Cora *really* felt brave, having no longer to fear being murdered and tossed down a mine. She turned on the family and divulged three extra murders the authorities did not know about. In 1895, Cora said, Mike and Ed had murdered an Italian peddler and, later, two girls. The peddler had come to the house selling his wares, including pencils, jewelry, linen, and lace. While he was there, one of the women sold him *her* wares. When he was asleep, Ed tried to pick his pocket. But the Italian woke, and Mike and Ed killed him with a club and a pistol and threw him into one of those expedient abandoned mine shafts.

As for the two female victims, a couple of days before the peddler arrived, the Stafflebacks found two young women living in a tent nearby and invited them to take up residence in the family's house, an offer the campers unwisely accepted. About a week after the peddler's murder, Mike came home and was outraged to find one of the new tenants sitting in a stranger's lap. (One wonders what he expected, since the family cabin doubled as brothel.) Mike chased away the stranger—presumably, a paying customer!—and then turned his wrath on the woman. She tried to run away, but Mike throttled her into unconsciousness. Her friend objected, and Mike broke her skull with the butt of his pistol. Figuring he might as well finish what he started, Mike struck both women repeatedly until they were dead. When his brother Ed came home, the two had tossed the remains of their guests down a shaft.

While Cora was in a confessing mood, she also told authorities that, in 1892, when the family was living in Joplin, Missouri, the Staffleback brothers murdered their mother's then-suitor for his pension money. He was an aging soldier named Rodebaugh, and the family got $31.50 as their spoils. They tossed his body down a mine shaft, which may have been when they got the idea for this novel method of corpse disposal. Upon hearing about Cora's blabbing, her husband, George, decided that the life of a stoolie was the safest course for him as well, and he turned state's evidence against his family.

Meanwhile, the entire pack of Stafflebacks were in the jailhouse in Columbus. It was a small jail, measuring twenty by fifty feet, yet into it were packed Ma Staffleback; the brothers Ed, George, and Mike; and forty-two *other* prisoners. The place must have made the Black Hole of Calcutta seem downright spacious, but at least Ma Staffleback got to stay in a separate cell with one other woman. The matriarch spent her sixty-fifth birthday in jail on August 16, weeping over her fate and no one else's.

As the family learned the true meaning of togetherness in that tiny jail, the town's citizens—including, according to one account, "leading Galena businessmen and property owners"—were said to be ready to form a vigilance committee at a moment's notice should Cora's story be corroborated by the discovery of bodies. Note that the vigilantes wanted proof first; in some communities, the custom was to lynch first and ask questions later.

On September 14, as citizens lowered grappling hooks into the mine, hundreds watched and undoubtedly secretly hoped they would see something horrible. Vendors set up booths to sell melons, apples, cider, cold drinks, and lunches to famished rubberneckers. The excavators found a woman's shirtwaist, "a pair of men's drawers with particles of decayed flesh adhering to them," and also "bunches of human hair and several pieces of bones." When a pump was applied to the shaft on September 16, investigators found a club and a pitchfork handle entangled with human hair. No complete human bodies were discovered, but it was thought that Mike Staffleback removed the bodies from the shaft and hid them in a better location after the tourist first saw the floating Galbraith. In any case, the family had already been convicted of murder, so finding the remains of the peddler and the two young women simply would have been the gruesome icing on a homicidal cake, to coin a phrase.

The constant threat of lynching took its toll on Edward Staffleback. It was reported, on September 25, that he had gone insane and had to be restrained with a straitjacket. The law handed down the family's sentences on October 2: life sentences for George and crazy Ed; twenty-one years for their mother, Ma Staffleback; and seven additional years for Mike after he finished his five-year term for burglary. Charles Wilson, who had been located, arrested, and tried, also went to prison for twenty-five years. All were sent to Leavenworth.

Years later, Ma Staffleback, aged nearly eighty, came down with pneumonia in her cell in the women's ward. Her son George and her paramour, Charles Wilson, were brought from their cells to see her in her last hours. Ed had died in prison in 1905; Mike served out his term but was arrested again for an undisclosed crime and, by 1909, was in prison in Jefferson City, Missouri. Ma Staffleback died on March 9, 1909, with George and Charles by her side. This comforting family reunion was more than the Stafflebacks' innumerable victims received at the close of their lives, when they fled their bodily tenements with a little assistance.

Willie's Poor Conduct

Mr. Mendel lived eighteen miles northwest of Osage Mission. (Some accounts give his name as Mendall or Mendells.) At around one o'clock in the morning of March 8, 1886, a human scream outside his door disturbed his slumber. Finding the circumstance interesting, he opened the door and saw Willie Sells, the son of his neighbor J. W. Sells. Willie was sixteen years old but often was mistaken for being younger, since he was "sickly" and "undersized," as unkindly folks put it. The quiet Kansas farm boy was soon an object of intense interest to people as far away as the readers of the *New York Times*.

"Mr. Mendel!" cried Willie, "A man is at our home with a hatchet and has hurt father and mother. I don't know how badly."

Mendel hurried to the Sells farmhouse with Willie and, not being a fool, along the way, he got backup from another neighbor, J. L. Rice (Reece in some accounts), in case the hatchet-wielding maniac was still in the house. Once at the Sells residence, Mendel and Rice went in while Willie stayed outside.

(A possibly relevant aside: FBI profilers John Douglas and Mark Olshaker note in their book *The Cases That Haunt Us* that domestic murderers often manipulate the situation so that someone else discovers the bodies.)

Researchers who use old newspapers as sources know how graphic those nineteenth-century journalists could be when describing a circulation-building murder, a picturesque suicide, or an imagination-provoking accident. The Sells case is no exception. The wire services tell us exactly what Mendel and Rice saw when they cautiously entered the house. First, the subheadline: "A Deed without Parallel for Fiendishness in the History of Blood-Stained Kansas."

And then . . . "In the bed in the north room lay Walter, Willie's eldest brother and bedfellow, aged nineteen, his throat cut and the entire top of his head chopped off, exposing the brain, and his left eye hanging upon his cheek."

Note that the reporter even told his details-hungry readers the exact geographical direction in which the room was located; presumably, he brought a compass. Next came the scenic master bedroom: "Passing into the south and main room, where a light was burning, they stumbled over the prostrate form of Mr. Sells, his head crushed and almost severed from his body. Nearby lay Mrs. Sells, a lady of forty-three years, her head mashed and a fearful gash in her throat. On the bed in the southeast corner of the room, lay Ina, Willie's sister, aged fourteen, killed in the same manner as the other three. Lying near Mr. Sells's head was a bloody butcher knife, and on a chair, a hatchet matted with hair and blood."

Even the usually starchy fuddy-duddies at the *New York Times* sounded like twenty-first-century gorehounds, stating, "The floor was covered with blood in which [Mendel] fairly had to wade. The ceiling was spattered and the walls stained."

Mendel and Rice asked Willie exactly what he witnessed during this mayhem. Willie said that something had awakened him, and when he looked up, he had seen a short, heavyset man with closely cropped dark hair standing in the doorway. The man stepped into the room, and, instead of striking Willie, who was closest and therefore the most opportune victim, he had reached over Willie and whacked brother Walter in the head with a hatchet.

One might expect that after this rude awakening, Willie would have sounded the alarm and awakened his family—or tried to fight off the attacker—or fled. He chose the third option. One can hardly blame him; but—but *first, he got dressed*, evidently thinking he might meet ladies while in flight for his life.

By this point in Willie's "very gauzy story," as one paper called it, Mendel and Rice were probably looking at each other through narrowed eyes. Let's hear it in Willie's own words: "I got my clothes off the foot of the bed and was putting them on when the man turned, looked at me, and then ran out into the yard. I did not try to arouse my brother, but put on my pantaloons and went into the room where my parents were sleeping to get my boots and my overcoat. I saw my father on the floor with blood on his face but thought his nose was bleeding, as he was troubled that way."

A nosebleed?! The reader will recall that when Willie first rousted Mendel in the middle of the night, he said a man had hit his father with a hatchet. Anyway, having asserted to the contrary that he was not in the least alarmed after seeing his father lying on the floor in a pool of blood (although the stranger had just killed his brother) and that he had taken time to fully dress, including his boots and overcoat, Willie said that the mysterious man ran outside. Willie followed in hot pursuit, so it was a good thing he had troubled to put his shoes on. He chased the man half a mile when the villain approached another man on horseback, who was holding a second horse's reins. The attacker jumped on the free horse and the dastards galloped away. Seeing there was nothing more he could do, Willie went to Mr. Mendel's house for help, and, well, here we are!

The youngster's tale did not fill his listeners with confidence in his veracity. Mendel noticed that Willie was strangely untroubled by the carnage, showing no more reaction than if his family were asleep rather than slaughtered. Additionally, socially backward Willie couldn't understand why the neighbors were horrified when he tried to put on a pair of his late father's pants for size. Rice took the boy back to his own house—ostensibly to let him sleep after the trauma of seeing his family murdered, but more likely, one suspects, so Rice could keep an eye on him.

When the coroner's jury convened hours later, jurists made it no secret that they did not believe Willie. Investigators had found a washbasin containing bloody water on the Sells family stove. Willie testified under oath that he had *not* washed his hands since the massacre. An inspection proved that his hands and wrists were spotless, but when his shirtsleeves were pulled back, dried blood was on his forearms. Willie had no good explanation for this; his hyperactive imagination failed him. A closer examination revealed dried blood under his fingernails.

The coroner ordered Willie to remove his pants, and the jury saw his blood-smeared underwear. He also had blood on the soles of his bare feet, which perfectly fit bloody footprints at the crime scene. Speaking of which, police found Willie's footprints clearly imprinted in the muddy yard—but no other prints, despite his fancy story of chasing the family's assassin through the yard. There were tracks of neither man nor beast in the half-mile area through which Willie said he had pursued the villain, who supposedly got away on horseback with an accomplice. Even Willie's tracks were missing.

After the examination, Police Judge Cambern and Deputy Sheriff Locke smuggled Willie in a buggy to the jail in Erie, since a number of men seemed to have no philosophical issues with lynching a sickly looking sixteen-year-old. Despite the stout denials he had just made in the courtroom, on the ride to jail Willie made a statement to Cambern that could not have been more incriminating if he tried: "Those fellows tried to get me to say that I did it, but I thought it would be better not to admit it."

Willie's trial for quadruple murder began on July 19. "The youth of the criminal, the number and relations of the victims, the entire lack of provocation, and all the circumstances of the case make it almost unprecedented in the annals of crime," commented the *New York Times*, showing that Willie's callousness, youth, thoroughness, and body count had made an impression back east. Faced with the circumstantial evidence against him, Willie offered a novel triple-tiered defense: I didn't do it; and if I did do it, I must have been temporarily insane; or maybe I did it in my sleep. One of Willie's most consistent character traits is that he appears to have thought everyone else was an idiot.

The motive was a mystery. There had been no robbery of the victims; the so-called assassin had not purloined $100 in gold, $100 in paper money, or three watches belonging to Mr. Sells that were out in plain sight. The *Kansas City Journal* noted that there was no evidence that Willie's parents or siblings had abused him in any manner. However, a modern profiler might suggest that most of Willie's rage was directed at his brother Walter, since he took the most drastic punishment, the other three family members having received "merely" a crushed skull and a cut throat. In 1886, however, authorities and reporters thought the chief culprit, other than Willie, was dime novels, which they felt had put toxic ideas in his impressionable, immature head: "It is said that he was a constant reader of dime novels and had several times expressed a desire to become a hero," remarked the *Times*. On the other hand, the bodies were not yet cool before Willie happily announced that he would inherit the house, the farm, and all of his father's money—so maybe his motive was simply greed.

Or maybe his total lack of concern after his family's deaths, his open delight when considering the property he would inherit, the fact that he enjoyed being a spectacle in jail, and the indifference he displayed at his trial point to his being a sociopath. Physicians declared him sane, so if their diagnosis was correct, he could not even claim insanity as a fig leaf to explain his conduct.

The verdict, which came on July 27, was no surprise: guilty of first-degree murder, four times over. On August 25, he was sentenced to be hanged. Because he was but a callow youth, the sentence was automatically changed to life in prison.

And so, the jail doors clanged shut on youthful, bloodthirsty, enigmatic, emotionally stunted Willie Sells. Over the next several years, it became the goal of many to see him pardoned, generally based on his tender years and his model behavior in prison. Petitions circulated now and then; one prison warden after another thought he should be released. Willie himself thought it was a swell idea. As early as 1897, the Kansas State Board of Pardons recommended an unconditional pardon. The residents of Erie showed what they thought about that on July 12, when they hanged Sells and his attorney C.A. Cox in effigy.

Another decade passed. On April 9, 1907, Governor Edward Hoch granted Willie, a "model prisoner," an unconditional pardon. He had been so youthful when he went to jail that, even after serving twenty-one years, he was still only thirty-seven when he got out. He moved to Nortonville, where he worked at a drugstore. The record indicates that he never so much as jaywalked for the rest of life.

Sometimes Everyone Else Is Right

By all accounts, Samuel Purple of Pennsylvania was a mean drunkard; by all accounts, he was not a good match for Johannah Lauber of Buffalo, New York. They met in Kansas in 1881. She fell in love, and—by all accounts—her parents and everyone else warned her not to marry this man. She did anyway.

The couple lived near Marena, Hodgeman County, Kansas. In 1886, after a few years of domestic turmoil, Sam was thirty-two years old, Johannah was thirty-one, and they shared their home with four children and Johannah's sister Ottilie ("Tillie").

On the morning of October 29, Johannah told Sam to get out of bed and eat his breakfast. Something about this annoyed him, and he immediately shot her through the body with a revolver, killing her instantly. Then he shot and killed their three-week-old baby and one of their older children.

Sam shot sister-in-law Tillie. The bullet passed through her arm and lodged in her shoulder. He turned his attention to another child but, finding his revolver empty, loaded his shotgun. By accident, he put the shot in one barrel and the powder in another, so when he fired at the child's head, he inflicted only a bad powder burn.

Sam failed at these last two attempts, but galloped away on his horse, exclaiming that he would kill Johannah's parents. Tillie survived her wound, however, and alerted the neighbors. Such a mob gathered at the elder Laubers' house that Sam surrendered to the authorities at Jetmore, knowing his evil plan was thwarted and not particularly wishing to face a mob.

He lengthened his life by only a few days. On the night of November 9, a crowd of over a hundred men—allegedly, many related to Johannah Lauber—walked to the jail and demanded that the lawmen hand over Sam. The officers didn't have the heart to argue, and, within moments, the crowd was on the way to the Purple farm with Sam in tow. According to the local paper, the *Jetmore Reveille*, Sam made many bizarre statements as his lynchers tied a noose around his neck and forced him to mount a barrel: "I am the man that jars the world. Oh, I wish that I could shake it . . . Men, if I had the thing to do over again, I would not do it. I am going to my wife and children . . . I can't pray. If I did wrong I want to die for it . . . I am too good a boy to hang; I am too good a man to be hung." Whether his incoherence was born of fear or drunkenness, we cannot know.

From this point, accounts vary wildly as to details, so believe whichever version you prefer. According to one report, the mob hanged Sam from a tree; according to another, in a barn; according to the third and most ghoulish rendition, they hanged him from the doorway of the house where he tried to exterminate his family.

Another mystery concerns not the exact location where Sam left this world—whether tree, barn, or residence—but rather what happened to his body afterward. One source states that he is buried in an unmarked grave in Fairmount Cemetery in Jetmore. A competing legend affirms that he was buried in his own yard but was exhumed by his family and reinterred in a secret location to prevent grave desecration. Some folks say Sam was buried under a road so people could walk on his remains. For that matter, Johannah's final resting place is also unknown.

Only two members of the Purple family survived the massacre—the child with the burned face and a little boy who escaped harm by hiding under the bed when his father lost it. Tillie, who also lived through the ordeal, died in Los Angeles on August 1, 1902, aged only thirty-five. She is buried among other members of the Lauber family in Hillside Cemetery in Kinsley, Edwards County, Kansas. Some think sister Johannah rests nearby in an unmarked grave.

6

MINNESOTA MASSACRES

Wayward Hayward

On the night of December 3, 1894, a melancholy and lonesome horse returned to its home, a livery stable in Minneapolis. It was pulling a bloody buggy containing bloodstained cushions. But there was no trace of the woman who had rented it earlier that evening, unless the blood counts as a "trace."

A passerby found her fully clothed body lying on a road beside the shore of Lake Calhoun (now known as Bde Maka Ska), a few miles from the city. There was a bullet wound in the back of her head but no gun. It wasn't a case in which the murderer didn't want his victim's identity known; in fact, it was essential to his plan that she be identified, and quickly. Police spoke with the livery stable owner and learned that she was the buggy's renter, Catherine Ging.

Alarm bells went off in the head of Minneapolis resident Levi Stewart when he heard the news. Three days before, a nervous friend named Adry Hayward told him that a scheme was in the planning stages to murder a woman for her insurance money. Adry didn't know any further details, but the mastermind was his brother, Harry T. Hayward. Stewart dismissed it as nonsense. When the real-life killing occurred, he immediately informed the police about what Adry had told him.

The tipped-off police discovered that Ging's life insurance payout did, in fact, go to Harry Hayward for no apparent reason. He was neither her spouse nor her relative.

On December 8, detectives with a search warrant examined the rooms of the Hayward brothers, both living in the Ozark Flats Apartments, owned by their wealthy father, W. W. Hayward. (The building still stands; it is called the Bellevue. Harry Hayward's ground-floor apartment is now a restaurant.) They also picked up Adry Hayward, who kept silent until they took him to the office of his friend-turned-informer Levi Stewart. Adry lost his nerve in Stewart's presence and confessed that the insurance-murder scam involved three men. Harry, the leader, insured Ging's life in his favor and planned her removal from the earth. Harry did not deign to sully his own hands and hired Claus A. Blixt, janitor at the Ozark Flats, to do the murdering. Workhouse inmate Ole Ericsson's job was to destroy Blixt's bloody clothing. Little did Harry realize that the more people involved in a plot and the more responsibilities delegated, the higher the odds someone will talk, get caught, or make a mistake. Adry said that Harry had magical powers of hypnosis—many others would soon make the same claim—and almost convinced him to join the gang. But Adry resisted and, instead, told his friend Stewart what he knew.

"How long have you known about this conspiracy?" asked detectives.

"Several months," admitted Adry.

"And you warned no one? Can you explain that?"

"Well, frankly I was afraid of my brother. He even threatened to kill me if I didn't go along. I did try to talk him out of it. He had a hypnotic spell over me. But I did tell Levi Stewart, who didn't take me seriously."

Chillingly, Adry told investigators that his brother had visited his apartment on the evening of the murder and warned him that he'd better have a rock-solid alibi as to his whereabouts.

On December 8, Blixt and Ericsson were arrested, and Catherine Ging's body began its long, lonely journey to Cold Spring Cemetery, in her hometown of Auburn, New York, where her twin sister, Julia, lived.

Gradually, the details of the conspiracy and murder came out. In times past, Harry Hayward had found Blixt a useful stooge in setting fire to insured buildings, but arson seemed small potatoes. Why not insure a human being to the limit and have Blixt kill her? The subject Hayward chose was Catherine Ging, another resident at Ozark Flats—unmarried, thirty years old, frankly plain, almost supernaturally naive, and a milliner. Harry was rather a handsome bounder, and Ging was delighted to receive attention from him. Gradually, he worked his way around to the fascinating topic of life insurance; did she know that if she took out a large policy on herself, she could borrow money against the policy? Tempting! And then Harry loaned her $10,000 to improve her millinery shop with the stipulation that she insure herself for the same amount and make her old pal Harry the beneficiary. After all, it was only good business! Perhaps he did not realize that one would hardly expect a hatmaker to be so lavishly insured, and the amount would be certain to draw suspicion. (In modern currency, the ten grand would be equivalent to over $260,000.) Ging agreed to Harry's idea.

How did Hayward make so many people bend to his evil will? As has been noted, there was considerable talk that he had some sort of "mesmeric influence"—that he could hypnotize unwitting pawns to do things like sign their insurance over to him or join a murder conspiracy. Taking a less mystical point of view, it seems the charming and affable Hayward was simply adept at convincing otherwise intelligent persons to do stupid things.

Harry should have waited a while before putting his evil plot in motion, but greed overcame his common sense. On the night of December 3, merely *ten days* after Ging signed that extravagantly generous insurance policy in his favor, he drove her to Thirteenth Street in the buggy that he insisted she rent so there would be no record of his having hired it. To Ging's puzzlement, they picked up Claus Blixt, whom she may have recognized as the janitor at her apartment. When the three were on Calhoun Road—far enough from the city to have privacy, but not too far—Blixt shot Ging. Hayward hurried back to town on foot and made sure he was spotted at the theater for an alibi. He even met a date there, a society lady who ended up with a great story to tell her descendants—if she chose to tell it.

After committing the murder and dumping the body, Blixt hoofed it to Minneapolis and gave his blood-soaked clothing to conspirator Ericsson, who did something remarkably dumb: Tasked with disposing of this damning evidence, he threw some of it in a furnace immediately. But avarice got the better of him, as it had for his puppet master Hayward; the more valuable clothing he saved, and, the next morning, he traveled to Iowa Falls, Iowa, to see his wife and asked her to wash it! When Ericsson returned to Minneapolis with the laundered clothes, he reasoned that he could sell them in a Washington Avenue pawnshop.

Harry Hayward and Claus Blixt were arraigned on December 17. Surprisingly, Blixt—who had admitted he committed the murder—pled not guilty. He was hoping against hope that he would be charged with manslaughter rather than murder and get a lighter sentence than the hanging he fully expected. Blixt's attorney claimed his client had been temporarily insane, thanks to a drug *some villain* (Hayward was meant) slipped in his alcohol, and said he would prove it in court with medical testimony, a promise he never fulfilled.

As Hayward awaited his trial, certain of his other sins were exposed to the public. In addition to dabbling in arson, insurance fraud, and murder, he was unmasked as a member of a "green goods gang." To modern ears, this might sound like he was a vegetable thief, but it meant that he pushed counterfeit money.

On Christmas Day came another story that harmed Hayward's case: it was said that he tried to bribe Sheriff James Ege to murder "that coward Blixt" or at least allow his former henchman-turned-stoolie to commit suicide if the mood struck him. Perhaps Blixt could be pushed into it! Just give him a loaded gun and tell him a lynch mob was on the way, and—

Sheriff Ege told him *no*.

On January 21, 1895, Hayward's trial began in Minneapolis. The public was so eager to see it that every seat in the courtroom was taken within five minutes; had it been a vaudeville show—which in some ways it was, since the defendant spent much time ostentatiously chewing gum and playing with his pet spaniel—it would have been considered SRO (standing room only). Adding to the strangeness, prosecutor Frank Nye was a brother of noted humorist Bill Nye. It must have made Hayward nervous when Blixt's defense attorney sat on the prosecution side, a sure sign that his lackey was about to turn on him. Predictably, Hayward's attorneys said they would enter an insanity plea. If taken at face value, this would mean a *genuinely* insane Hayward had doped Blixt's liquor to render him *temporarily* insane, and therefore neither of them could be held responsible for anything.

It was a protracted trial by the standards of the era, lasting seven weeks. Hayward seemed determined to do everything he could to make people ache to see him swing. Not only did he try to bribe the sheriff to kill Blixt, on March 2, he also threatened his brother Adry in court. When Harry saw him leaving, he "accosted his attorney and insisted that he be allowed to swear out a warrant against his brother" and emitted "oath after oath." As Adry passed, Harry shouted, "You'll be wearing stripes inside a year! I'll see if I get the worst of this and you go free! I know enough about you to send you up for ten years! I can show that you are a highwayman, and that you have had five fires, [and] set them yourself!"

Adry sadly muttered, "Harry, I don't wish anything against you. I don't want you to wear stripes, and I sincerely hope you will be a free man."

"If I am, you had better keep a deputy with you the rest of your natural life!"

Harry had the good sense to pitch his tantrum after court had adjourned and the jury was gone for the day, but reporters heard it, and, when it got in the papers, he looked less sympathetic than ever.

On March 8, the jury found Hayward guilty as sin. They didn't even vote twice. His sentence was fixed as death by hanging, to the surprise of absolutely no one. The date was set for June 21, but, due to the usual legal delays, it was rescheduled for December 11.

Claus Blixt turned state's evidence to save his own skin or, to be anatomically precise, his neck and testified against Hayward. Nevertheless, he went on trial for murder in April, when he again said Hayward's strange hypnotic power had completely overshadowed his will. Blixt received a life sentence at Stillwater State Prison and was considered darned lucky to get it. I don't know what happened to the third conspirator, Ole Ericsson, who thought it a good idea to clean up and sell incriminating evidence in a murder case to earn a few coppers, but undoubtedly his punishment was less serious than that meted out to Blixt and Hayward.

Especially Hayward. His attorneys appealed to the governor for a reprieve but were met with a chilly refusal. The governor signed the death warrant on December 7, giving Harry Hayward four days of life. Seeing that the jig was up, he confessed. He seemed proud of his villainy, although his carefully crafted, would-be nefarious scheme began falling apart almost as soon as it was perpetrated. He was mouthy in those final days, refusing all religious advisers and revealing that he originally planned to murder Blixt and make it look like suicide to eliminate a witness, but he had gone soft and changed his mind. He cursed Blixt, his brother Adry, and everyone else who, in his judgment, had gotten him into such a predicament—everyone but himself, that is.

As his hours turned to minutes, Hayward indulged in gallows humor, saying he felt so good "I would like to be hung every day." He remarked,

"When Harry Hayward is hung, his ghost will turn around and say that it is ashamed of his body." He put on the suit he was to be hanged and buried in—a snazzy black cutaway, with a turn-down collar and a white silk tie—and refused to remove it. He said he wanted his barber to attend the hanging. But despite the display of bravado, the death watch noticed his lips quivered from time to time and that he constantly wiped his hands.

Hayward recovered his nerve, and jailhouse officials were astounded by his foolish nonchalance in the face of death. Evidently, he forgave Adry, as he shared a last dinner with him. To his brother Thaddeus, he said, "You know I am a great believer in Spiritualism. If I get safely on the other side I will send a message to you." Just before two o'clock on the morning of December 11, he made a five-minute speech on the gallows, asking for three cheers—a speech so larded with absurd witticisms that his own attorney finally requested that he knock it off. He refused to pray in his cell, yet it appeared that he changed his mind about God as he stood on the gallows. Turning serious for a few moments, he hoped the deity would pardon his wicked deeds: "O Lord, for Christ's sake, forgive me my sins." But then he said to the officials—"with a sneer," according to the *New York Times*—"Keep up your courage, boys, pull her tight. I 'stand pat.'" The trap was sprung. Just how painless was his trip to the nether regions is uncertain; some sources state that he lived only "for several moments" after being hanged, while others say he kicked the air like a colt for fifteen interminable minutes.

The body was placed in a temporary vault at Lakewood Cemetery. Mother Hayward made a spectacle of herself at the grave site, shrieking things such as "Poor dear Harry! My baby boy! God has forgiven him!" Poor Adry was there too. The reason for Harry's short-term storage was revealed the day after Christmas, when his body was sent to Chicago for cremation. Hayward (and his family) had a mortal fear that grave robbers would seize him—no idle worry, since body snatchers were especially pleased to acquire the remains of notorious criminals. In fact, there were signs someone had tampered with the vault; whether it was a medical student or someone who wanted to put Hayward's carcass on public display, no one could say. Harry's ashes were given to his brother Thaddeus (*not* Adry!). Who knows where they are now.

After Hayward's death it was learned that—if he told the truth, always a matter for debate—he was even worse than previously realized. During his ridiculous oration on the gallows, he said, "The people think that I am a kind of a devil, and if they knew my past life they would be well aware of that fact. I have made a shorthand confession of some of my deeds to Messrs. Mannix, Goodsell, and Mabey [his attorneys], which is true to the best of my recollections." The contents were made public on December 19. Within its twenty thousand words, written in a "careless, flippant style," according to a reporter, Hayward confessed to four unsuspected murders: Carrie Hass of Pasadena, whom he claimed to have robbed, shot, and buried in the woods of the Sierra Madre Mountains; an unnamed tubercular man in Long Branch, New Jersey, whom he shot and dumped in a river; a Chinese man he killed brutally after "a gambling quarrel"; and a Mexican in El Paso. Suspiciously, he didn't include many checkable details such as dates and named only one alleged victim. There were no follow-up stories in the newspapers. Most researchers then and now think he invented the extra murders to increase his notoriety.

(Those with an interest in serial killers may note that Hayward's infamous contemporary H. H. Holmes also wrote a confession—his was for the newspapers—in which he acknowledged more murders than he probably committed; he claimed twenty-seven victims, and some trusting souls have credited him with more than two hundred, but only nine were confirmed. Holmes wrote his memoirs in April 1896 and was hanged on May 7, 1896, six months after Hayward preceded him to hell; possibly Holmes modeled his false confession on Hayward's and made himself out to be worse than he actually was, though certainly he was bad enough.)

What happened to the $10,000 in insurance money for which Catherine Ging was sacrificed? Harry willed the money to his father—which means that the good-natured folks at Travelers Insurance Company actually gave Harry the payout! But the grieving father relinquished it, so, on December 14, 1895, the murdered woman's twin sister, Julia, filed a claim to it. On January 8, 1898, she lost her lawsuit against Travelers; the judge followed the bizarre logic that Julia was not entitled to the money since Catherine Ging was not killed by accident and "was not killed in defending her own life." Presumably if Catherine had put up a struggle, Julia would have struck it rich.

A final droll note: in April 1896, the nation's newspapers ran an advertisement with a triple-barreled headline: "MISS GING'S AVENGER. The Prosecutor of Harry Hayward Breaks Down Under the Stress of That Great Trial. His Nerve, Strength, and Sleep Restored by Dr. Charcot's Kola Nervine Tablets." This was followed by a testimonial from Frank M.

Nye. Manufactured in La Crosse and Boston! Only fifty cents at your local druggist's! Write for a free sample!

Barrel of Fun, or: The Scenter of Attention

The date was November 5, 1889—and it was nighttime, which likely made the following event worse. Hunter and trapper Theodore (or Timothy) Delaney was in the forest on Lake Johanna's west shore. Not far from a schoolhouse, Delaney found something he had not been hunting for: a man's hand, not exactly in mint condition, protruding from the ground. He left for his home in St. Paul, thirteen miles away, with understandable haste.

On November 8, Coroner Quinn came to the lake and, after some difficulty, found what Delaney had described to him, with a bloody hatchet nearby. The coroner dug up the torso of the unlucky fellow two feet below the surface. A piece of wool carpet covered the dismembered legs. The nude remains were in sorry shape, and the odor, as one might imagine, was indescribable. Quinn really had his work cut out for him, but these were his findings:

- The top of the skull was sawed off.
- The scalp was lacerated in several places and removed from the skull.
- The left arm was fractured.
- Two upper right ribs were crushed in.
- There was a gash over one eye.
- Under the body lay a tar barrel, burned on the inside.
- The body was bisected crudely at the hips, probably with the hatchet left at the scene.
- The heart and lungs were in place, but the liver and intestines had been removed and placed in the bottom of the barrel.
- Part of the brain was missing.
- For a finale, whoever buried the body also carved the words "A traitor" on a plank and nailed it to the barrel.

The seeming murder was, overall, an unnecessarily extravagant production. Quinn noted that the unknown man was about five feet, nine inches tall and between thirty and thirty-five years old. He was clean-shaven and had good teeth and small, delicate hands.

So, who was the poor fellow? Locals remembered a riot at a Swedish immigrants' picnic at Bass Lake, after which a participant named Andrew Johnson disappeared. Problem was, the fight occurred over a year before, and Coroner Quinn estimated that the body had been dead three or four months. Scratch Andrew!

The favorite theory in town, for a while at least, was that Charles Kemper, son of former Virginia governor James Kemper, was the victim. Charles disappeared from his Wabasha Street apartment, not far from the state capitol building, the previous June. The twenty-three-year-old had come to town to recover his health; he was described as a young man "of exemplary habits" who stayed out of trouble, was not in debt, had many friends, and spent his evenings reading rather than in dissipation. However, one afternoon, Kemper went for a walk and was never seen again. Some thought the body's description matched Kemper's. However, when the remains were brought to St. Paul on November 9—so that all and sundry might take a peep at and a sniff of them—Kemper's friends saw that the deceased had blondish hair, while their missing companion had dark hair. An operative of the Pinkerton Detective Agency, hired by Kemper's family to seek him, agreed that it was not he. Scratch Charles!

The coroner considered other mysteries besides the victim's identity. Why was the makeshift forest grave so shallow? Why was a hand poking so ostentatiously out of the ground? Why had the killer left a hatchet in plain sight rather than take it with him? It was almost as though someone *wanted* the body to be found!

These circumstances led Sheriff Bean, along with Coroner Quinn, to theorize that the whole thing was just a practical joke played with a rotting human corpse as a prop instead of a rubber spider, a whoopee cushion, or fake vomit. But who had pulled off the funny, and where had he procured a real human cadaver? The authorities dusted off the standby explanation whenever bodies turned up in inappropriate public settings: medical students did it. The sheriff thought the "murder victim" was really a train accident fatality whose body was given to a surgeon and his students, who shared a sick sense of humor. In fact, it *did* appear that surgical instruments were the tools used for the mutilations described above, and the top of the skull had been sawed off autopsy style. Bean said he knew the names of the surgeon and students but refused to divulge them. The *St. Paul Globe* pointed out that even if this were the case, the perpetrators were still guilty of the crime of burying the body in violation of state and city laws. (One might add that they had committed abuse of a corpse, and how.) "A gross outrage upon common decency has been committed," said the paper. "But it is hard to believe that intelligent young men could be guilty of such an offense against the laws of nature."

Why would anyone pull off such a hoax, anyway? St. Paul authorities said a clue lay in the words carved on the barrel: "A traitor." Fellow Irish immigrants murdered Dr. Patrick Cronin in Chicago the previous May for being *a traitor* to the secret Irish organization, the Clan na Gael, which he accused of embezzlement. This led reporters to conclude that the Minnesota hoaxer, whomever he was, was copycatting the Chicago murder for publicity. (Or whomever *she* was—let us not be sexist; let us assume that a woman is equally capable of hauling a decaying body into the forest and cutting it into pieces for a laff.)

On the other hand, the conspiracy-minded and people who just love a good juicy murder insisted that the man had been slain, and the killer had mutilated the body as a false clue to cast suspicion on those ever-handy scapegoats, medical students. Adherents to this theory argued that surgeons in training wouldn't toss away such a usable anatomical specimen merely after removing part of the brain and that the body had not been dissected so much as hacked into fragments. If a killer had cleverly shifted blame onto medical students, kudos to him for at least coming up with an original idea.

When first reporting the story, a *Globe* subheadline called the body's discovery "A Mystery That May Yet Rival Chicago's Big Sensation"—a reference to Dr. Cronin. It sounds as though journalists in St. Paul were secretly hoping for a first-class murder to compete with Chicago. If so, their civic pride was deflated when the truth came out, not unlike a ripe body from an unhallowed grave, on November 12.

On that day, *Globe* readers learned, in a story bearing the delightful subheadline "The Story of a Stiff," that the sheriff and coroner had been partially correct: the body was not a murder victim. However, medical students were not responsible for the disrespectful disposal of the remains. The newspaper confirmed that an anonymous tramp had been killed in a train accident back in the summer. After students performed a cursory autopsy, they buried the corpse in a tar barrel so that they might retrieve it later and reassemble its skeleton for a handsome display. They interred it at Lake Johanna, outside of city limits, and employed a mercifully unnamed high school lad to help.

The youth saw a rare opportunity to manufacture a sensation. He came back to the burial site later and single-handedly exhumed the hapless hobo. His first impulse was to boil the body and keep the skeleton himself, but then he had the happy notion to cut the body into pieces with a hatchet and replant it in such fashion that it was sure to be found eventually. This he did, after attaching the plank reading "A traitor" to the barrel. Who says all teenagers are lazy? Given the amount of physical labor and secrecy it must have taken to perpetrate his practical joke, one does not know whether he deserved congratulations or a spirited ear boxing. A disgusted doctor reported that the same precocious young ghoul once turned a bagful of snakes loose in a Jackson Street restaurant with an effect that likely beggared the facility of language to invoke.

So, in the end, St. Paul could *not* compete with Chicago in bloodiness. It was fun while it lasted.

Irresistible

Professor Oscar M. Olson was thirty-five years old and a respected instructor at the University of Minnesota's Farm School, for which he was superintendent of demonstration farms. Farmers and Olson's colleagues thought highly of him, but his life was not all haystacks and combines. Olson had suspected for some time that his wife, Lillian, was having a fling with Clyde Darling, a married laundry-van driver with a richly comic surname under the circumstances. On June 16, 1912, she admitted it. As the professor recounted later, "When I returned from my office my wife told me Darling had hugged and kissed her. I saw Darling one day later in the presence of the man for whom he was working. When I accused him of insulting my wife, he turned pale. Then he recovered himself and said, 'I admit it. It's all my fault.'"

Olson warned his adversary to stay away from his house but to no avail. Mrs. Lillian Olson—described by a reporter as "tall, dark, good-looking, affable"—simply could not resist Darling. She insisted that his hypnotic hold on her psyche influenced her to do naughty things against her will.

She begged her husband to help her fight those urges. For example, when Olson was in Clearbrook on November 12, she sent a message asking him to return home immediately. She met him at the door crying, "Oscar, do I look demented? That devilish laundryman is haunting me again. He has been here several times and I can't resist his overtures. Please help me to keep him from me."

The finale came on the night of March 5, 1913. According to his account, Olson was staying alone in his house at 21 Nourse Street when he heard someone enter the summer kitchen. He crept in and found Darling standing there with a bundle of laundry in his arms, as though he owned the place. Darling seemed distinctly disappointed that Mrs. O. wasn't at home. "Oh, it's *you*," he said, with superfluous profanity for emphasis, and took what the professor interpreted as a threatening step forward.

(To be fair, some press accounts suggest that the professor was more an aggressor than a victim. For example, the *St. Paul Pioneer Press* of March 7 headlined a story "Was Clyde Darling Lured to His End?" Some theorized that Olson tricked his rival into entering the house by sending a false invitation in his wife's name. Such a note could not have come anytime recently from Mrs. Olson, who had been visiting relatives in Montevideo for the past two weeks. Darling's apologists even suggested that he innocently came by the Olson house to collect a bill—but at night?)

Olson shot Darling twice in the chest. The Irresistible expired, clutching that bundle of laundry. A few minutes later, the professor ambled over to his neighbor Andrew L. Anderson. "There has been some trouble over at my house and I want you to come over there," he told Anderson. The neighbor assented, and the two walked to the residence in silence. At the doorstep, Olson laconically told Anderson what the hubbub was all about, "I shot a fellow. He's dead."

He showed Darling's corpse to prove he wasn't rousting his neighbor out at night for trivial reasons. Anderson asked, "Should I call the police?"

"Yes," said Olson. The cops arrived and took him to the Prior Avenue station, where Olson took a long, untroubled nap.

The theory that the professor had lured Darling to the house with a fake note gained traction with the revelation that a postcard in the dead man's pocket was addressed to "the little tottie man" from "the little brown hen" and written in a distinctly feminine hand. However, the laundryman's widow, Viola Darling, admitted, no doubt with no small embarrassment, that she was the little brown hen in question. She had written the note to her husband as a Valentine's Day joke.

Investigators examined a notebook in which Olson kept track of his daily expenses and travels. They discovered that he took a trip to Montevideo on February 27, a few days before he shot Darling and while his wife was in the same town visiting relatives. She professed to know nothing about his trip. Why had he gone to the town without telling her? It seemed an exciting discovery at first, but it was preposterous to think that Olson would keep a careful written record of his trip if he were up to something sinister. Most likely, he made the unannounced, secret journey to find out whether his wife was seeing family members as she claimed or was gadding about with Darling.

The grand jury indicted Olson on a charge of first-degree murder on March 10. He was taking another refreshing nap when the news broke, and jailhouse personnel didn't feel it worth waking him to tell him. Meanwhile, the University of Minnesota's Farm School published a pamphlet including an article by Professor Olson on the topic "Testing Seed Corn," in which he persuasively argued that "money is saved by testing corn before it is planted."

In early April, Olson sat in a St. Paul courtroom explaining his actions before a roomful of intensely interested spectators. He pled the "unwritten law"—a defense used since time immemorial, yet not codified in any law books, holding that an aggrieved married person had a perfect right, perhaps even a *duty*, to injure or kill a home-wrecker because he or she had it coming. If the reactions of court attendants were anything to go by, Olson had made a canny choice. According to news reports, onlookers wept throughout the testimony, as did the professor and his wife.

To save her husband, Mrs. Olson took the stand on April 4 to lay bare her secret sins and assure the jury that something about Darling annihilated her natural defenses and good sense. The judge cautioned her that she did not have to answer self-incriminating questions, but she said bravely, "I will tell all."

And she did: "I told Darling I was not a bad woman and begged him to discontinue his visits to our home, but he persisted in coming and when he pressed me closely in his arms I could not resist."

The professor added, "My wife said, 'Darling has a superhuman power over me. I can't resist him. He hypnotizes me. I am afraid of him. Please keep him from me.'"

Mrs. Olson said Darling threatened to kill the professor if he separated them and then would "tell all the neighbors what I was." During one unsolicited visit, she had commanded Darling to get out and never return, to which he replied, like a stage villain, "You're in the game now, and you are in to stay. Olson always has stood in our way. I'll put him out of the way if you tell him."

(It appears that Darling had had the run of the house. One wonders if the Olsons ever considered buying better door locks.)

Lillian must have had a lot to confess, since her testimony did not end until the night of April 7. As soon as she finished, she collapsed to the floor in a melodramatic faint. Spectators no doubt were secretly hoping she would and probably would have felt cheated if she hadn't.

As though the jurors were not sufficiently thrilled, the defense asked the professor to re-create the shooting, just like in the movies. "Grasping the same revolver with which he killed Darling and fairly shaking with emotion," wrote a reporter, "Olson trained the weapon upon one of the jurors and stepped slowly forward. He hesitated a moment, then quickly retreated and pulled the trigger of the empty weapon."

Darling's widow, Viola, took the stand and contradicted nearly everything Lillian Olson said, claiming that her husband had been at home on the nights when Mrs. Olson said he had been making his unwanted, yet badly wanted, social calls.

The jury evidently didn't believe Mrs. Darling. On April 8, they found Olson not guilty. "There is going to be a happy reunion at the Olson home tonight," announced the happy professor. Just the two of them!

It was all too sordid, to be sure, but the Olsons were interesting enough to grace the front page of the *New York Times*. How many of us can say that?

7

IOWA EXTERMINATIONS

A Dying Man's Love Letter

It was a cold Midwestern day, January 8, 1927. Charles Elrod, a twenty-eight-year-old widower, electrician, and World War One veteran from Lewellen, Nebraska, lay ill on his rented bed in a Marshalltown hotel. Convinced that the Reaper was tapping on his shoulder, Charles composed a mondo weird love letter to his fiancée, local nineteen-year-old high school senior Veda B.

Charles suspected she had poisoned him, as depicted in a dream—but even if she had, well, he would forgive her because he loved her so darned much:

Dear sweetheart: Last night I dreamed that I had come to see you and that you had got mad at me and gave me poison for revenge. Although you have been so mad at me that you have threatened my life, I don't believe you would do a thing like that after the living hell I have gone through for you. If I could have you for my own, without all this grief, I would be the happiest man on earth . . . Honey, I went out in the kitchen tonight and got a drink. Have been getting sick ever since. Could see stars when I left you, dear. If I don't feel better soon I will go. I sure wish tomorrow night would hurry up and come, dear. You surely know that I love you with all my heart and soul. Dear, I don't feel like I will get to give this letter to you. I hope you or no one else has poisoned me, as I dreamed you did. But if you have, I will forgive you with all my heart. I feel like we will never see each other again . . . If I don't the last words are—forgiveness for all. Will rest a while, dear.

At its conclusion, Charles's letter became increasingly discursive: "If anything happens let all be known, and the paper has got full authority to print and [has] the right to use all there is in the room. Sick, oh God, how I feel now . . . Print the pictures and everything for something is sure wrong. I feel it coming on—I am almost blind now. I am a World War soldier—will have to rest some more."

He never finished. Charles's hunch that he was on his deathbed proved correct. He died on January 9. The accusations in his premortem love letter to Veda attracted the interest of the Marshalltown coroner. This official sent Charles's viscera to the University of Iowa at Iowa City for examination. Their chemists reported that they found no poison.

Nevertheless, the unsatisfied coroner wanted a second opinion and had two other doctors examine the viscera. They said there *was* evidence of poison and that "the appearance of the vital organs . . . gave evidence of death from an unnatural cause." The doctors theorized that Charles met his end from one of those untraceable poisons so beloved of mystery authors.

Some thought the poisoner might have been Charles himself. Veda admitted to having played a foolish little trick on her fiancé to test his love: she had written letters to him, using a male pseudonym, to make Charles think he had competition for Veda's hand. (She had gotten this inane idea from a magazine story.) The schoolgirlish ruse to provoke Charles's jealousy had an unintended consequence: he took the letters seriously and developed a paranoid obsession that his nonexistent "rival" might kill him. He wrote a letter to the police telling them he feared for his life. Had Charles imbibed poison to escape his imaginary adversary?

Veda was embarrassed that her silly prank had gotten so out of hand. When Charles's final letter was read aloud in court, she muttered, "I can't stand any more," and appeared on the brink of a nervous breakdown. She wept throughout her testimony but emphatically declared that she did not know Charles to be suicidal; to the best of her knowledge, he had not owned any poison; and he had not seemed to believe in dreams.

In light of the professional opinion of the two doctors who said they had detected poison, on January 19, the coroner's jury determined that an unknown person had slain Charles. This was all too ambiguous for the authorities, who ordered Charles's grave opened and a second autopsy performed. The coroner wanted the University of Iowa to take another crack at it. Meanwhile, police stood guard at Veda's home to kick out nosey reporters who saw nothing wrong with pestering a teenage girl about the possible murder of her fiancé.

Charles was again exposed to daylight on January 25. His vital organs were removed and taken to his examiners in Iowa City. He must have had the most closely scrutinized intestines in all of Iowa. The results were announced on February 5: scientists *still* found no traces of poison. There were no other signs of violence, and they opined that Charles's cause of death might never be determined. Some persons (not the scientists) suggested that Charles had died of a broken heart, triggered by his jealousy over Veda. If so, it was interesting that his heart broke right after he had that drink in the kitchen.

The amateur sleuth will enjoy knowing the reason why Charles, who lived in Nebraska, was in the Marshalltown hotel room in the first place. (Were you wondering?) He was in town to see if he had Veda's parents' permission to marry her. But before they could give their yes or no, he had entered his everlasting rest.

One cannot help feeling the key to the mystery lies in that strange, rambling letter Charles wrote while dying, since he considered it his last statement to his fiancée. It suggests that he was peeved with her despite his fulsome proclamations of love. Unfortunately, since it was composed in a possibly poison-fueled frenzy, the most intriguing parts are incomprehensible. For example, was he referring to newspaper reporters when he wrote, "The paper has got full authority to print and [has] the right to use all there is in the room"? (All of *what* in the room?) What did he mean when he urged that the newspapers (presumably) "print the pictures and everything for something is sure wrong"—pictures of *what*? Had Veda actually threatened his life, as he stated in the letter, or was that just the delirium talking?

These questions and many others must remain unanswered. Despite the contradictory scientific opinion as to whether Charles was poisoned and the bizarre statements in his letter, the authorities shrugged their collective shoulders, said, "Oh the hell with it," and let the matter drop forever.

By a Dirty Coward

James O'Day was proprietor of the Coal Chutes restaurant outside of Tama, so named because the establishment was located near the Chicago and Northwestern Railroad tracks, on which coal trains ran day and night.

In January 1913, O'Day hired a newcomer to town, sixty-three-year-old George Taylor, as a cook. Taylor proved to be a good short-order chef, and he made friends among townspeople and trainmen.

A few months later, O'Day tired of the restaurant business. Taylor took over as owner and cook of the Coal Chutes.

The ordinary life of the ordinary Taylor ended on the rainy night of July 19, 1913. At 9:00 p.m., Taylor closed the restaurant and started walking home along the railroad tracks. As he strolled into the darkness, William Puize and Elmer Lewis entered the train yard, intending to hop a freight to Belle Plaine in search of work.

As they waited, they heard three quick shots not far away; then a pause, and two more shots. Badly spooked, they hurried to Tama, figuring they could catch a train there. Their hasty departure became even faster when they noticed an object lying in the gloom beside the south track, an object that, upon closer inspection, proved to be a dead man. Once in Tama, Puize and Lewis reported their discovery.

Dr. Benjamin Thompson examined the body of George Taylor, that embodiment of ordinariness, and found the cause of death to be a bullet wound in the chest. Jessie Traviss, a friend of Taylor's, testified at the inquest that Taylor had visited him three hours before the murder and had had $700. The money was gone except for a few coins, so the official verdict was that a person or persons unknown had shot and robbed him.

The victim had no known family and, seemingly, no close friends except the ones he had made in Tama over the last six months. There is something sad about the local newspaper's observation that Taylor had few mourners when he was buried in Tama's Oak Hill Cemetery on July 22.

However, the few friends he had were fiercely loyal. They must have felt determined to avenge his death in some fashion and so bought a monument for him, the epitaph on which has since become famous: "Assasinated [sic] by a Dirty Coward Whose Name is Not Worthy to be Mentioned Here."

The murder was unsolved then and remains unsolved now, and it is unlikely that the dirty coward's name ever will be known.

Bones in the Basement, or: Razing the Dead

When demolition crews tear down old houses, they probably have two subconscious thoughts: (1) *Hey, maybe I'll find treasure!* (2) *But what if I find a body?!?* Workers razing an old building in East Dubuque had the incomparable thrill of undergoing the second experience—five times over.

By 1888, this section of Dubuque, a boomtown only a generation before, was prey to what we now call urban decay. Instead of the thousands the neighborhood had once housed, there were only a few hundred occupants. On July 30, workers tore down a building known as Farmers' House, which stood in a neighborhood where there were once more than twenty hotels and many boardinghouses. As they excavated the cellar, they found no fewer than five skeletons.

All but one skeleton was laid to rest facing east, so it is nice to see that whoever buried them followed tradition and social niceties. Everyone assumed the bodies were surreptitiously buried murder victims. After all, it is difficult to conceive an innocent scenario in which five persons who die of natural causes might be interred in a cellar. This conviction was strengthened when Dr. Campbell found a bullet hole in one skull.

They were the remains of middle-aged men. Some old-timers noted that twenty-five years earlier, the house "where they were found had been a combination saloon and boardinghouse, where gamblers and wicked women congregated." One remarkable feature was the brevity of its tenants' occupations. The brief tenancy did not draw much comment at the time, since East Dubuque was a popular stop for pioneers on their way to the California goldfields. Visitors did not remain in the area long, and no one was suspicious if they abruptly vanished.

In those days, "money was plenty and gambling and dissipation were the order of the day," commented a reporter. "Most of these old hotels, once regarded as magnificent in their proportions, still stand, grim monuments of the past, the abode of rats and tramps."

The one-time proprietors of the boardinghouse had long since absquatulated, and the skeletons' identities never were confirmed, but longtime residents of the town came up with a couple of intriguing possibilities. One was a man named Dixon, who had sold a valuable Vermont farm many years earlier to finance his search for gold. Possibly, he let the wrong people know he had several thousand dollars in cash on hand. One day he disappeared; a boy who had traveled with him insisted to all who would listen that two thugs had killed and robbed Dixon. They, in turn, insisted that Dixon had been drunk and had gone for a pleasure trip on a skiff that overturned, sweeping his body away. His drowned body never turned up—nor did the accused, who vanished the day after the boy named them and never were seen again.

Another candidate for victimhood was a butcher named Baron who came to Dubuque around 1863 from Grant County, Wisconsin. He, too, was indiscreet about the inordinate amount of cash he carried and, like Dixon, checked into the boardinghouse that recently had fallen to the wrecking crew. However, Baron was described as "young," and the five cellar skeletons were those of older men.

The victims never were identified, and the killer, or killers, never caught. But we can say with confidence that a skeleton buried in a cellar is indicative of the laxest housecleaning, and four more only compound the issue.

8

INDIANA IMBROGLIOS

Charles McGalliard Gets a Twofer

On Halloween night 1911, the community of Muncie, Indiana, held a masked costume party in Franklin Hall, located at 113–117 North Mulberry. It was a great civic-minded idea to give the youngsters something to do other than smash pumpkins, soap windows, and knock over outhouses. It would discourage mindless violence, right?

One young man among the revelers was unhappy: Charles McGalliard, a twenty-four-year-old painter who already had been married and divorced once. He had been dating Alta H. for six weeks, and he was just silly in love. His buddies at the pool hall complained about his putting on airs lately, getting all "slicked up," and no longer spending much time with them. Why, the dandy even bought new clothes! Charles told all his pals that Alta promised to marry him on Christmas Day, which her father later hotly denied, with excellent cause.

But back to the Halloween dance. Charles was peeved because Alta went without him. He turned up at the function late and intoxicated. He was heard to remark, "No one else will take her home tonight." He and Alta had just started a midnight waltz when bystanders overheard their angry dialogue.

"I won't," hissed Alta.

"You will," said Charles.

"I won't," Alta reiterated and started to pull away from her dance partner. The circular argument ended when Charles produced a .38-caliber revolver from his hip pocket, aimed it at her breast, and pulled the trigger three times. It fired the third time, and the bullet went entirely through Alta's body. She had only enough time to say "Oh, I'm shot."

For a few seconds, the other partygoers thought they had witnessed a sick Halloween prank. Then they realized the truth, and most stampeded for the exits. One was Alta's sister. "Costumes that a moment before were comical, suddenly, in the light of tragedy, became horribly grotesque," observed a reporter from the *Muncie Evening Press*. Partygoers carried Alta to Dr. Spickermon's office, where she died three minutes later at the age of twenty.

Instantly remorseful, Charles turned the gun on himself but was stopped by the few former revelers who were brave enough to stick around. Not that he could have harmed himself in any case; the bullet he had fired was the only one in the revolver. The police led Charles to a jail cell, where he spent a despondent night. After he left the hall, the dance band struck up a two-step, and a few straggling couples did some mirthless dancing, but the party was effectively over. The band finally gave up, played "Home Sweet Home," and departed.

The *Muncie Evening Press* described the community feeling after the murder in mysterious, almost occult terms: "The police are stirred deeply. It has been some time since there was a tragedy of the kind that happened at Franklin Hall and the people seemed to have believed that the reign of terror which had held the city in its grasp for some time had passed. There is a feeling over the city that there is yet more of the same nature to follow and the horror . . . grows with the conviction."

What "reign of terror" had gripped Muncie previously, and why? Unfortunately, the reporter did not explain for posterity. It appears from the context of other stories in the paper that there had been several recent murders in the city.

The editor of the *Press* placed the blame not necessarily on Charles, but on a society that encouraged youth to attend such decadent bacchanalias as Halloween parties where they danced their lust-inspiring waltzes. In an editorial titled "The Dana of Death"—that must be a typo for "dance"—the journalist went rather over the top and then some:

> Her fate might have been worse had she lived. . . . She was the product of just such affairs as that put on at Franklin Hall Halloween night. And what was the youth who killed her? He was a product of the same institution.

The dance in Franklin Hall was a dance of revelry. It was a dance of drunkenness and ribaldry, lust and destruction. . . . Had Alta H. been under the care of the virtuous instead of under the glare of the red light she would not have been killed by McGalliard. And had McGalliard been sober, it is not probable that he would have been fired with the spirit of murder.

There was more vitriol in this vein, coming within a hairbreadth of suggesting that girls who attended such functions were likely to become prostitutes and other things that surely did not comfort the grieving families of killer and victim. One can imagine the *Press* editor hiding under his desk if Alta's father came calling.

Alta's funeral was held at First Methodist Protestant Church on November 3. The house of worship was so crowded that many mourners had to listen to the services standing outside. But they weren't all bereaved friends and family. A reporter observed that some were morbid curiosity seekers who had neither seen nor heard of Alta in her short lifetime. She was laid to rest in Beech Grove Cemetery.

Charles McGalliard was in a world of trouble, to be sure, and nearly indefensible, as his crime was committed before many witnesses. McGalliard's attorneys refused to tell journalists their strategy for defending him. One strongly suspects they had none, since, over the ensuing months, they, to say nothing of local gossips, offered every farfetched argument known to the law, the imagination, and (perhaps) dreams:

1. Charles didn't know his gun was loaded. After all, he pulled the trigger three times before it went off, and, after he killed Alta, he shouted, "I didn't mean to do it." (On the other hand, skeptics argued that Charles believed his gun was fully loaded and did intend to kill her. After he was arrested, he said, "I knew what she was," which suggests that he thought her too flirtatious, and his motive was jealousy.)
2. He aimed it at Alta but was juuuuust kidding.
3. He aimed it at Alta but was "only bluffing the girl," that is, trying to scare her—it *was* Halloween, after all!
4. He should be shown leniency because he was so very, very young.
5. He should be shown leniency because he was so very, very intoxicated at the time and didn't know what he was doing, a precursor of today's "diminished capacity" defense.
6. He felt so very, very remorseful.

When McGalliard went on trial in early January 1912, his legal team polished off the creakiest of all defenses: Charles should be shown mercy because he had "mental epilepsy." In other words, the insanity defense. At least they combined it ingeniously with the diminished capacity defense: Charles took a drink of a "mysterious brand of liquor" that triggered epilepsy and unseated his reason. It does not appear that Charles had epilepsy before Halloween night 1911, so that must have been some really potent brew! Even his facial features were transformed fearsomely, said one of McGalliard's attorneys, who strained credulity to the snapping point by adding that the boy had "never had a quarrel in his life" before the dance. Skeptics noted that Charles spoke rationally with police officers minutes after the shooting, so the temporary insanity must have been fleeting indeed.

The same lawyer offered as proof of Charles's mental instability that he was "unable to remember" what had happened that night and, thereby, could not aid in his own defense. He had to take Charles's word for it concerning his memory loss, naturally, as this was not exactly an objectively provable claim. In a further display of dubious logic, the attorney argued that when a man killed out of jealousy, he usually killed his rival, not his beloved. He maintained further that the angle of the bullet's track through Alta's body proved Charles could not have fired the shot—a bold statement, as dozens of witnesses saw Charles. He literally had a smoking gun in his hand, and he shouted, "I didn't mean to do it." It is possible that an assassin who could move at the speed of light invaded the dance, grabbed Charles's gun from his pocket, shot Alta, pressed the weapon into a conveniently intoxicated Charles's hand as witnesses turned in the direction of the noise, and then fled, making McGalliard his befuddled patsy. But it somehow strains belief.

On the other hand, the prosecutor had his own moment of high silliness when he displayed Alta's bloody clothes in the courtroom and, in his stentorian voice, urged her spirit to reveal what *really* happened at the dance. Strange to say, she didn't, perhaps having not been properly subpoenaed. Ah, for a time machine and ventriloquism lessons!

The jury retired on January 20. The next morning, they declared that they found McGalliard sane and guilty of second-degree murder. They sentenced him to life imprisonment. Charles hardly blinked at the news. Nobody was surprised except his overly optimistic attorneys.

Franklin Hall is now a parking lot, which somehow seems depressingly fitting. Most of the motorists who use it are unaware of the tragedy that took place on such a mundane site—in fact, it was a *double* tragedy. Similar dramas have been played out thousands of times: jealous young man loses his temper and his reason and kills the object of his affection, leading to a wasted lifetime of punishment and regret. But one additional detail makes this case unique. Thirty-eight-year-old Mae Leonard, who also attended the Halloween party, was so terrified when she saw the shooting up close and personal that she died of heart failure four hours later, likely caused by fright. McGalliard caused two deaths: an intentional murder and an unintentional manslaughter.

"Kill Da Umpire!"

We often hear the angry cry at sporting events and in cartoons and movies—*especially* in cartoons and movies. When the umpire makes what fans of the penalized team perceive to be a bad call, someone shouts "Kill the umpire!"

But, in the long history of this great republic, have any fans actually killed an umpire? Thanks to the magic of backbreaking research, this question can be answered with a resounding *yes*. Following are real-life examples from across America, including two especially memorable events that happened in the Midwest, which I am saving for last, as one might save marshmallow-laden gelatin treats for after the main course.

On September 4, 1889, a baseball game was held in Darlington, South Carolina, between the hometown team and a team from nearby Wadesboro, North Carolina. The umpire was William M. of Wadesboro, described as "a clever young man." At the end of the eighth inning, the score was Wadesboro eight, Darlington four. The mood was ominous; the surly home crowd displayed violent tendencies when things didn't go their way. "One of the Darlington men in attempting to steal third base ran over," said a *New York World* correspondent, "and was clearly and fairly put out" of the game by William the umpire. The crowd howled in protest. Leon Dargan, Darlington's shortstop, ran up and clubbed William upside the head with a bat. William "lay senseless on the ground with blood freely oozing from his mouth, nostrils, and ears," according to the reporter, who knew his readers wouldn't want to be shorted a single detail. The wounded man was carried home and died there. Leon was summarily arrested, but research has failed to disclose his punishment. The nation's newspapers dropped the story after a few days, but I'm sure the fact that Leon was the son of the congressman from the Sixth Congressional District of South Carolina had nothing to do with it.

Two black baseball teams were competing at the Spain plantation near Quitman, Georgia, on June 27, 1903, and there was considerable enmity, if not hatred, between the teams. "The game was a contest between the Spain Negroes and those of a neighboring plantation," explained a press report, "between whom there has existed a fierce rivalry dating back to the times of slavery." In the sixth inning, the Spain plantation team was ahead four to three; one of their star players, Sam J., was about to steal second base. A fan of the rival plantation displayed poor sportsmanship by emptying a load of buckshot into Sam just before he reached second. The shooter fled. Amazingly, rather than call off the game or alert the police, the players continued as Sam expired on the sidelines. In the eighth inning, when the score was tied and everyone's temper was up, the umpire ruled in favor of Spain's hated enemy team. This time, violence came from one of Spain's players, who shot the umpire three times, killing him instantly. *Even then* the game was not ended, and fans of the teams joined in an invigorating riot, during which the murderous baseball player escaped. Several hours later, the police finally heard about the twice-fatal game, but, by then, the assassins, representing each of the teams, had escaped in the swamp south of town.

In June 1907, two baseball teams representing Springfield, Massachusetts, and New Haven, Indiana, played at the New Haven field. The umpire became suspicious when he noticed eccentricities of the ball in flight and unwisely opined that the New Haven pitcher cheated by greasing the ball. Somebody shouted, "Kill the umpire!" After hearing this clarion call, every man and boy who rooted for New Haven had a poke at the poor umpire. They failed to kill the man but not from lack of effort. They broke out his front teeth, gashed his face, and tore his clothes. When the dust settled, he resembled "a shapeless mass painted red." The *Louisville Courier-Journal* told the tale in an editorial plaintively titled "Let the Umpire Live," but which included these bloodcurdling lines: "No baseball-going human being with red blood in his veins can say that he has not experienced a burning desire to beat the umpire into a soft pulp.

The desire is perfectly natural. . . . The desire to dabble in the gore of the umpire and to smear his anatomy into the diamond is altogether human, but it should be curbed—even when he accuses the home team pitcher of having greased the ball."

There was bad blood between Robert N. and Herman D. to begin with since the latter had been paying unwanted attention to the former's daughter. Robert and Herman crossed paths on June 14, 1913, at a baseball game between teams from Nelson County and Bullitt County, Kentucky. Robert was the umpire. He got into a profane dispute with a shortstop. Herman happened to be among the spectators and, perhaps seeing his chance to settle an old score, ended the fight permanently by striking Robert on the head with a bat. He was sentenced to life in prison. His attorneys appealed, but the court of appeals affirmed the verdict on January 15, 1915. Kentuckians apparently considered the cold-blooded, public murder of an umpire a trifling matter, and many citizens signed a petition urging Herman's freedom. The signers included the original jurors, attorneys for the prosecution and defense, the county officers, the usual "prominent citizens," and even one of the dead referee's relatives. "Petitioners said [Herman] was incensed at the umpire's conduct and rulings," said one account, "but had no idea of seriously injuring him." Indeed, how could one expect to deliver a serious injury with a bat to the head? Governor Stanley surrendered to this nonsense and pardoned Herman on June 19, 1916.

Two Missouri teams, Fenton and Valley Park, played a game in August 1922. A Fenton fan was outraged when the umpire ruled for Valley Park after a play. The fan grabbed a bat and hit a homer with the arbitrator's head. The hot-tempered fellow was charged with murder, it is true, but, on the other hand, his action may have won the game, as described by a press account: "The game ended in a score of 11 to 0 in favor of Fenton, the adverse decision of the regular umpire having been reversed after the umpire had been removed in an ambulance to a hospital in St. Louis, where he died." Maybe the second official was wary of crossing Fenton's boosters after that little display. The dead umpire left behind a widow and four children. Once the fan's temper cooled down, he was big enough to admit that, perhaps, just *perhaps*, he had overreacted and insisted that he hadn't intended to bludgeon the umpire "that hard."

As a finale, and for a refreshing change of pace, let's review two Midwestern cases in which beleaguered officials refused to take abuse meekly. (Dare we call these events "The Umpire Strikes Back"?)

On July 14, 1902, Arthur D. was refereeing a baseball game held at Cannelton, Indiana, between the local team and a team from Owensboro, Kentucky. In the last inning, Arthur got into a verbal argument with Owensboro's pitcher, William W. The argument came to blows, whereupon the umpire produced a pistol and shot the pitcher in the back as he ran away.

The big game between the towns of Paulding and Oakwood was taking place in Paulding County, Ohio, on October 13, 1929; the "champeenship" was at stake, and seventeen-year-old Jack S. could *not* resist catcalling, abusing, and ridiculing umpire Clyde C. The referee already had had two face-to-face confrontations with Jack that day, sufficiently serious that bystanders had to separate them. Then came the last half of the eighth inning. When Jack, with the impetuousness of youth, pushed his luck for the third time, the umpire killed him instantly with a blow to the face. This distressing story made the sports page, and there we learn that the final score was Paulding four, Oakwood two.

Dias Gets the Hang of It

The earliest accounts give his name as Samuel Dias; later ones call him Henry Dyas. Whatever his true name was, he lived in Otter Creek Township, ten miles from Terre Haute. He needed to take an anger-management class, had such a thing existed back in 1843. In those days, "anger management" generally consisted of cooling your temper after someone gave you a (usually well-deserved) swift warning kick in the posterior.

On October 16 of that year, Dias attended a social gathering at Mrs. Brady's home—at least, that was the impression given by the genteel newspapers of 1843. It was not until 1902, many years after the initial squeamishness died away, that certain facts made it to print. Mrs. Brady's residence was a house of ill fame, which she comanaged with her daughter, so Dias was not exactly attending a top-hat-and-tails soiree.

George Brock, an Illinois cattleman, was also gracing Mrs. Brady's establishment with his presence. A Terre Haute paper stated in 1902 that Dias and Brock got into a controversy over a liquor bill. During the argument, Brock "let drop some expression offensive to Dias," as a journalist phrased it in 1843. Exactly what Brock said has been lost to history. The papers of the era do not favor us with even an approximation. Perhaps he suggested that Dias had canine ancestry on his mother's side, a common enough insult at the time.

In any case, what matters most is not what Brock said, but rather Dias's reaction. He immediately went outside and found a handy ax. Dias struck Brock several times as his insulter sat in a chair, nearly decapitating him, a scene that caused perturbation and dolor among the others present. Dias, his fury spent, was captured easily.

Scarcely more than a month later, Dias went on trial for chopping Brock up like cordwood. Interestingly, the court docket, as reported in the *Wabash Courier* of November 18, 1843, states that a woman named Hannah Gilman was indicted for Brock's murder, along with Dias, but her connection to the atrocity—if any—evidently was not established, and the press dropped references to her. Most likely, she was one of Mrs. Brady's employees.

The case against Dias was ironclad and copper riveted, which is the usual outcome when one commits a grotesque murder before eyewitnesses. Alexander Mars testified against Dias; another witness, Asa Fenton, was not quite as helpful to the prosecution, since he went insane during the trial, perhaps a result of having seen a man chopped to pieces.

After three days, the jury inevitably found Dias guilty and scheduled his hanging for December 22. Equally inevitably, his attorney called for a retrial, but it was to no avail. A second jury found Dias guilty, and, on May 11, 1844, the delightfully named Judge Law set the execution for June 14.

Somehow, Dias won another month of life, but, on July 5, he sat on a coffin in a wagon as it bounced its way to Strawberry Hill. There he became the key focus at an outdoor social event that truly could not have been held without his participation. It was customary for condemned men to wear a fine suit to the gallows, but Dias showed up wearing his white burial shroud.

Dias did not pass away as easily as he might have wished. The rope slipped as he plunged, and he died of strangulation rather than a broken neck. He was the first man hanged in Vigo County, so at least he had that going for him.

Homicidal Honeymoon, or: Cupid's Arrow, Jane's Ax

Long ago, Moses Rush married a young woman named Jane in Brown Township, Montgomery County. (Historical accounts give the year as

1836, but newspaper reports originating from within days of the unpleasant events that followed the wedding say it took place in June or July 1839.) It is said that Moses was a notorious outlaw and bully. He took Jane to live in his cabin, located, according to historian H. W. Beckwith in 1881, "just below where Deer and Canine's Mill now stands." Writing in 2015, Stephen J. Taylor gave a more precise location: "This is the Deer Mill covered bridge at the edge of the park near Pine Hills."

The marriage was unhappy right out of the starting gate. Moses tried to choke his bride on their wedding night. She fought him off, and, thereafter, the nuptials were strained by his uncouth wedding-night behavior, not to mention his perpetual domestic abuse.

After two weeks, Moses informed Jane that he had murdered his first two wives, had also killed a man for his money, and intended to make her his fourth victim.

"Oh, please don't kill me until morning!" she pleaded.

Moses cogitated. He replied, "Very well, I will wait a while."

He lay down in the doorway with an ax under his arm, vowing that he would make quick work of Jane at the first opportunity. He then made the grave error of falling asleep. Jane slipped the ax out of his grasp and did something that generally is not done in a marriage, at least not during the honeymoon phase.

Jane immediately surrendered to the justice of the peace, who jailed her. She was not there long. The authorities released her on a writ of habeas corpus. A few days later, Jane had the distinction of becoming the first woman tried for murder in Montgomery County. Judge Naylor discharged her after hearing her testimony, ruling it a case of self-defense. The public heartily approved the verdict, the general feeling being that Jane should have been rewarded for removing a public menace.

According to historian Virginia Banta Sharpe, Moses was buried right there next to his cabin/murder site under a beech tree on which was carved his name, visible as late as 1898. At some point, picnickers, possibly wanting healthy physical exercise after eating too many pies, dug up Moses's grave and beheld his skull, which bore the three-inch cut Jane put there. Accounts do not state whether they reburied the skull or carried it away as a smiling souvenir.

Did I mention that Moses was eighty years old and Jane about a half-century younger? If he were an octogenarian outlaw, as legend has it, he was plenty old enough to have been ashamed of himself.

Concerning Murder, Dubious Insanity, and Patriotism

Willard Schray of New Albany ambled into a Pearl Street saloon on the night of January 17, 1914, and told acquaintances, "Well, I killed my wife an hour ago." He added that he had done the deed at her parents' home. Such a statement was bound to attract attention, but most patrons assumed he was drunk and full of stories. Curious folks went to the Richard Adams house at 39 West First Street to see for themselves. They found Rosa Adams Schray, age twenty-eight, lying dead in the yard by the front gate, with the left side of her head crushed and a cut in her throat so deep that she nearly was decapitated. Schray's fellow drinkers repented of their skepticism.

The police found an eerily calm Schray still at the saloon. He was quite an accommodating fellow and confessed in detail. He had seen Rosa talking to another man, so naturally he had to kill her. After following her to the Adams home, he hit her in the head three times. Then he went inside to retrieve his brother-in-law Ben's shaving razor, which he tossed in the river after cutting Rosa's throat. He had intended to give himself up immediately at the police station, he said, but thought he would drop by the saloon first for a tall frosty one. Even before that, he had called his sister, Mrs. William McAfee, to let her in on the news. Despite this eager confession, he fibbed on at least one point: he claimed he had struck his wife only with his fist, but a bloody iron pipe lay under her head.

Next day, Schray admitted using the pipe—you know, lest anyone think the worse of him for telling a lie. "Yes, I murdered my wife with an iron pipe and a razor and I'm willing and ready to hang," he told reporters. "I loved her, but I was racked with jealousy when I saw her taking to another man. I don't regret what I have done. I expect to pay the penalty and I will do so without hesitation when the time comes." If Schray actually did expect execution, he was in for a most pleasant surprise.

Schray's behavior, bizarre to begin with, became even more so as he sat in his jail cell. He repeatedly took a picture of Rosa out of his wallet and gazed at it. He expressed a wish to go see the corpse he had made, but police refused to let him leave his cell. They were sort of funny that way.

Looking into Schray's background, investigators found that he had gotten out of the Indiana Reformatory a year earlier after serving two years for grand larceny. He could have served up to fourteen years, and it would have been better for Mrs. Schray and society if he had. (A newspaper editorial criticized the overly generous parole system, suggesting that Schray, and many others like him, got out of jail too soon simply by "obeying prison rules and making themselves agreeable to wardens. . . . The parole system, therefore, lets out a goodly number of calculating criminals whose freedom is a positive menace to public welfare.")

Police also learned that Schray's father, August, was an inmate of the Southeastern Hospital for the Insane at Marion.

Despite Schray's open confessions of murder to anyone who would listen, he pled not guilty when arraigned on January 20. The judge granted his attorney a change of venue, and the police moved him to Corydon for trial. At the end of March, Corydon's health officer, a doctor, declared Willard Schray a lunatic. What had convinced the doctor of his patient's lunacy? Well, for about ten days, Schray had bellowed for his wife night and day; he had refused to eat; and, when his mother, Sallie, came to visit, he did not recognize her. Or, at least, he *said* he didn't. As the weeks passed, he continued to "act in a strange manner," as one report had it. The suspicious reader may think these so-called symptoms of insanity would be very easy to fake.

Schray's trial for first-degree murder was scheduled to begin in May, but, first, his defense attorney filed a petition asking that a panel of three doctors determine the killer's mental soundness. The judge complied, as Indiana law required. There seemed to be three options open for Schray: if the doctors found him sane, he would be tried; if deemed insane, he would go to the Indiana Colony for the Criminal Insane in Michigan City; but if he went to the colony and regained his sanity later, he could still be tried for murder. As we shall see, Schray thought of a fourth, unsolicited option.

Upon examining Schray, the panel believed he was insane, since he had been acting *so* peculiarly, and, besides, his father was insane, wasn't he? The judge considered the testimony of the doctors and jail attendants and, on May 18, ruled Schray officially non compos mentis.

Police took Schray to his hometown, New Albany, for an overnight stay on May 21 on his way to the asylum. He did not seem to recognize any of his old attendants at the New Albany jail, nor did he seem to know any former acquaintances who dropped by to say hello. That's what he said, anyway. He paced his cell and continued his old habits of shouting "Rose, oh Rose!" and refusing to eat, although—observe!—he *would* eat if spoon-fed.

The uxoricide seemed content at Michigan City's asylum for nearly three years. He also seemed insane. Yet, on April 17, 1917, three weeks after a fearsome tornado struck New Albany, Schray—who had somehow gotten hold of a saw—cut a bar in his cell's window into a hook shape and lowered himself to the ground by climbing down a rope made of bedsheets, just like in the cartoons. He fled the grounds, along with four other inmates. Let's be charitable and say that hindsight makes it easy for us to see that Schray gulled assorted judges, attorneys, jail attendants, and doctors with his hunger strike and foolish talk.

The folks in Michigan City didn't much like the fact that five men from the asylum, at least some of whom had to be genuinely crazy—remember, it was called the Colony for the *Criminal Insane*—were free and in the vicinity. Three were recaptured within a day, leaving Mr. Charles Hull, late of Vigo County, and Schray on the loose.

I do not know what became of Hull, but the question "Where is Willard Schray?" was on the minds of worried Hoosiers until December 4, 1923, when the fugitive turned up in Milwaukee. Police found him after getting an anonymous letter from Chicago revealing his whereabouts. It was sent special delivery rather than by ordinary post, so evidently the tipster wanted Schray off the streets as quickly as possible. The reader will note that would-be raving maniac Schray—who would not eat or cease babbling when observers were around—held down a job, got married a second time, and remained unobtrusive and undetected for years.

Indiana police nabbed Schray as he and his second wife drove through Michigan City, the very town from which he had escaped. Was he taking a sentimental journey to revisit the scene of his former triumph? When police inspected Schray's car, they found nine cases of whiskey, so it appears he was a bootlegger on top of everything else. Willard Schray went to prison at Michigan City—a real prison, not an asylum—and Mrs. S. went back to Milwaukee, no doubt very surprised to learn the fate of the first Mrs. Schray.

To recap the highlights of the Willard Schray story: he bludgeoned his wife, Rosa, with an iron bar in a fit of jealousy and then slashed her throat; he dodged the electric chair almost certainly by faking insanity; escaped from the asylum, scaring the community witless; was not caught for over six years; and, at last, was jailed for murder. He sounds like the kind of guy you wouldn't parole in a thousand years—and yet, he received a second one in 1933. The early parole system had favored Schray once before, and now it had come to his rescue again.

He thanked the justice system for its act of leniency only days later in his own idiosyncratic way. On January 5, 1934, a now middle-aged Schray was hitchhiking near Chicago. Motorist Clifford J. Brown gave him a lift. At Lake Forest, Schray pulled out a revolver, shot Brown three times in the head, and stole his benefactor's coat, car, and fifteen dollars. Although left for dead, Brown survived and went to the hospital soon after he was found.

At almost the same time, an officer, who was unaware of the shooting, spotted Schray wearing a bloodstained coat in a restaurant in the Chicago suburb of Lake Bluff. The officer arrested him on well-founded suspicion, an act that must have evoked strong feelings of déjà vu in Schray. There were two striking parallels between his latest crime and the one from twenty years before. Both times, he was arrested within two hours, and he confessed to the point of becoming a blabbermouth. He even volunteered to the officer that he was the fellow who had killed Rosa Schray back in 1914.

Clifford Brown positively identified Schray as his attacker. Did Schray finally go to jail permanently after this crime? Or did he again crazy-talk his way out of it? There appear to be no records confirming a conviction, nor any records of Schray's death, so it is possible he changed his name and went on to commit mischief somewhere else.

On the other hand, records at Ancestry.com reveal that a Willard Louis Schray, living in Zion, Illinois, was drafted to serve in World War Two in 1942. At first glance, it seems unlikely that this is the murderer Schray, as he would have been in his midfifties that year—too old for the draft, as age forty-five was considered the limit—and it is improbable that the military would accept a man with a prison background, especially a convicted murderer also on record as being a lunatic.

On the other hand, the 1930 US census featuring the definite Schray, serving time in Michigan City before his 1933 parole, reveals that he had had military experience: he was a World War One veteran. He had escaped from the asylum in April 1917 and so must have immediately enlisted in the military under an assumed name, which may explain why he couldn't be found in Indiana. (The United States entered the war on April 6, and Schray escaped on April 17. The timing leads one to suspect that he broke out *intentionally* to join the war effort.)

The 1900 US census says the definite Schray was born in May 1888 in Indiana and, at age twelve, was living in New Albany; the World War Two draft card gives the Illinois Schray's birthday as May 14, 1888, and his birthplace as New Albany.

The 1942 draft card includes the line "Name and Address of Person Who Will Always Know Your Address." The fifty-four-year-old Schray included Mrs. Nora Renshaw of New Albany (no relation stated); the 1900 US census reveals that the definite Schray had an older sister named Nora.

The conclusion seems inescapable. Despite his many failings, Willard Schray was at least patriotic enough to serve in two world wars. What became of him during, or perhaps after, World War Two is a mystery.

9

OHIO OBLITERATIONS

Tragedy of a Tree

William R. of Elyria, Ohio, was very poor and jobless—as were many people, the Great Depression being in full swing, despite several years' worth of the government's tinkering with the economy to end it. To make things worse, it was Christmastime. Thanks to careful saving, he had presents for his two daughters, Geraldine, age eleven, and Sarah, age eight. But he did not have a Christmas tree. He thought of a way to get a free one. There was that elderly man, Will C., who had a tree farm. Local children called the eighty-four-year-old "Santa Claus" because he had a long white beard and gave them nickels for Christmas every year. He was generous—right? He wouldn't miss just *one* tree—would he? On December 24, 1938, William and his wife, Mae, drove the family car to Will's farm in the dark of night to pilfer a pine.

There were a couple of circumstances they did not count on: for one, people had been stealing trees from Will for a long decade, and he was sick of having his livelihood taken. For another, he intended to stay up late this time and keep an eye on his property. He was just waiting for someone to trespass so he could ambush them.

William and Mae arrived at the farm and stealthily got out of the car. They cut down a tree and started hauling it to their auto. Will C. saw them and fired his shotgun without warning. The first blast killed William; the second wounded Mae. Then, completely ignoring them, Will went to a neighbor's house, nonchalantly talked about what he had just done, and went back home to get a good night's sleep.

His slumber was disrupted when the police arrested him and took him to jail. Will demanded to be set free: "I must stand guard over my Christmas trees again tonight!" He told reporters that he had been annoyed by the authorities' inability to protect his trees from being stolen, so he took action himself. "I was shooting to kill," he said. "For ten years people have been coming to my farm along about this time. I've got some dandy big evergreens just right for Christmas trees and every crook hereabouts seems to know it." He added, "I would have given them a nice tree if they had asked me."

The next day a reporter stopped various citizens on the street and asked about their reactions to the shooting. One shopkeeper, Joseph K., seemed to think Will C. should go to Ohio's electric chair just for being ungenerous: "I can't see killing a man, particularly at Christmastime. I'm opposed to capital punishment but I'm also opposed to Scrooges. That's one time I'm afraid I'd be for capital punishment of a man who would shoot an unemployed man trying to get a Christmas tree for his children."

Mrs. A. of Maryland Avenue said, "The man who did the shooting certainly would have been better off if he had a little Christmas spirit."

Others called the act "terrible" and "shocking." But one respondent, a student nurse and a winner of a recent popularity contest, expressed an unpopular attitude: Will C. had displayed "poor judgment and a lack of Christmas spirit. But the father had no right to steal the tree and the fact he was unemployed doesn't have anything to do with it." The author of a letter to the editor agreed: "I agree that [Will C.] should not have shot the man for taking a tree, but what right had [Mr. R.] to take a tree from a man eighty-four years old, who had spent his life raising trees that he might have something to live on when he was unable to work?"

In sum, opinions about Will C. seemed to fall into three major categories: (1) Some felt he should have been generous enough to have given William a tree—or at least sufficiently generous to have given a warning before firing. (2) Others argued that just because one is poor, that does not confer a right to take someone else's property. (3) Some people believed (and many still believe) that it's okay to steal something as long as the victim has a *lot* of it.

Public opinion was mostly against the tree farmer, as these quotations indicate, but the Elyria prosecutor admitted that criminal action was not likely for the simple reason that when sentimentality and anger were stripped away, William R. and his wife had been trespassing, and the law permitted persons to protect their property. A few days later, the prosecutor charged Will with manslaughter and noted that the grand jury might change the charge to murder.

William's daughters had a bleak Christmas indeed. "To think Daddy died to get a tree for us," they were heard to say. "He must have thought a lot of us." Neighbors gave them more than forty presents, not that it helped very much. Meanwhile, even Will C. received two jailhouse gifts: a cake and a box of candy.

When the grand jury heard the case against the elderly tree farmer in April 1939, emotions had cooled down, and people recognized that there were only losers in the tragedy and that the principals would gladly take back their actions if they could. Even Mae R., by then recovered from her wounds, urged the jury not to indict Will C.

On April 20, the jury announced that it would not indict. The farmer, who had taken ill, said, "I guess I am getting ready to die, but I want to stick it out until next Christmas." He didn't. He died on June 18.

In a final, bitter irony, surveyors took measurements of Will C.'s land and found that the tree William and Mae R. had cut down wasn't on his property after all.

Ohio State Campus Poisonings

The toiler in academia can be certain of one thing: the common cold will ravage campus at least twice a semester, and, thus, many students at Ohio State University in Columbus were sick at the end of January 1925. Students needing medicine went to the health service office. Doctors there wrote prescriptions, which were then filled at the College of Pharmacy's dispensary.

Timothy J. McCarthy of Fremont, varsity football player, was one of the afflicted. He got his prescription for cold medicine (capsules containing quinine and aspirin to relieve fever and aches) filled at the campus dispensary on Thursday, January 29. Instead of getting better after taking a capsule, however, McCarthy got much worse. He developed excruciating muscle pains and cramps. He pulled through and probably thought it was the worst cold he had ever had.

On January 31, two other ill students, sophomore Harold E. Gillig of Tiffin and Charles H. Huls of Logan City, took cold medicine they had received from the dispensary. Both became violently ill immediately afterward. Gillig survived, but twenty-one-year-old Huls died in convulsions in his room at the Phi Gamma Delta fraternity house on Seventeenth Avenue. Officials believed that he had died of tetanus.

David I. Puskin, age twenty, a student from Canton, also got cold medicine capsules at the university dispensary. He died on February 1, twenty minutes after swallowing one. Official cause of death: meningitis. Doctors were so certain of their diagnosis that they placed Puskin's friends in quarantine.

On February 3, student George Delbert Thompson of Canton felt under the weather, so he took cold medicine from the dispensary. Soon afterward, he became sicker than he ever could have imagined. His fearsome illness at last drew official suspicion to the recent events at OSU. An analysis of Thompson's stomach contents revealed strychnine. His remaining capsules were examined and found to be poison-free; it was his very bad luck to have taken the one in the bottle that had been tampered with.

Now college authorities knew what Huls and Puskin had *really* died of. It might seem incredible that officials weren't suspicious from the start when the students died within a day of each other, one allegedly of tetanus and the other of meningitis. But as dean of the College of Medicine E. F. McCampbell explained, the two diseases have similar symptoms— and they also match the signs of strychnine poisoning: fever, severe muscular pain, rigid muscles, and spasms. "Any one of the three might be mistaken for the other, unless all the facts in each case were definitely known," said a newspaper. No tests to detect poison had been undertaken at first because there was no reason to suspect it—and besides, it seemed like everyone on campus was sick.

Four additional students were stricken with violent illness after taking the dispensary's cold medicine, but none died. The poisonings were bad news for the university—and then the news got worse. A careful review of the evidence on February 4 made it clear that the attacks were not the work of an outsider. OSU officials stepped aside and left the investigation to the Columbus Police Department.

Had the poison been added to the cold medicine capsules in a ghastly mistake? Dr. Clair Dye, dean of the College of Pharmacy and in charge of the dispensary, observed that if it had been an accident, the strychnine should have been mixed in more than just a few capsules. He further pointed out the unlikeliness of an error, since strychnine powder was heavier than the quinine the capsules were supposed to contain.

Had the poison originated on campus? As it happened, a number of departments at OSU had supplies of strychnine. "But," a reporter noted, "in each instance it was learned that the faculty members personally kept it at all times under lock and key, and could account for practically all that had been in their possession for some months." In addition, detectives found that while fifty-nine prescriptions for the cold medication had been written in the past week, only thirty-four had been filled at the dispensary. Could students have had their prescriptions filled in town? No, because the campus health service physicians wrote prescriptions in code. The unsettling conclusion was that while the poison likely came from off campus, the assassin lived and/or worked at OSU.

And he or she probably worked at the dispensary, for how could an outsider have gotten access to the medicine? One of the most baffling mysteries of the case was the difficulty that *anyone*, insider or outsider, would have had tinkering with the capsules. A reporter explained the security at the facility: "Medicine compounded at this dispensary is always made up under the direct supervision of faculty members in the College of Pharmacy, all of whom are registered pharmacists."

The hypothesis that the killer worked at the dispensary did not significantly reduce the number of suspects. Sixty-four students worked there the week before the poisonings. Twenty-four, including seven women, were questioned by detectives on February 5. Not a single clue turned up, the workers having nearly unanimously testified to the strict supervision by faculty that they underwent when filling prescriptions. Only one worker admitted laxity, as a reporter explained: "[She] said that she had dispensed the 'R' and 'W' (red and white, for aspirin and quinine) capsules so many times in the last two years that, of late, she had not troubled to consult instructors when that particular prescription was presented. The two kinds of capsules, she explained, were already made up. The two bottles containing them always stood together in the same place and there was no danger of error."

City prosecutor John Chester said that after questioning the students, he was convinced the deaths had not resulted from the university's negligence. The school's president, W. O. Thompson, issued a statement reassuring understandably nervous students and parents that there was no need to withdraw from classes. He also ordered that the remaining stock of cold medicine in the tainted bottle be chemically tested. By February 4, two-thirds of the capsules had been examined and found innocuous—except one, which contained 100 percent strychnine. It was not found in the bottle but was in the batch given to football player Timothy McCarthy. This discovery put a permanent end to the theory that strychnine might have been mixed accidentally with the quinine or aspirin.

Naturally, students who had been prescribed capsules for their colds turned over all their unused medicine—*promptly*, and with no complaints—and among these, mingled with the late David Puskin's remaining medicine, investigators found a second strychnine-filled capsule on February 5. It contained enough grains to kill four people. Taking into consideration the two dead students, the ones who were merely sickened, and the two unused capsules, officials estimated that of the three hundred capsules that were originally in the bottle—dubbed the "death bottle" by the sensation-seeking press—eight had contained poison:

Two capsules went to Puskin (deceased); one was not swallowed.
One to Huls (deceased).
Two to McCarthy (survived); one was not swallowed.
One to Gillig (survived).
One to Thompson (survived).
One to an unnamed student (survived).

A female student collapsed in class and was taken to the University Hospital. She was not the next victim but had fainted from extreme tension and hysteria, since, like everyone else, she was terrified of the campus's faceless mad poisoner.

Charles Huls was buried in Lancaster on February 4. His parents refused permission for an exhumation and further analysis. Perhaps they were afraid to face what investigators might find. "We do not wish to take any part in the investigation," said the dead student's father. "We are satisfied that an infected tooth led to his death." (Huls had a tooth removed earlier in the day before he took the cold medicine.)

The State Pharmacy Board investigated legal sales of strychnine in Ohio in the past year. They found nothing that shed light on the mystery. Dr. Dye, troubled by the shadow that fell over his university and unable to sleep, went to the OSU dispensary on the night of February 4 to inspect the place personally, top to bottom. To his surprise, he found a forgotten, square-shaped bottle of strychnine pushed to the back of a shelf in the chemical storeroom. But it did not appear to have been opened recently; it was dust-coated and nearly full. Dye did not recognize the blue-penciled handwriting on the label. The next day bore a mundane explanation for what briefly seemed like a possible clue: the bottle belonged to William Keyser of the pharmacy's faculty. Records showed that Keyser had taken strychnine from the container twice in the past fifteen months, ten grams in November 1923 and an ounce in April 1924. Both times, he had used the poison in his classes.

On the third day of the investigation, Prosecutor Chester questioned eighteen more of the sixty-four students who recently had worked in the dispensary. They found that Joseph M. of Columbus was the student on duty when Harold Gillig was given his medicine and that Armond W. of Baltimore, Ohio, had given the still-recuperating George Thompson his.

They also uncovered Nelson R., a pharmacy student from Cleveland who, in the words of a reporter, had been "using tablets containing a minute quantity of the same poison as was in the 'death capsules' as a stimulant."

The reader may be wondering what the reporter meant that the student was using one of the deadliest drugs known to humankind as a "stimulant." Small doses of strychnine could be used as an upper, like amphetamines—a sort of pep pill for the very reckless. (*Please* do not try this at home.) Nelson R. admitted to the prosecutor that he had purchased a dozen tablets of the poison off campus. He had been using it to keep up his concentration while studying for tests. He still had eight left. Another strange matter: Nelson told investigators that a bottle of strychnine had been left out in plain sight in a basement laboratory where anyone could get at it. Furthermore, he insisted that other students knew of it. But not only did his fellow students deny knowledge of the bottle, police couldn't locate it. Nor could Nelson himself when the authorities asked. Presumably, Nelson R. assured detectives that he was not out to poison his fellow students, and they accepted his explanation.

A portent of how the investigation was going, or rather not going, came on February 7, when officials admitted that, despite a week's hard work, they were no closer to solving the mystery than when they started. On that day they had interviewed, and learned nothing new from, twelve additional students who had worked in the dispensary during the time period when the poison must have been added to the capsules.

Nevertheless, detectives and the prosecutor plugged on. On February 8, Prosecutor Chester made an unannounced visit to the OSU pharmacy students' fraternity house to take a closer look at Nelson R. and his potentially deadly "stimulants." Intriguingly, one of the dead students, David Puskin, had spent time at the fraternity house the night before he took that deadly capsule, but no connection was established.

On February 9, Chester questioned the last of the pupils who worked in the dispensary and four pharmacy instructors. He was rewarded with a confession of sorts. Nineteen-year-old Louis F. of Canton, a pharmacy student, nervously admitted that he had dispensed the fatal capsule to his pal David Puskin. In fact, he had "entered the college dispensary without authority" and filled the prescription health services had given Puskin. Louis admitted that when attendants at the dispensary wouldn't let him enter, he had sneaked in through another entrance. He swore he had only done it to help his friend save money. He assured investigators that he got the capsules only from the "death bottle."

And why hadn't Louis come forward with this information from the start and saved everyone a lot of trouble? Well, he said, he had not desired the notoriety of being mixed up in a high-publicity murder investigation. The prosecutor learned that Louis had been "the first student to work in the dispensary the week when other strychnine capsules were issued" and that on the night of Friday, January 30, just before his fellow students started dropping left and right, Louis had left campus and gone home to Canton—a distance of about a hundred miles. As soon as he got there, he turned around and drove right back to the OSU campus. He could offer no good reason for this strange action except "I didn't want to stick around Canton."

Louis was under arrest while his story was checked out. It was noted that while he had been acquainted with Puskin, he didn't know the other poisoning victims. The next day, he was released and called a "victim of unfortunate circumstances." His story seems suspect, but it must have satisfied Prosecutor Chester. Perhaps convincing additional details were never released to the press.

There the investigation screeched to a halt until February 20, when Governor Donahey—who openly suspected carelessness on the part of the university dispensary—ordered the case reopened by the Ohio State Board of Pharmacy.

Well over a year later, on July 2, 1926, the State Board released its findings: the poisonings were deliberate, the strychnine had originated from an off-campus source, and "the poison capsules could not have gotten mixed with the quinine capsules through accident or carelessness." And there, the official inquiry sputtered and died permanently.

The report failed to answer the biggest questions of all: Who did it, and why? Only one person (presumably) knew in 1925, and no one knows now. Did the poisoner intend to kill at random, like the Tylenol Killer who terrorized Chicago and the nation at large in 1982? Or did the OSU poisoner have a particular victim in mind and didn't care how many died as collateral damage, as long as he or she succeeded? In the final analysis, only eight of the three hundred capsules in the bottle were ascertained to have been contaminated, and since the capsules were dispensed by sheer chance, this would seem a haphazard, if not thoroughly idiotic, method of murdering a selected victim.

But never underestimate the power of incompetence! In 2000, the *Columbus Dispatch* interviewed celebrated forensic psychiatrist Dr. Park Dietz about the 1925 poisonings. He opined that the killer had intended to kill only one person and perhaps even hoped others would die to mask his or her true intentions. Dr. Dietz thought it probable that the assassin failed to poison the true target.

According to Ohio State University Archives, "The University investigation did change how the dispensary and pharmacy program at OSU operated. OSU became the first school in the country to offer a four-year program for pharmacy students. Tighter regulations and better training measures were put in place at OSU and quickly adopted across the country."

As the Tylenol Killer changed forever the way over-the-counter medicine is packaged, the OSU poisoner's rampage resulted in improvements in the nation's campus pharmaceutical distribution system. As too often seems to be the case, anonymous maniacs force progress.

Buckeye Bluebeard

Alfred A. Knapp was born in Greensburg, Indiana, in 1862. When he was forty, he and his wife, Hannah Goddard Knapp, were living in Hamilton, Ohio. By early winter 1903, however, Hannah's brother-in-law Edward F. King was getting worried. He hadn't seen her since December 21, 1902, and no one had seen her since December 23. His suspicions were heightened when Alfred married Anna May Gamble of Indianapolis on February 3, 1903, and left town. That Alfred had been able to inveigle someone to marry him was remarkable since, at the time, he was a jobless loafer who worked sporadically in a livery stable and was so impoverished that Anna May's relatives had paid for the ceremony. Not only that, but Alfred Knapp had a criminal record, well known to his new bride and her family. On February 24, 1903, King alerted Hamilton police to his suspicions.

Detectives discovered that on December 22, 1902, the day before Hannah disappeared, Mr. Knapp had rented a horse and wagon at a livery stable, loaded a cumbersome box in the wagon, and driven away. Both the box and Knapp had vanished. That was interesting in itself, but then the detectives remembered that eight years before, the body of a woman named Jennie Conners had been found in a Hamilton canal. She was Knapp's second wife.

Hamilton police requested that their brethren in Indianapolis, the city where Knapp had formerly lived, do a record search. He had an impressive criminal career going back as far as 1882, when he had been sent to prison for burglary while living in Terre Haute. Altogether he had served five terms in various state penitentiaries, three times for larceny and twice for rape. Two jail terms had been spent in Jeffersonville, Indiana; one term in Columbus, Ohio; one term in Joliet, Illinois; and the most recent one in Michigan City, Indiana, for molesting a girl in Indianapolis in 1896. To say that Knapp was a "person of interest" in Hannah's disappearance would be understating it.

Indianapolis police quickly determined that the missing man and his new wife, Anna, were living in town. On the frosty morning of February 25, the cops went to Knapp's home at 630 Indiana Avenue and ordered him to get out of bed, although he was still on his honeymoon. Regardless, they hustled him over the state line and back to Hamilton to answer pointed questions concerning Hannah's whereabouts.

Perhaps Anna was angry when police insisted on spiriting away her brand-new husband. Very likely the officers had just saved her neck. There were facts—*lots* of facts—she hadn't known about her groom since he was reluctant to share inconvenient details apt to spoil a romance. For starters, she was actually Alfred's fourth wife; the others, in chronological order, were Emma Stubbs, Jennie Conners, and Hannah Goddard. He was the number-one suspect in Hannah's disappearance and Jennie's murder, and police were still searching for Emma, whom Knapp had married in Terre Haute in 1884 when she was seventeen and he had just gotten out of Joliet after serving a term for burglary.

To give Knapp a modicum of credit, once he saw the jig was up, he immediately confessed rather than waste everyone's time. He said that on the morning of December 22, 1902, he had choked Hannah to death, as charged. The penitent Knapp hinted none too subtly that he could tell a lot more if he had a mind to: "I may tell it to you in the morning, but I will not tell anything about it tonight. I cry every time I think of poor Hannah, and I feel like crying when I think of this *other* thing."

The next morning Knapp proved as good as his word—another point in his favor, or so some might have it. The "*other* thing" he confessed was that he had strangled not only wife number three (Hannah) but also number two (Jennie). Then he surprised everyone by admitting to three more strangulations he had not been suspected of committing, those of a young woman and two little girls. He described his five murders in a lavishly detailed document, which he wrote with C. F. Borsch, mayor of Hamilton, as a witness.

On January 21, 1894, he had strangled twelve-year-old Emma Littleman in a lumberyard on Gest Street, Cincinnati: "I met the Littleman child in the lumberyard and assaulted her and choked her to death when she made an outcry." Although she had been raped and strangled, at the time police reached the risible conclusion that she had committed suicide.

He had strangled Mary Eckert on Walnut Street, Cincinnati, across from the YMCA, on August 1, 1894. He confessed, "I went into the room with the Eckert girl and sat down with her. She cried, and I strangled her with a towel and hurried from the house."

Less than a week later, on August 7, 1894, he had strangled his second wife, Jennie Conners Knapp, whom he had married at Lawrenceburg, Indiana, in 1886: "I was mad at my wife . . . We were walking along Liberty Street. I sat her down under the bridge, on a pretext, and choked her to death . . . After she was dead I threw the body into the canal." (At the time, Cincinnati police concluded that she had strangled herself and thrown herself into the water. Somehow suspicion did not fall on Knapp, despite his having served many terms in prison for a smorgasbord of crimes.) Knapp vehemently added in his confession, "I deny that I poisoned her. I never told anyone I did." Because, you know, he didn't want anyone to think poorly of him.

He had raped and murdered a child named Ida Gebhardt (or Gebhart) in Indianapolis on July 19, 1895, and stashed her body in a West Indianapolis barn, where it was found several days later. Knapp denied remembering specific details about this murder: "Ida Gebhardt I killed, but my memory is not clear as to what I did." One wonders if he felt too remorseful to own up in full—or perhaps it was because he had been threatened with a lynching the day before.

In 1896, as mentioned, Knapp had gone to jail for a few years after being convicted of child molestation. After a seven-year hiatus from murder, on December 22, 1902, Knapp had strangled his third wife, Hannah Goddard, in their home at 339 South Fourth Street, Hamilton. He had hauled her body out of town on a rented wagon, exactly as surmised by the victim's brother-in-law Edward King, and had dropped her in the Great Miami River, a tributary of the Ohio, at Lindenwald.

Knapp ended this remarkable document with an assurance that it had not been forced or coerced: "I make this statement by my own free will and not by the request of any officer or anyone else."

Journalists compared Knapp to those industrious murderers Jack the Ripper and H. H. Holmes. But Knapp stressed the point that at least he had not murdered his first wife, Emma! She had divorced him after living with him for only a few months, which indicates that she had a wise head on her shoulders. She was presently living in Louisville, or so Knapp had heard.

Once the confessing bug bit Knapp, he could *not* stop talking. Torrents and torrents of details about his crimes spilled from his lips. When investigators asked how he felt when he strangled women, his answer could all too easily have come from a modern serial killer:

> I can't tell. I was seized with an irresistible desire to choke them, and I can't help it. I could not let go when I once began even if I wanted to. I never feel any remorse, only a feeling of satisfaction when I know that they are dead. I used my hands in every case except that of Mary Eckert. I choked that woman with a towel, but I could have done it with my hands. I got acquainted with Mary in Dayton, Ohio, through an advertisement, and when she went to Cincinnati I visited her at her room and choked her to death one night.

Knapp was so penitential that he even admitted to comparatively minor crimes, such as a number of highway robberies back in December. Indianapolis police believed he had committed two arsons in that city in December 1902. With good cause: when Knapp had been convicted of child molestation and sent to prison back in 1896, he swore revenge on those who had convicted him. No sooner had he returned to Indianapolis when, like night following day, a barn belonging to former Sheriff

Womack, who had arrested Knapp, was burned down. Soon afterward—and only six weeks before Knapp was arrested for the final time—a barn owned by a member of the jury was also burned.

Leon Reinhold, an Indianapolis attorney, came forward with a disturbing story. Knapp's last victim, Hannah, evidently had feared for her life. In October 1902, she had gone to Reinhold's office to ask if she could secure a divorce, since Alfred had been threatening her. Reinhold informed her that she had not lived in the city long enough to file for divorce. It was as good as a legal death sentence: within two months, the Knapps had moved from Indianapolis to Hamilton, where Alfred made good on his threats.

The public saw another side of Knapp on February 27, when the press published a gushy letter to his very lucky fourth wife, Anna, written after his bloodcurdling confession. He referred to himself as "Allie" and "your kid" and included cloying sentiments such as "Don't forget your kid and he will never forget his little sweetheart as long as he lives." The gist of the letter was that Knapp, self-admitted strangler of little girls and women, optimistically thought he would get off easy with a life sentence at worst. (Similarly, he told a reporter, "I guess that they will send me up for life. Now don't try to scare me by saying that I will go to the chair. They won't do that to me, will they?") For her part, the fourth Mrs. Knapp stood loyally by her husband in his moment of trouble. One wonders what she thought when her husband admitted later that he had considered strangling her too.

The day after his epic confession, Knapp's lawyers warned him to cease talking, or he would be certain to have a few very interesting seconds in a certain chair that was the property of the state of Ohio. He disregarded their advice and kept up his chatter; one of the defense attorneys retained by his family was reportedly "greatly annoyed" by his motormouthed client. It occurred to attorneys on both sides, much too late, that every time Knapp spoke with a reporter, his words were read by thousands, which would increase the difficulty of acquiring an impartial jury when he went to trial. On February 28, for example, the press released an interview with Knapp in which he was far too candid for his own good, especially regarding the murder of Mary Eckert. She had been his mistress, Knapp revealed; when a reporter asked why he had killed her, he responded, "I was afraid she would tell something she knew." (The reporter added, "His utter calmness was appalling.")

"*What* did she know?" asked the journalist.

"I was married then to Jennie Conners, the one I threw in the canal, you know, and I was going with Hannah to this house on Walnut Street in Cincinnati to Mary Eckert's room. That night Hannah and I went there and Mary Eckert went out, and when she came back she got mad because we were there so long and she said, 'I am going to tell your wife on you.'"

In other words, although Knapp had been married to Jennie at the time, he claimed he was cheating on her with Mary Eckert *and* Hannah Goddard, whom he later made his third wife. According to Knapp, Hannah had restrained Mary's hands as he strangled Mary with a towel. ("When I think of Hannah and the rest I feel bad. I don't know why I killed Hannah. She was a good wife to me.") Was the story true or just Knapp's attempt to blacken two dead women's reputations? Who knows? In any case, it didn't exactly endear him to the newspaper readers, twelve of whom soon would have his life in their hands. It was noted, however, that some details *had* to be true: Knapp knew exactly what Eckert had been wearing when throttled, what the towel used in the commission of the crime looked like, and the location in the house where her body had been found.

Then Knapp was so foolish as to tell the reporter the precise details of his preferred method of strangling, even re-creating his moves and mincing about like a stage actor! His attorneys must have been beside themselves.

Meanwhile Knapp's family, understandably but misguidedly, tried to leaven his evil reputation—one he insisted on spreading himself—by declaring that he was insane. His sister claimed he had been kicked in the head by a colt in Twenty-Mile Prairie, Illinois, when he was five years old. He had not been quite right since. His parents added that he had been struck by lightning in Terre Haute. But, they added, they thought their son would be better off dead.

The legal system was embarrassed on February 28 when reporters found that Knapp had been released early from the Michigan City prison for good conduct despite the seriousness of the child molestation charge. Worse, while there, he had confessed a couple of his murders to a fellow prisoner—Knapp had even written and signed a confession!—but no one followed up on it. Had he served the full ten years' sentence, Hannah Goddard would have lived.

As Knapp waited for his court hearing, he finally wised up and shut his yap when reporters were afoot. Journalists, deprived of a chance to speak with him directly, perhaps took out their frustration by describing him as a craven who feared lynching more than he feared the electric chair: "He is very apprehensive of lynching or some form of violence and those who watch him say that he is really cowardly. The least noise that is not an ordinary jail noise startles him and causes a shudder to run through his frame . . . Though the taking of life to him was a mere pastime, he himself is afraid to die. He wants to live, even though he is behind prison bars. In the hope of saving his life his family says he is insane, and insanity will be his plea for his life."

On March 1, the prisoner was confronted at the jail by Herman Littleman of Cincinnati, father of Knapp's first victim (that we know of). Mr. Littleman glared and said, "I have never seen this man. I don't care to look at him anymore." Bystanders thought Knapp seemed truly remorseful. He was badly shaken and sniveled, "I am just as sorry as can be that little Emma is dead. She had hair and eyes like yours."

Ever since Knapp's arrest, the frustrated authorities had searched for the body of Hannah Goddard, which he had placed in the river. Many weeks had passed; her body could have floated downstream, possibly hundreds of miles, and gone anywhere. But they kept dragging the river, knowing the body could provide evidence to convict Knapp. A reward was offered to no avail, and the search was all but abandoned by the first of March. By coincidence, or by a mysterious dispensation of providence, if you prefer—because, as we shall see, the timing of the discovery could not have been more fortuitous—three deckhands on the steamer *Bellevue* saw Hannah's body floating in the Ohio at the foot of Fourth Street, New Albany, on March 2, the same day Knapp was arraigned in Hamilton. Her body had traveled from Lindenwald to near Louisville, a distance of about 130 miles on our modern highways—a longer journey for her, taking twists and turns and curves and being snagged occasionally down the Great Miami and then the Ohio.

Though Hannah's body had been in the river for over two months, the icy water had preserved her appearance to a surprising degree. Reporters did not spare the grim details they knew their readers secretly craved. The corpse was hairless, swollen, green as you please, and naked except for black stockings with white feet. Could this horrifying vision be positively identified as Hannah Goddard Knapp? Yes, because her diabolical mate stupidly failed to remove distinctive jewelry: gold wire earrings and an octagonal ring, given to her by her uncle Charles Goddard as a birthday gift, bearing the images of three birds and an owl. The body also had a bandage wrapped around its right ankle, and Knapp had mentioned in his confession that his wife had injured her ankle shortly before he murdered her. She was further identified by Major George Kuemmerling, Hamilton's chief of police, and two relatives, Uncle George Goddard and brother-in-law Edward King; both recognized a scar on her forehead and a deformed fingernail. Coroner W. L. Starr determined that the woman was dead before being placed in the river and that she had been strangled, since her lungs were collapsed and waterless.

Mr. Goddard told reporters that he was dumbfounded at how such a shiftless man as Knapp had won the love and loyalty of Goddard's "good, honest, hard-working" niece, finally concluding that there must have been something paranormal about it: "She was never of the foolish and frivolous kind. It is all the more mysterious that such a girl as she was should have yielded up everything in life and finally life itself to such a creature as Knapp. He must have supernatural powers to have worked on the passions of his victims as he did. He is a fiend incarnate, there can be no doubt of that."

The relatives took Hannah to Greenwood Cemetery for burial, but not before hundreds of men and women had trooped through Shrader's undertaking establishment to see the victim of Hamilton's latest sensation. Even children came, no doubt storing up a lifetime's worth of nightmares. "The body had been embalmed and wrapped in a white shroud," wrote a detail-oriented reporter, "but the most careful attention from the undertaker was insufficient to prevent decomposition, and in order to preserve the remains it was necessary to have a metallic casket." Her funeral was attended by two relatives and a throng of reporters.

When prison officials informed Knapp of the discovery, his spirits dropped sharply—and strangely, considering his multitude of rambling, almost boastful admissions. The man who had seemed only too pleased to confess to murder changed his tune once the body turned up. He had given the police a good story, but now the details could be corroborated. Knapp denied it was Hannah, saying the body could not have gone over the falls near Louisville, since the water was not high enough. When the officials countered that the body wore jewelry like Hannah's and had an ankle injury like hers, the formerly too-talkative Knapp clammed up.

At his arraignment—which was held in secret, since the authorities did not want to attract a large crowd—Knapp pled not guilty due to insanity.

He reminded everyone within earshot that a horse had once kicked him in the head, and, therefore, it followed, he could be held responsible for nothing now. In a bitter irony (bitter for Knapp, that is), his sister had requested earlier that his examining trial be delayed because she wanted to be present with an attorney. She got her way, but if the examining trial had been held *before* the body was found, Knapp likely would have been set free due to lack of evidence. All the police really had was his story, after all, but now they had smelly, bloated proof that he had committed at least one murder.

When the murder trial opened in Hamilton on June 23, Knapp, "looking very well groomed," turned up wearing black crepe to commemorate his father's recent death. (The old gentleman had died of a broken heart a few weeks after his son's arrest.) Finding a jury acceptable to both sides was such a slow process that the trial proper did not begin until June 29. Knapp's defense team faced an uphill battle since their client had confessed openly to his misdeeds. Their genius strategy was to try to prove his confessions were false—that Knapp was bloviating and making up stories, simply for the sake of being entertaining, one assumes. The reader will immediately detect the critical flaw in the defense's logic: if Knapp had merely lied about murdering Hannah, how came it to pass that when her body turned up, its condition so closely matched the details in his imagination? Not only had she been strangled and dumped in a river just as he said, Knapp had described her ankle injury, her stockings, and her jewelry *before* the corpse was discovered.

Nevertheless, the defense tried its very best, which is all anyone can do. Their task was made even harder when the state put on witnesses who testified that just after Hannah Knapp disappeared, her husband had disposed of her worldly goods and told curious people that she was gone, never to return. One witness, furniture dealer David Loeb, said that the day after Christmas 1902, Knapp had told him that Hannah had gone to Indianapolis. Conversely, at around the same time, Knapp had told his friend George Cooley that Hannah was in Cincinnati.

There was always the insanity defense, and, on July 1, the strangler's mother, Susan (Martha in some accounts) Knapp, testified about the head injury he had received in his youth. However, the press tells us, "Prosecutor Gard greatly weakened Mrs. Knapp's testimony on cross-examination, involving her in repeated contradictions and errors as to the date of accidents and other circumstances." Over the next couple of days, relatives and friends testified that they considered Knapp crazy because of "his absurd statements and conduct." Their evidence for Knapp's insanity was unconvincing—downright paltry, in fact. The prisoner's brother testified that when he had visited Alfred the day before the murder, Alfred had declared that he was an actor and was destined to be the next mayor of Hamilton. Longtime friends recalled that the accused used to put worms and bugs in his mouth, threw rocks at girls, enjoyed "showing off," and walked around in cold weather without coat or shoes. All of this may have shown that Knapp was eccentric, but it did not answer the important question of whether he could tell right from wrong. No one seemed very impressed with such testimony except Knapp himself, who thought an acquittal was as good as in the bag.

A doctor thought that Knapp might have "epileptic insanity," possibly triggered by that horse kick, but other friends and acquaintances of Knapp testified that they had never thought him insane. A warden who had charge of Knapp in prison said that he had kept his supposed raving insanity well in check for the seven years he was in jail.

The case went to the jury on the evening of July 15. They deliberated so long that many trial watchers thought they would deliver an acquittal or at least a verdict of guilty with a recommendation of mercy. When they returned to court on the evening of July 16, they announced exactly the reverse: they found Knapp guilty of first-degree murder; no mercy recommended.

In September, the judge refused Knapp a new trial. The prisoner was removed to the prison at Columbus, where an unenviable event awaited him, scheduled for December 12. On that day, Knapp was saved at the last moment when his attorney got news that the circuit court had granted an appeal to the Supreme Court of Ohio. Not nearly so lucky was Knapp's mother, who was said, on January 29, 1904, to be dying of grief because of her son's infamy—this, after "a lifetime spent in good deeds," said a news report. Knapp's official death toll was five, but considering that he also caused his parents' demise in a roundabout way, perhaps the count should be seven.

Or eight if you count Alfred Knapp himself. After his attorneys' dickering won him that coveted second trial, they nervously offered to enter a guilty plea for their client if the state would be so kind as to reduce his sentence to life imprisonment. The great state of Ohio responded with the legal equivalent of a horse laugh. On June 28, the Supreme Court affirmed the original verdict. The electric chair was now inevitable. On July 12, as Knapp was being shuttled back to death row in Columbus, a mob waiting at the train station in Middletown nearly saved the state the trouble.

Knapp's highly charged exit from this vale of tears was scheduled for August 19, 1904. Two weeks before, the press reported that the man who had lightly boasted of five murders lost his nerve and could neither eat nor sleep. Prison officials thought he might have to be carried to the chair.

Somehow, Knapp was executed a few minutes after midnight in the early morning of August 18 rather than August 19 as scheduled. Not sure why the rush, but he was in no position to complain. This man, so full of surprises, astonished everyone a final time by fully regaining his nerve at the end. He went to his death with the bravery of a gladiator, an aspect of his being that some would consider praiseworthy—especially in his own time, when a murderer who went to his execution without "dying game" was considered a coward and a disgrace and was likely to lose his social standing among his peers.

Prison officials were relieved that Knapp went out so easily. The press related, "The execution was one of the most successful in the history of electrocutions. Only one charge of the fluid was necessary." An electrocution is an event that you definitely want to come off without a hitch, although the end result is the same whether it goes perfectly or not.

On the other hand, some held that Knapp went to the chair with serenity only to get revenge on his executors *after death*. Two days after his electrocution, the prison warden died suddenly; at the same time, C. A. Marden, the prison's electrician, came down with typhoid. He died on September 3.

Another Woman in Another Furnace

Readers of my book *Horror in the Heartland* (Indiana University Press, 2017) may remember the extraordinary case of Elfrieda Knaak, who was found alive in the Lake Bluff, Illinois, city hall furnace on the morning of October 30, 1928. She survived a few days before succumbing to her horrible burns, without revealing who put her in the furnace, if anyone, as the matter of whether she was a murder victim or a suicide was never resolved.

The Knaak incident had a precedent in another Midwestern town, just a few years before. The earlier case also was full of unresolved, frustrating ambiguities.

The Sheatsley family lived at 2314 East Main Street in Bexley, a suburb of Columbus. There were four children. The eldest, Milton, was twenty and attended Bexley's Capital University. The others were Clarence Jr., age sixteen; Elizabeth, age fourteen; and Alice, age ten.

On November 17, 1924, Milton came home at 3:15 p.m., after college classes let out. Before entering, he noticed a distinctly unpleasant odor emanating from the residence, which he said smelled like "burned hair or flesh." He traced it to the furnace. Glancing in, he saw nothing but a pile of ashes. He did not investigate further. When the other children got in from their school, minutes after Milton's arrival, Clarence Jr. looked in the furnace too and evidently took a longer, harder look than Milton. He saw something more unnerving than mere ashes. Then he did something extremely incongruous, as will be detailed later.

Their father, Clarence Valentine Sheatsley, came home from Columbus around 5:00 p.m. He was horrified by the all-pervasive smell, which had become quite the family topic. He opened the furnace door and saw ashes—but, sifting through them, he found his fifty-year-old wife Addie's jewelry and pieces of skin the fire had not consumed.

Coroner Joseph A. Murphy gave his preliminary verdict the same day: he believed Addie had crawled into the furnace intent on suicide, locked the door, and burned to death. The reader, who undoubtedly has a mind finely trained by years of watching televised detective stories both fictional and true, may have noticed a flaw in the coroner's theory: How did Addie lock the furnace door from the inside? County prosecutor John R. King was dissatisfied with the verdict and announced that he would investigate.

Only two days into the probe, the press was calling the case "one of the most baffling in the history of the Columbus police department." King and Police Lieutenant Shellenbarger spent all of November 18 questioning Mr. Sheatsley and the four children. Another witness, bread wagon driver C. O. Strader, said he made a delivery at the house at two o'clock in the afternoon the day before. No one answered when he knocked, so he left the bread outside. Strader neither saw nor smelled anything unusual, although the odor of the burning corpse was discernible outside the house when the eldest boy, Milton, returned home at 3:15. If Mrs. Sheatsley were in the heater by 2:00, the smell should have been detectable via the chimney when Strader dropped by.

Milton told King that when he came home, the delivered bread was sitting on the kitchen table. Who had brought it inside? If Mrs. Sheatsley had retrieved the bread, how was it possible—assuming all witnesses were telling the truth or not mistaken—for her to have done so after two o'clock and been reduced nearly to ashes in the furnace in less than three hours, at the most, before Mr. Sheatsley arrived home? It hardly seemed possible. It should have taken many hours and crematorium-style temperatures far beyond the capability of a common household furnace to destroy a human body to such a degree.

Prosecutor King asked Milton why he did not inspect the ashes. Milton explained that he thought the smell came from a rabbit pelt (his father was an avid rabbit hunter) or from burning trash, as the family used the furnace for handy garbage disposal. King replied, bluntly and tactlessly, "Didn't you know that the body of your mother was in that furnace? After you knew that the odor that attracted you was the burning flesh of your mother, did you go to the furnace and look at the body?"

"I did not," said Milton.

"Why didn't you?"

Milton replied sensibly. "I didn't want to see my mother burning in a furnace."

All four Sheatsley children testified that they had lunched at home that day and their mother was alive at noon. Milton said that he and his sisters departed at 12:15, leaving his mother, father, and brother Clarence Jr. alone in the house.

Clarence Jr. later said that he left home at 1:30 p.m. Under King's questioning, he mentioned a possible clue: the family kept a bottle of deadly carbolic acid in the medicine closet, but it was missing.

Some locals were convinced a lunatic was on the loose. Mrs. George Allen, who lived on Oak Street, about two miles from the Sheatsley residence, came forth with a weird story, an inevitable feature of any mysterious, unsolved death—but this time, there may have been something to it. She told investigators that on the morning of Addie Sheatsley's death, a strange man, "having the appearance of a maniac," came to her house and asked for an overcoat. When Mrs. Allen refused, the man asked, "May I see the furnace room?" Then he jumped off the porch and ran with what Mrs. Allen deemed "a funny little trot" in the direction of the Sheatsley house. Police didn't think Mrs. Allen's story was worth very much, but they gamely sought the strange fellow. One detective even fruitlessly searched a blacksmith shop, a hundred feet from the Sheatsley house and unused for three years, on the chance that someone had hidden there. The coat-begging, wannabe furnace-inspecting madman never turned up.

It was a while before Bexley residents ventured outside at night or stayed at home alone—especially after a second person, and then a third, reported similar encounters with a stranger. At 1:00 p.m. on the day of Addie's death and only five blocks from the Sheatsley residence, a housewife heard frightening sounds coming from her basement. She shouted, "Who's there?" No answer. In a panic, she tried to flee through the rear door and found that someone had secured it from the outside. She heard someone coming up the stairs to the first floor. Luckily for her, the door was locked. The intruder gave up doing whatever he had planned and left the house through the cellar door.

In addition, Christine Roller, housekeeper for Mrs. Nelson Sims, reported that on November 24, a week after Addie's death, a man came to the door asking if he could have an overcoat. When she told him no, he inquired, "May I go down to the furnace to get warm?" She refused *in no uncertain terms.* Not only did the man resemble the weirdo Mrs. Allen claimed she saw, he too ran away "in a half trot."

In cases involving a wife who dies under fishy circumstances, detectives usually consider the husband the number-one suspect. However, Mr. Sheatsley was not just an average suspect; he was *Reverend* Sheatsley, the eminently respectable pastor of Bexley's Christ Lutheran Church and professor of religion at Capital University. In fact, the family's home was the church's parsonage. As far as anyone knew, the couple had no domestic trouble. The police carefully emphasized that no family member was under suspicion.

Reverend Sheatsley publicly supported the coroner's original verdict of suicide. This represented an abrupt shift in his thinking. On November 18, he indignantly denied that Addie killed herself; on November 19, he agreed that she had. His reasoning was not exactly a model of clarity, perhaps due to grief. Although the furnace door was only fourteen inches square, he thought his slender wife could have wiggled through it. He pointed out that she was afflicted with "chronic nervousness" and was menopausal to boot, which he thought could have made her "violently insane." (The reverend seemed to think the miseries wrought by the "change of life" could encourage a woman to burn herself alive.)

One of Reverend Sheatsley's strange theories was that his wife might have imitated the Hindu women of India, who purged themselves of sin by self-immolation. (He had done missionary work there in 1920 and published a book in 1921 called *Our Mission Field in India*.) He said she had "brooded over imaginary sins," such as forgetting to supply drinking glasses at a church bazaar and, on the morning of her death, had remarked, "I have committed a grievous sin; I wonder if I will go to Heaven." He seemed to be implying that she thought entering the heater was the only way she could atone.

Possibly to support his father, Milton changed a critical detail in his story. Previously, he swore the furnace door was closed when he had first approached it. Since the door could not be shut from inside the furnace, a closed door would indicate murder. However, on November 20, he wrote, in a signed letter to Prosecutor King, "When I went into the cellar with my sisters I saw the little door open (i.e., the door above the one where you put the coal in), and closed it."

Investigators interviewed Addie's elderly mother, Lydia Sponseller, who lived with the family for eighteen years and moved out in June 1924 to live with her son at Paris, Ohio. She said that relations between the reverend and Addie always were superb, and, in her opinion, her daughter, indeed, killed herself.

Prosecutor King, on the other hand, stood by his first opinion: suicide was impossible. He conceded that small-boned Addie could have squeezed through the furnace's narrow aperture, but also said it had been "definitely established" (how, the newspapers do not tell us) that she had entered the furnace feet first, which would have made entry impracticable unless she had held onto some object for support. No such bracing object was anywhere the furnace, King said. In addition, the door was thirty inches from the floor, so climbing in would have required some high-stepping. It was far likelier, said King, that someone had crammed Addie, dead or alive, into the furnace.

Supporting King's point of view was Dr. C. B. Wells, the Sheatsleys' family physician, who offered his professional opinion that Addie had a normal mentality and was not suicidal—she was "a woman of extraordinary balance, not given to fits of nerves." The doctor was sympathetic to Sheatsley, whom he had known for thirty years: "I think perhaps Dr. Sheatsley is groping for an explanation of the tragedy." So Dr. Wells depicted Addie as a rock of inner strength; her husband said she was an obsessive bundle of nerves, bent on self-destruction. One of them had to be wrong.

On November 23, Reverend Sheatsley's parishioners released a unanimous resolution affirming their belief that Addie was murdered. Undertaker Edwin Abbott, who removed Addie's remains from the furnace—all in a day's work!—related that her skull was intact but cracked. However, he could not say if the crack originated from blunt force or heat.

Some investigators wondered if Mrs. Sheatsley had been drugged before her cremation. Her stomach's contents were too badly burned for analysis, though the lining was intact. Scientists hoped her lungs and esophagus might reveal the truth. Chemist T. C. Long dropped a bombshell on November 21: He had extracted three ounces of blood from Addie's lungs. Analysis showed no signs of poison—but also, no carbon monoxide. Had she been alive in the heater, her lungs and blood should have borne traces of the gas. Long's verdict: Addie was dead before her placement in the parsonage furnace. Her lungs were "intensely congested," suggesting strangulation or suffocation. Other recoverable vital organs—the stomach wall, thorax, and esophagus—were turned over to Dr. H. M. Brundage for pathological, as opposed to chemical, testing. Because there was no poison in Addie's system, police called off the search for the missing bottle of now-irrelevant carbolic acid.

One of the oddest aspects of this odd case was teenager Clarence Sheatsley Jr.'s seeming determination to draw suspicion. Some authorities theorized that Addie's death was the result of a suicide pact—that she had killed herself, and then someone shoved her body into the furnace to hide the evidence, thus sparing the family disgrace. Allegedly, when a detective offered this suggestion to Clarence, the boy replied, "Maybe she got him to put her in." Could "he" have been Clarence, referring to himself in the third person? It was his father's chore to take care of the furnace, but, on November 17, when the reverend came home, Clarence did not ask where his mother was, as one might expect. Instead, he told his father not to bother with the furnace because he already tended to it. Detectives pointed out that, if that were the case, Clarence must have known his mother's body was in the heater before the reverend discovered it.

Clarence Jr. confirmed as much: "I knew something was wrong. It looked like she was in there to me. I didn't know what to think." Instead of alerting anyone, Clarence just went to his room—and took a nap! When asked about this singular behavior, Clarence said: "I went down and looked [in the furnace] and saw something black. I let things go for a little while. I didn't say anything. I thought it might have been my mother, but did not want to believe it."

He added philosophically, "She was dead already. What good would it do?"

Inexplicably, the police appear not to have further investigated Clarence's assertions. Several days later, Reverend Sheatsley tried, not very successfully, to rationalize his son's weird statements: "The boy probably saw the form in the furnace but his heart said it can't be mother. There is a possibility that he was excited when he made the statement, due to his age. You know how a boy is."

On November 24, a *whole week* after Addie's body was found, Prosecutor King thoroughly scrutinized the parsonage while Sheatsley and his children were staying with relatives in Paris, Ohio, and found what appeared to be damning evidence. One wonders why he delayed this essential step in the investigation; furthermore, if any family members had anything to do with Addie's death, why had they not cleaned up such telltale clues before they left town?

Specifically, in the basement, police found three fingerprints on a white-covered pipe that led from the furnace to a heating register. The prints were so obvious, they conceded, that it was unthinkable a murderer who knew his business would have just left them there. More likely, the prints were those of an investigator who helped retrieve Addie from the furnace, or perhaps undertaker Abbott. Searchers opened a closet for preserves, located fifteen feet from the furnace, and found what seemed to be dried blood in an upside-down jar lid. Also, a hammer (some accounts say a hatchet) in a corner had a suspicious smear, a small piece of something resembling bloody flesh adhered to a panel on the kitchen door, two small pieces of tissue were on the cellar steps, and another piece was on outdoor steps that led from the kitchen to the rear churchyard. Detectives theorized that Mrs. Sheatsley was killed in the backyard and then dragged up the rear stairs, through the kitchen, and down to the cellar and its awaiting furnace. The church itself would have blocked onlookers from seeing any nefarious activity.

On the second floor, they found stained blue trousers in the corner of a bedroom closet. In another closet, they found a spotted tablecloth. Amazingly, someone—an oblivious police officer?—removed ashes containing human remains from the furnace and dumped them in the edge of the yard near the hedge. Detectives combed through the pile and found bone fragments and Mrs. Sheatsley's dress buttons.

Outside, detectives discovered a burlap sack that seemed bloodstained in a hedge.

The strangest clue, if it was a clue at all, was that someone had restored the formerly missing bottle of carbolic acid to the parsonage medicine chest—and that someone could not have been a family member, since Sheatsley and his children had been out of town for the last several days. When reporters in Paris informed Reverend Sheatsley about these findings, he released a statement from his relative's home: "I believe the spots of blood will be found those of rabbits rather than those of a human being. I had cleaned four rabbits in the cellar. I am perfectly in accord with Mr. King combing the house for anything that may lead to the solution of the mystery. Anything they want they may have. I have removed nothing from the house except a small tin box, which contained my insurance papers and other legal documents."

Investigators sent these suspicious items to chemist Long and pathologist Brundage for analysis. Sheatsley was correct: the scientists reported that the various stains were not human blood. So much for evidence found in the house and on the grounds; Brundage had yet to release his report on evidence from the furnace.

On November 26, the reverend's congregation greeted him when he returned to Bexley. Facing reporters from the parsonage doorway, he reiterated his belief that Addie killed herself. He hated to admit it, saying, "I would rather believe she was murdered—foul as the deed may be—rather than to believe she took her own life, but until such evidence has been definitely established I will think she took her own life." Sheatsley asked the public to be fair, noting that some people enjoyed thinking the worst of a minister: "There is a certain element of the public which seems to delight in getting something on a preacher, so to speak. I think perhaps that fact is responsible for the insinuations that have been made." Speaking to students and faculty at Capital University on December 1, he again referred to the rumor campaign against him: "The excited populace was astir, suspicion was aroused. The voice of the slanderer was heard."

It seemed that citizens of Bexley were glad to have the reverend back. However, just to play it safe, six football players who were teammates of Milton's guarded the parsonage.

On November 28, Prosecutor King questioned Reverend Sheatsley, Milton, and Clarence Jr. for over six hours. They did not divert from their original statements. "We gained nothing which might be of any value in clearing up the case," said King.

Chemist Long and pathologist Brundage released their long-awaited report on December 2. By throwing, uh, live guinea pigs in the parsonage furnace and dissecting their remains, Long and Brundage found that large quantities of carbon monoxide gas "literally saturated" the poor critters' blood, proving that Addie had been murdered.

And yet, in the face of this outwardly conclusive evidence, on December 4, Coroner Murphy stubbornly insisted that Addie had put herself in the furnace, and he filed his official verdict as suicide caused by "immediate asphyxiation." Murphy argued that when Addie climbed into the furnace, the intense pain caused her lungs to fill with blood and her heart to dilate. Her heart was bloodless, proving that it continued to beat while she was in the furnace. Had she been murdered, her heart should have had blood in it. But why was there no carbon monoxide in Addie's blood? Murphy reasoned that "the reflex action caused by the heat probably halted breathing and consequently there could have been no carbon monoxide, smoke, dust, or other debris in the blood or lungs." Instant asphyxiation meant no buildup of smoke in the lungs or gas in the blood. By rendering this verdict, Murphy disregarded the experts' opinion and gave Prosecutor King the legal equivalent of "In your face!" King refused comment before reporters.

One question appears not to have been answered: Regardless of whether Addie was dead or alive in the heater, how did her body get cremated so thoroughly and so quickly in a home furnace? And there were other loose ends. Who returned the carbolic acid to the medicine chest? Can we reconcile the radically differing assessments of Addie's mental health from her husband and her doctor? What are we to make of Clarence Sheatsley Jr.'s curious statements to the police?

On December 21, Reverend Sheatsley returned to the pulpit. Despite his seeming vindication, rumormongers still found him an irresistible target. Authorities, reporters, and common gossips offered sundry bone-headed solutions to the mystery, based on nothing stronger than fertile imaginations. For instance, a story spread that years before, when Reverend Sheatsley worked at a Pittsburgh orphanage, he had reprimanded a boy who swore he would "get him" someday. The reverend countered that the story was nonsense, as he never had rebuked a boy there, nor would doing so have been part of his duties. Others remembered that, after his return from India, Sheatsley had gotten into an argument with a Hindu after making a speech in Detroit. The reverend admitted that had happened, but said the disagreement was trivial. He discounted the theory that the Hindu had murdered his wife and crammed her in a furnace for revenge. Some busybodies even found deep significance in that Sheatsley had neglected to give his wife a good-bye kiss as he left the house on the fatal day.

Then anonymous letters came to Sheatsley, claiming to come from members of his own flock. Some were printed in Columbus newspapers. The writers demanded to know why he had not made any public statements from the pulpit about his wife's strange demise. If there was a murderer on the loose, why had he not offered a reward, they wanted to know. The situation became so intolerable for the reverend that, on January 11, 1925, he broke his silence in church and urged his parishioners to give him a break.

"Several anonymous letters, purporting to have been written by members of my congregation, have asked why we have not mentioned the tragedy that took place in our home," he began.

One listener, Reverend Dr. Edward Pfeiffer, rose to his feet and asked Sheatsley to stop. "What do the people want?" Pfeiffer upbraided the congregation. "Did our resolutions [in support of Sheatsley] carry no weight?"

No new evidence was ever uncovered, and Prosecutor King finally accepted Coroner Murphy's verdict. So, it appears, Addie Sheatsley officially committed suicide. Unless she didn't.

There the matter stands, unless we take the Knaak furnace death in Illinois four years later into consideration and make the preposterous suggestion that a serial killer was wandering the Midwest, stuffing women into furnaces. On the other hand, perhaps we should not be as quick to dismiss, as the police did at the time, the stories told by the three women living near the parsonage who claimed that a young man seemingly fascinated by furnaces tried to break into their homes—two on the same day as Addie's death, the other a week later.

The Things We Do for Love

Back in the old days, train personnel faced robbers so often it was considered an occupational hazard, similar to modern taxi drivers. It wasn't merely a Wild West phenomenon, as Charles Lane's fate illustrates. The twenty-eight-year-old worked for the Adams Express Company on the Pennsylvania line's train Number Eight. His job involved protecting valuables that passengers and companies stored in the train's safe. When the train arrived in Columbus on the night of August 10, 1900, crewmen found Lane dead on the floor of the express car. He was riddled with three bullets in his back, one in his left side, and four in his right leg.

His revolver lay by his side, missing two bullets. The safe was empty, its key still in the lock. The train robber was not content with pilfering the safe and also stole the dead man's knife and money.

The brave expressman was last seen alive when the train stopped at Milford Center; therefore, the thief attacked somewhere between there and Columbus. Investigators thought the bandit abandoned the train either at its Marble Cliff stop or as it slowed down near its destination, Columbus's Union Station.

The Adams Express Company was understandably reluctant to say how much money was gone, but journalists estimated the take at $45,000 (the equivalent in modern currency would be over $1.4 million).

Officers searched the railroad track between Columbus and Urbana, investigated "dozens of stories and rumors," and placed a number of suspicious persons under surveillance. The search involved the entire Columbus detective force, railroad detectives, and police departments in towns within a fifty-mile radius of Columbus. Despite the combined effort, the police emerged clueless. Nevertheless, they arrived at a valid conclusion: whoever masterminded the robbery and murder was "perfectly familiar with the train and the customs of the people on board." The thief left behind valuable silver bullion, perhaps because he knew it would be difficult to resell without incriminating himself. Or perhaps it was just too heavy to carry.

By August 12, the mystery was no more. Columbus detectives arrested Charles Rossyln Ferrell, age twenty-two, originally from Steubenville and a fine-looking devil indeed, described as being six feet tall with a "splendid physique," having "dark hair and an attractive face," a "gentlemanly and refined appearance," and being "finely dressed." They collared him at his fiancée's parents' home, which must have been a pretty awkward social situation. At first, he played it nonchalant, but as the questions became more pointed, he gave up the pretense and told all. His conscience must have troubled him, as he confessed before he even made it to the police station. Just to show how quickly the course of one's life can change, a few hours before detectives came to the house, a vocal quartet had been rehearsing the wedding songs, and Ferrell had been ordering invitations.

As detectives had predicted, Ferrell did have insider knowledge. He was a former Adams Express Company employee and was acquainted with train schedules and the company's inner workings. He had had no accomplices. The murder was premeditated and heartless as could be: the victim, Lane, had been a friend of Ferrell's, but Ferrell was not about to let sentiment get in the way of easy money.

He had boarded the express car when it stopped at Urbana and told Lane, "Say, I'm a little low on money. Mind if I ride with you all the way to Columbus?" The affable Lane agreed, unaware that he was making the mistake of his life.

As the train rolled along the track, Ferrell waited until Lane turned his back. He fired his six-shooter at his friend until it was empty and then shot Lane twice with his own gun. He opened the safe with Lane's key, put the money in a satchel, and sneaked off the train when it made its Plain City stop. He spent the night in a hotel, where he was silly enough to hide Lane's revolver within the bedsprings and leave it there. The next morning, wanting to get the empty express bags as far away as possible, he stuffed them in a package and mailed it to a fictitious address. Then he took a train home to Columbus, where the murder and robbery was the talk of every person he met. The publicity made him nervous, but he kept his composure.

Meanwhile, as Ferrell tried to maintain a veneer of calm among acquaintances in Columbus, detectives inquired at the hotel in Plain City, a railway stop. The proprietor remembered that a young man had checked in and forgotten to sign the register and had left for Columbus the next morning. When detectives searched the stranger's room, they found Lane's gun and incriminating documents Ferrell had forgotten to take. From here, they trailed the fugitive to his fiancée's parents' house.

Ferrell's motive: he had needed money—and *soon!*—because in less than a week he was to marry lovely young Lillian Mae Costlow, whose father, Patrick, was an engineer on the Pennsylvania train line. The Adams Express Company had fired Ferrell back in May after three customers had complained about broken packages, so one wonders if a thirst for revenge did not also factor into his decision.

Ferrell had given $1,000 (modern equivalent would be roughly $3,740) of his ill-gotten money to Lillian to keep for him, claiming it was his own savings. This statement was not exactly believable, but love will blind us to the obvious. Taking into consideration that the average American worker in 1900 made slightly less than $700 annually and that Ferrell had been unemployed for the past three months, Lillian really must have strained to swallow this lie. However, she did believe him, and so did her parents. They were distraught when they found that he was not the "model young man" they had thought. The *Courier-Journal*'s editorialist wondered why Ferrell simply didn't delay his wedding if he had no where-withal to pay for it: "He thought the sacrifice of Lane's life would be better than the postponement of his own marriage."

Since Ferrell had shot Lane as the train exited Milford Center, he would go on trial in Union County. When police took him to Marysville on August 14, a reporter noticed that his dashingly handsome physiognomy reflected his inner ordeal: "Ferrell is losing his nerve and beginning to show deep lines of care on his face." Before he left Columbus, Lillian came to see him. The visit "was very pathetic," said a reporter. "It was at once a meeting and a parting forever." She had to be placed under a physician's care afterward.

Ferrell was arraigned two days later. Despite his full confession and the plentiful evidence against him, he pled not guilty. In his cell, he cried for his mother, behavior hardly in keeping with his manly-man appearance. Jailhouse personnel placed him on suicide watch.

Ferrell spent a good deal of August 15 writing to Lillian, asking her to be faithful to him and avowing that, eventually, he would make his way out of his little difficulty.

The trial started in October. Lillian took the stand on the 19th, telling the court how Ferrell had given her his "savings" and how he was arrested before her very eyes two days after the robbery-murder. She said what you would have bet she would say, had you been there—that she believed fervently in Ferrell's innocence, was certain he would be acquitted, and would plead to the jury to save "her boy"—but she also admitted, surprisingly, that she would prefer to see her dear Charlie go to the electric chair than spend his life in prison.

Just as predictable as (most) of Lillian's assertions were the defense team's: they declared that Charles Rossyln Ferrell was crazy as a bedbug.

To be more precise, it seems they could find no evidence that Ferrell *himself* was insane, so they tried to prove he had insane family members, thereby arguing something along the lines of insanity by osmosis. They asked the jury to consider his good reputation before he murdered someone. Therefore, he was a nice, but insane, fellow.

As the trial unfolded, the flinthearted *Courier-Journal* editorialist wondered what sort of husband he would have made, anyhow: "The man had deceived her by holding himself out as a careful and provident man who saved his money, and so might be expected to be able to support a wife, though temporarily out of work . . . Had he escaped arrest long enough to marry, the girl he married would either have deserted him as soon as the stolen money was exhausted, or he would have depended upon her for support."

On the day before Halloween, the jury found Ferrell guilty of first-degree murder, with no recommendation of mercy. He must usher in the new century by going to the chair on March 1, 1901. The following night, Ferrell tried unsuccessfully to suffocate himself with his bedclothing.

"Miss Costlow's grief was pitiable," commented a reporter.

Ferrell was sent to prison in Columbus to await the end. He sought a commutation to life imprisonment rather than a confrontation with the chair, so he had very different ideas from Lillian on that particular topic. The governor called a special meeting of the Board of Pardons on January 10, 1901, to debate whether Ferrell was worthy of such.

Despite the vicissitudes in their relationship, Ferrell *still* wanted to marry Lillian if she was willing. Shooting a man in cold blood eight times and going to jail, and very likely to the electric chair, must have seemed to him a concrete declaration of love. The warden said he would have no problem with it if it were okay with Lillian. Ferrell perhaps should have been tipped off to her cooled passions by the fact that she had visited him in jail only once, and, even then, she brought her mother.

The Board of Pardons turned down Ferrell's request, and, for the next couple of months, he had little to do but contemplate the transient nature of worldly pleasures. The prisoner's final meeting with Lillian and his mother was on February 21.

On March 1, Ferrell went to the death chamber right on schedule. He muttered, "I have nothing to say," and then the executioner pulled the switch. The apostle Paul said it was better to marry than to burn, but this wasn't what he had in mind.

According to records at Ancestry.com, Lillian married William A. Nunn on November 28, 1901—slightly less than nine months after Ferrell's execution. She got over him, it appears, quickly. She died in Cuyahoga County on September 22, 1963.

10

WASTED IN WISCONSIN

Blackmailers' Bloodbath, or: The Hun Also Rises

Siblings William and Hulda Hille ran a two-hundred-acre farm called Ravensholme, which bordered the Fox River, six miles southwest of Waukesha, Wisconsin. They inherited the land and the farmhouse from their father, who had emigrated from Hanover, Germany. When the United States entered World War One in April 1917, William was fifty-nine and Hulda was sixty-three.

It is well known that Americans' fury against Germany in general and the kaiser in particular was so pronounced that citizens of German descent were singled out for harassment or worse. Mobs vandalized homes and stores. In some cases, persons with names that sounded a little too Anglo-Saxon changed them. My voluminous files of weird Americana include many examples of persecution—sometimes for foolhardily praising the enemy nation and its allies, sometimes for no better reason than that the targets or their ancestors had emigrated from *das Vaterland*. Here are a few tragic, typical, or preposterous cases:

- After Germany sank the British ship *Lusitania* in 1915, residents of German Township in Bartholomew County, Indiana, circulated a petition to change the town's name to American. Similarly, in May 1917, the folks in Berlin, Wisconsin, started a movement to change its name to Mascoutin. Ditto in Bismarck, North Dakota, where signs erected in July 1918 read, "Change the name of the city to something decent." All of these motions failed after tempers cooled.

- In April 1917, citizens of Winchester, Kentucky, persecuted a shoemaker of German descent, Charles Balmut, for making "disloyal utterances," which he denied. Matters grew so ugly that he sought police protection.
- Also in April 1917, someone in the Swiss settlement of Helvetia near Elkins, West Virginia, raised a German flag. It was torn down, and riots commenced. News reports are vague as to whether the fighting was over the raising or the tearing down.
- In March 1918, the famous vaudevillian team Weber and Fields announced that they would cease doing German dialect comedy. Some commentators wondered what their new act could possibly consist of, since gentle mockery of Germans had been their only shtick for years.
- Sammy K. Harrington of Columbus, Indiana, did not like his middle name—*Kaiser*—for a too-obvious reason. In August 1918, Harrington announced that he would use the middle name no more. He was only nine years old!
- In August 1918, a sign inside the Warsaw, Kentucky, courthouse read, "No German language talked in this town. If you can't talk United States don't talk at all."
- Lest we mistakenly believe only rednecks were agitated by the German presence in America, consider that at the end of April 1918, federal agents arrested Miss Agathe Wilhelmina Richrath, instructor in the German language at New York's Vassar College. The charge was "circulating Hun propaganda," apparently including the belief that the *Lusitania* deserved to be sunk and rooting for the invasion of Belgium. One might think she could have gotten a few years in jail just for her name alone.
- One of the more serious manifestations of the prevailing attitude occurred at Collinsville, Illinois, on April 4, 1918, when a mob of 350 dragged Robert Prager (or Praeger), whose parents were German, from the city hall basement and hanged him for making "disloyal remarks." In June, a jury acquitted all eleven members of the mob who had been identified and charged. Nevertheless, perhaps the mob's leader felt pangs of guilt. He shot himself to death in Collinsville on January 11, 1919.

- In January 1919—after the war was over!—the stockholders of the German Mutual Fire Insurance Company of Louisville, Kentucky, overwhelmingly voted to change the corporation's name to the American Mutual etc.

These vignettes, and had space permitted I could have included dozens of others, show why persons such as William and Hulda Hille were so jumpy at the prospect of being thought disloyal to the United States. In the face of this anti-German reaction, it is ironic that fellow German Americans, looking to make a quick buck by exploiting the nation's anger, were responsible for the tragedy that ended the Hille siblings' lives.

On April 1, 1918, the Hilles hired teenager Ernest Fentz, a neighbor's stepson, as a farmworker. William Hille was fond of the boy and even bought a car so Ernest could go for rides.

For unknown reasons, the Hilles fired Fentz in June. For a replacement, they hired a Milwaukee man named Elder Krause, who purported to be, like the Hilles, the son of a German emigrant. On July 11, the hired man told them that he was actually a secret service agent working for the US government. He told them, in effect, "All I have to do is report you for disloyal activities, and you will go to jail." Then he probably added those words that seem never to go out of fashion: "Of course, I can make this all go away if you make it worth my trouble."

To back up his threat, Krause brought Ernest Fentz with him. (The teenager's stepfather must have sensed that Krause was bad news, as he urged Fentz not to go.) Fentz told the gullible siblings that he witnessed them planning espionage. He had, in fact, seen no such thing. The naive Hilles did not realize that Krause and Fentz were lying like *hunds* and that, even in an America rife with hatred for Germany, they could not be imprisoned without evidence and a trial. A later investigation proved that they were not merely verbally loyal to the United States; they also contributed to the war effort by purchasing Liberty bonds and war stamps and donating to the Red Cross and the YMCA. Nevertheless, to stay out of trouble, William reluctantly paid Krause thirty dollars "for protection against exposure," as the receipt said.

Krause was not satisfied and threatened to search the house for more money. William's mind snapped, and his tormentors soon learned a harsh lesson about the perils of greed, lying, and blackmailing. Krause, Fentz, and William Hille argued so vehemently that Hulda, afraid it would turn violent, called their neighbor Mrs. William Dingeldine (also spelled Dingeldein) and urged her to come over.

Mrs. Dingeldine's visit was brief. No sooner had she sat down in the kitchen with Hulda than a shotgun blast in another room shook the house. Hulda knew all too well what that meant. William entered the kitchen toting his gun. He offered his neighbor a hearty handclasp, but Mrs. Dingeldine declined and tried to coax him to hand over the weapon. Hulda stopped her, saying, "Let him go. It is for the best. They are after us anyway, and you cannot prevent this." By "they," did she mean their blackmailers or the government agents the Hilles dreaded?

Hulda told Mrs. Dingeldine to run away as quickly as she could but first gave her a wooden box in which she stored important papers and keepsakes, evidently afraid that Krause might seize it. Mrs. Dingeldine fled the farm, as Hulda's final words to her echoed in her mind: "We will be dead before anyone can get here." As she ran, she heard two more shots in the Hilles' barn. She also witnessed a panic-stricken Elder Krause lamming it across a field. She paused long enough to see that William was shooting his horses. When she begged him to cease, he replied in words similar to Hulda's: "They are after me." That was all Mrs. Dingeldine cared to see, and she ran home to call the police.

When the law arrived, they found that William Hille had left them with several crime scenes to process and many serious messes for someone to clean. Ernest Fentz's body sat in a rocking chair near the dining room's front door, with a considerable portion of his head decorating the wall. After killing Fentz, William had shot five horses and his dog.

Hulda knew she was next in line. To avoid her brother's wrath, she climbed in bed and swallowed arsenic. (Her sisters later denied that there had been poison in the house and said that weakhearted Hulda actually died of shock. Nevertheless, the coroner's report notes that a glass of poison was on a chair. There was a razor next to Hulda's right hand, evidently as insurance in case the arsenic did not work quickly.) Likely, she was dead before her brother made it back to the house.

Seeing that his sister was dead or dying, William went to his own bedroom and pressed the barrels of his shotgun against his chest. Police found him dead on the floor.

Elder Krause escaped with his life. Evidently, he didn't stop running until he got to Saylesville, even wading across a river in his fear. He joined the army in St. Paul. Police arrested him a few days after the massacre when he was en route to a North Carolina training camp. His thirty dollars were certainly hard-earned.

Officials never divulged the contents of the box Hulda gave Mrs. Dingeldine. Only one document was made public. On July 25, a local paper, the *Waukesha Freeman*, reprinted a largely incoherent letter by Hulda, notable for its eerily casual tone. She started by referring to the old superstition that a mysterious knocking sound portends imminent death and ended by listing who she wanted to be her pallbearers:

> Say, girls, the other night there was a slapping noise on the wall. I knew what that meant, so good-bye. All be good with Eliza. There are only these three left [a reference to her three sisters, the only Hille family survivors]. We will try our best to get our rights. Don't take it hard, because Bill would have to be in prison for life; he [Krause?] was telling Bill about the Japs coming over and how they will come. And then Bill—we would go in the house and shoot them. Give the machine to H. and A. That is W.'s wish. Ally and John, Arthur and Willie, Jamy and Will Werning for pallbearers.

Since Hulda gave this document to Mrs. Dingledine just before the latter ran from the farm, Hulda must have written it in the few minutes between her brother's argument with Krause and Fentz and the commencement of the bloodbath. Many have speculated about her remark that William would have been "in prison for life" had he lived. Did she mean that her brother would have gone to jail on false charges of disloyalty? More likely, Hulda feared that William would have been convicted for killing Fentz (and Krause too, had he been less fleet of foot).

Naturally—or rather, supernaturally—the Hille farm has a reputation for being haunted. Curiously, the apparition allegedly spotted there is neither bitter William nor frightened Hulda, nor the demolished Ernest Fentz, but the Hille siblings' father, John. Rather than undergoing a spectacular demise, John Hille died of natural causes when he was nearly ninety. There has also been much talk about a "curse" and a "force of evil" that permeates the farm, due to the number of accidents and premature deaths that have occurred there over the decades. However, no house or tract of land is free from mishap and death—and, as the number of such calamities will accumulate impressively with the passing of years, it seems unnecessary to credit such incidents to an exotic curse.

An Early Serial Killer . . . Perhaps

According to the Grant County Historical Society, Robert B. Turner's father, Albert, was from Tennessee, and his mother, Margaret, from Kentucky. Turner was born in Illinois around 1839. The family migrated to Grant County, Wisconsin, where Albert made a meager living as a lead miner before his death in 1857.

Robert fought in the Civil War in Company H, enlisting in the Twenty-Fifth Wisconsin Infantry in December 1863. That he was a veteran was about the only nice thing anyone could say of him in later life. A reporter described Robert when he achieved notoriety seven years after he was mustered out of the service: "He is a heavy-built man, five feet six inches high, and weighs about 160 pounds; is thirty-six years old and unmarried; is dark complexioned, with a full round face, which he usually kept well-shaved except the upper lip." His most disconcerting features, evidently, were his eyes and his reluctance to maintain eye contact: "He has sharp, piercing eyes, which are never still. One cannot get his eye for a moment."

Robert returned to his family in Potosi after leaving the army in June 1865. Like his father, he entered the lead mining industry along with brothers Albert Jr. and Newton. As the Grant County Historical Society notes, they had to support themselves, their mother, and three sisters. They were so impoverished that Robert spent time as an inmate at the county poor farm.

Robert was impoverished morally as well as financially. He had an unexplained grudge against his brother Albert. On December 6, 1873, Robert waited until Albert emerged from a mining hole and then took a swing at his neck with an ax, nearly beheading him. Albert's corpse fell limply to the ground.

Seeing that this strategy was successful, Robert called out, "Oh, Newton!" The second brother came out of a separate shaft, saw Albert lying on the ground, observed an ax in Robert's hand, and arrived at the logical conclusion. He tried to run for it. Robert grabbed his arm, shook the bloody ax at him, and told him that he would face the same fate if he did not help bury Albert. This well-reasoned argument convinced Newton that it would be wise to play along, but, after they buried Albert, Newton fled to Potosi and alerted the law. Officer Wilmot arrested Robert while he was on the run and clapped him in a cell. Robert earned further stern disapproval from his peers by trying to murder the jailkeeper and a fellow prisoner named Skellinger.

The ax murder got townspeople to thinking, as ax murders usually will. They remembered a strange missing person case from a few days before. On December 2, teenager Olney Neely had set out from Ellenboro to visit his mother in New California. En route, he had walked on a road that wound through a forest, and after Neely entered it, he was seen no more. Was it mere coincidence that, at the time, Robert Turner had been cutting hoop poles in those woods? Folks thought not and scoured the area for remains. On January 9, 1874, they found what they sought. The *New York Times* related that Robert killed Olney in the same way that he had committed fratricide: "The boy's head was nearly cut from the body, only hanging by a small piece of skin of the back and front of the neck." Olney was still clutching a parcel he had been carrying when the ax fell. The rest of his worldly goods, found on his body, were "a new jackknife, some marbles, and a fifty-cent stamp."

Police considered other unsolved murders that occurred where Robert Turner had been present. When Marshal Bennett asked him about it, Robert admitted, now that he thought about it, he *had* murdered two other men. One was a stranger he met in a ravine behind a poor farm, presumably the one where Robert had dwelt. The fellow had red hair, he mused. He had encountered the other victim on the road two miles from Muscoda and had struck him twice above the eyes with a four-pound weight. This murder had been in self-defense, Robert added primly. Then his confessional floodgates really burst open. After admitting the two hitherto-unknown murders, he said that over the years, he killed and buried around forty persons. Why had he massacred such a multitude? The best explanation he could give was that "there are too many people in the world," and he was determined to reduce their number as best he could, one at a time.

The inquest into Albert Turner Jr.'s murder was held in Milwaukee on January 16. Robert's reported motive: there were just too darn many people to feed at home, and there would be more vittles to go around if Albert were out of the picture. This was as dubious as his motive for killing teenage Olney Neely, which he explained earlier: the boy tried to kill him first with a club. Robert seemed normal when conversing on any topic, said a *New York Times* reporter, except murder, a subject that rendered him "possessed with a strong desire for blood."

A number of Badger Staters, particularly in Ellenboro, declared that if Robert escaped jail time for his deeds, they would carry him to the nearest tree and help him take a load off his feet.

After his prompt conviction, Robert did not have to worry about the death penalty. Since Wisconsin's founding in 1848, the state had executed only one murderer, Kenosha County farmer John McCaffary, on August 21, 1851. Life in prison was the expected verdict, and that was precisely what he got. He ended his days in Wisconsin State Prison at Waupun on May 28, 1902, a man brimful with many, many memories.

Was Robert B. Turner a genuine serial killer or just a lying blowhard, akin to H. H. Holmes in his time, or the Zodiac Killer and Henry Lee Lucas in ours—the sort of person who, once accused of murder, relishes in exaggerating his own reputation to seem the baddest of the bad? Robert certainly annihilated at least two of his fellow human beings, and he appears to have been amoral enough to do nearly anything. It seems that none of the skeletons of his alleged forty-odd victims has been found, so, if he were telling the truth, he hid them well. They may be out in the wilds of Grant County even now, just waiting.

Badly Misunderstood William

William John Mailahn (pronounced "Maylon") seemed troubled and was "acting strangely" to the townsfolk; but then, he was only twenty-one years old, so he was at the age when such behavior is to be expected, more or less. People thought he held a grudge against his father, Lewis, age sixty-six. Rumor held that he had grown to resent farm life. The large Mailahn family lived at Black Creek, two miles from Binghamton and fourteen miles from Appleton—the city where Harry Houdini grew up. Black Creek had its own claim to fame: it was the sauerkraut manufacturing capital of the world.

The notion that William was angry with his family seemed confirmed when he left home in autumn 1911, after an argument with his father, and didn't return until January 28, 1912. Some thought the problem was that William was his mother's favorite child, but after her death a few years before, he no longer got along with his father or siblings. A reporter later said that William was said to have "a fancied grievance over favors extended to other members of the family."

The problem, whatever it was, came to a crisis on February 2, less than a week after the prodigal's homecoming. While his younger brothers

George and Walter, ages thirteen and fourteen, respectively, were at school, William shot his father in the head, then cut the throat of his brother John, age eight, and left the body in a smokehouse, and then did the same to his sister Dorothea ("Dora"), age sixteen, as she lay on a couch. Afterward, William took a mirror to the woodshed and cut his own throat. With one sweep of the razor, he cut so deeply, he nearly decapitated himself. George found the bodies one at a time when he came home.

Just another youth turned mass killer after losing his temper over a fancied slight, right? So it seemed, but then a fuller, stranger picture emerged.

Five members of the Mailahn family died within the previous six years: sister Anna (March 1906, age twenty-five); sister Louise (March 1907, age fourteen); sister Alvina (June 1907, age thirteen); mother Augusta (January 1908, age forty-eight); and sister Carrie (June 1909, age twenty-seven).

That's a lot of fatalities in one family over the course of only a few years. Were they murdered? No—they all died of tuberculosis. William's father and siblings were also dying of the same disease, or at least William thought they were. The Mailahn survivors said that William often groused that they were all done for anyway, so they might as well just get it all over with. One night, he even spoiled everyone's meal by announcing at the dinner table, "We have been dying piecemeal for the last few years. I believe it would be a good thing if we could end this agony at once, all dying together. I believe I'll get some carbolic acid and kill the whole bunch."

So, it turned out, angst-ridden William really was anxious over the approaching deaths of himself and his family. His solution was to make their impending deaths even more so. To William's way of thinking, his mercy killings had saved his family from much trouble.

An uncle raised the three remaining Mailahn brothers. They went on to have productive lives—though, with one exception, not long ones. Edward was old enough to be living away from the homestead at the time of the massacre. He succumbed to the family scourge, tuberculosis, in the Riverview Sanitarium on October 1, 1914, at age twenty-nine.

Brother Walter, who was lucky enough to be in school on February 2, 1912, moved to Salem, Oregon. He died there of TB on November 29, 1932, at age thirty-four. His cremated remains are still at the Oregon State Hospital, waiting for a relative to claim them.

That left only George. He died in Chula Vista, California, in June 1970—probably *not* of tuberculosis, since he made it to age seventy-two.

Two Beheads Are Better than One

Twenty-seven-year-old Pasquale Marchesi lived at 681 Anton Street in Kenosha, Wisconsin, with his wife, Rosaria, and their two small children. Pasquale had lived there a decade and gained considerable wealth. In 1911, his nineteen-year-old cousin, also named Pasquale Marchesi, boarded with the family. After the incident that gave him coast-to-coast notoriety, the elder Pasquale claimed he had not suspected his wife of infidelity. However, on the night of November 25, 1911, he peeped through the bedroom window, which indicates otherwise. He saw his younger namesake in the bedchamber. In an instant fury, the man of the family committed what the *Wausau Pilot* termed "the most horrible [murder] in the criminal annals of this section of the state."

Before I tell what he did, note that the particulars vary greatly in several accounts.

According to his own version, Pasquale tiptoed to the woodpile and grabbed a tempting ax. Then this Italian merchant reentered the house through a window and did to his wife and formerly beloved cousin approximately what the New Orleans Axman had been doing to Italian grocers about a thousand miles away—only, according to the press, he surpassed the Axman's brutality by beheading both victims.

Pasquale took his unharmed, though blood-spattered, two-month-old infant, Michael, from the arms of his wife and cleaned him. He carried Michael to his brother's house on nearby South Oak Street and asked him to watch the baby as Rosaria was, uh, sick. Then Pasquale trudged home, dressed his four-year-old daughter, Josephine, and also took her to his brother for babysitting.

Well, what to do now? Pasquale returned to his cheerless home and hid the ax. Then he wandered the city, his conscience troubling him. Perhaps he had overreacted, after all? At daybreak, he hid in the basement of a Catholic church for solace. In these liturgical surroundings, his guilt bothered him even more. He later said that Rosaria's final screams kept replaying in his mind, and he had visions of headless persons approaching him.

Above him, the sounds of morning mass commenced. He thought he heard someone say, "Vengeance is mine, saith the Lord." At last, Pasquale could stand it no longer. He emerged from his hiding place, found a priest named Bandizonne, and confessed all.

The priest persuaded him to go the authorities and pay for his act. Marchesi melodramatically confessed to the police as he had to the priest, essentially saying that he was sorry now that he had axed his wife and cousin, but that it had seemed the thing to do at the time:

> I went home last night earlier than I had expected to return. I had no suspicion of my wife's unfaithfulness, but just for fun, I peeked in at her bedroom window. I was driven to senseless desperation by the sight that met my eyes. There, with all the confidence that I myself might rightfully exercise, was my favorite cousin, my namesake, wearing my night robe. My wife, with her two babies near her, was treating him with affection that was alone my due. I became as one insane. I ran to a woodshed in the rear and seized a lumberman's hand ax. I returned to the chamber window with only one thought—that of avenging myself. I carefully raised the window so as not to be heard. I crawled in unseen and crept to the bed. My arm strengthened by the sight, I chopped off my cousin's head at the first blow of the ax. He did not move, but the sound of the blow aroused my wife.

Unless the newspapers censored details, it seems that the younger Pasquale was doing nothing worse than wearing his cousin's bathrobe, and it strains credulity—though not necessarily to the breaking point—that Mrs. Marchesi would conduct a fling in the presence of her four-year-old daughter, who was old enough to tell on her. On the other hand, see the responding officer's version below.

To return to the thread of Pasquale's story, when his wife realized the trouble she was in, she dropped to her knees to beg forgiveness. Big mistake, said Pasquale later, because this defenseless position only made it so much easier to swing the blade at her neck. He had been very careful not to hit the baby she was holding. His anger still unspent, he chopped away at his cousin's body before finally coming to his senses and taking the children away from the scene.

On November 27, the coroner's jury charged him with first-degree murder. A partial transcript of the official court proceedings survived. Officer Fred Bradley, the first investigator to see the bodies at uncomfortably close quarters, provided details that differ in some respects from newspaper accounts. Bradley testified that the two corpses were in bed and covered with a blanket. Contradicting Marchesi's story about slaying his wife as she knelt in supplication, Bradley thought it looked as though both had been in bed when the ax fell. (If Pasquale's version of events were true, he must have lifted his wife from the floor and placed her in the bed before Bradley arrived.) In addition, there is some dispute as to exactly how Marchesi killed his victims. The press claimed that Pasquale decapitated both; Pasquale himself said that he beheaded his cousin, at least, with one swing. However, Officer Bradley swore under oath that neither was decapitated, although the cousin's head was cut in half, and the side of Mrs. Marchesi's head was missing.

The killer was arraigned for double murder the next day. "Marchesi himself seemed to be the least interested person at the inquest," wrote a reporter. "His attorneys would not permit him to go on the stand. He paid little attention to the evidence, and most of his time was spent watching the crowd."

Marchesi's lawyers said they would enter an insanity plea, while the killer said he would plead the unwritten law, which held that an adulterer or a seducer was open game for whomever he or she had wronged (see the chapter on Minnesota's Professor Darling). He denied that killing his wife and cousin was murder, strictly speaking: "We Italians are taught to believe that a man and his wife must be sacred to each other, and I believe that any jury will give me my freedom."

For whatever reason, the national press seemed to lose interest in the Marchesi story just as he went to trial. To discover his fate, we turn to the Wisconsin Senate's *Journal of Proceedings* entry for January 31, 1941, page 122, which informs us that Marchesi, who grotesquely slew two people with an ax in a fit of anger, was found guilty only of third-degree murder on May 23, 1912. The legal definition of third-degree murder varies from state to state, but it generally means that a murderer didn't *intentionally* kill his victim—he meant only to inflict bodily harm, a relatively less serious charge than deliberate homicide. The jurors evidently believed that when Marchesi sneaked through the window and belabored his wife and cousin with the blade end of that ax and perhaps sent their heads flying, he intended merely to rough them up somewhat. We might infer that the jury also felt he was justified. In other words, the unwritten law had won the day. Again.

Marchesi was sentenced to Wisconsin State Prison for merely two and a half years. The State Board of Control paroled him on March 26, 1914. The Wisconsin Senate restored his civil rights on July 26, 1939. A month later, he could have seen the Tin Woodsman swinging his ax when *The Wizard of Oz* debuted in theaters.

A final bonus—while there are notable differences between Marchesi's own account, the news stories, and the court report, for creative fiction nothing could surpass the version of events that appeared in a New Zealand newspaper in March 1912:

> Marchesi states that, coming home suddenly after announcing that he was going on a journey, he found his wife and cousin making love, and the spectacle so enraged him that he immediately took his revenge. He rushed forward and struck his cousin, felling him to the floor. He then bound him with rope before the eyes of his wife, who was too frightened to render her lover any assistance. He next bound his wife with rope, and going into the woodshed procured a log of wood and an ax. He then deliberately placed his cousin and his wife, one after the other, on the log and beheaded them with the ax. He buried the bodies in the cellar, and tried to burn the two heads. Marchesi declares that he has lived in the house since the murder, but the agonized death cries of the couple have sounded in his ears ever since, and he could neither eat nor sleep. The police immediately made search, and found the remains buried in the cellar. Since his arrest, Marchesi has gone raving mad and declares that he is haunted by the ghosts of his victims.

The story was wrong in nearly every detail, but Poe would have been proud!

Mayberry Meets a Mob

Back in the days when a *rapper* was a ghost communicating at a séance, a *deadhead* was someone who got permission to ride a train for free, *getting high* meant getting drunk, and a *reefer* was a Navy peacoat, two men in Wisconsin each made a deadly mistake. Andrew Alger's error was trusting stranger David Mayberry; Mayberry's blunder lay in killing Alger.

In 1854, horse thief Mayberry befriended a fellow convict named John Macomb (or McComb) in prison at Alton, Illinois. Macomb said that when they got out, Mayberry should travel to his father's farm in Rockford, where he would be certain to find work. When Mayberry was released in autumn, he worked on Macomb's family farm during winter 1854–1855. He might have taken the opportunity to rehabilitate himself, but, on June 15, he was tempted when, in Beloit, Wisconsin, he saw Farmington merchant Alger receiving $600 cash for a raft of lumber he sailed down the river. Mayberry jumped into his buggy and hurried down the road he knew Alger would have to travel on foot to get home. Then he slowed down and waited for the lumber salesman to catch up.

Feigning all the friendliness in the world, Mayberry asked, "Hey, would you like a ride?" Alger was not averse to the offer.

Near Janesville, Mayberry asked Alger if he would care for a pull on a bottle of whiskey. The raftsman had no objection to this either. As he drank, Mayberry took a second bottle from his coat pocket and shattered it over his guest's head. (Some sources say the weapon was a hatchet, newly purchased for this reason.) He dragged the unconscious Alger into the underbrush, cut his throat, and took his money. Mayberry stripped the corpse—except the underwear, which he didn't deem quite up to standard—and dressed himself in the stolen clothes, a detail that seemed to bother people as much as the murder itself. He made his way to the Macomb farm thirty-odd miles away, drunk as a boiled bandicoot by the time he got there.

Yet he kept on drinking and let down his guard. Sometime that night, he told his old pal, who probably wondered why he had come home in a different outfit, what he had done; "gloried in it," according to one report. Macomb sneaked away and brought back the sheriff. Mayberry was arrested with no difficulty. When he sobered up, he admitted the crime and said only that he wished he had not been arrested before he had killed two or three other unnamed people "upon whom he had his eye." Macomb the stoolie might well have been one of them.

Citizens of Rockford were so agitated that they almost lynched Mayberry. Officers extradited him across the state line from Rockford to Janesville for trial. No doubt he felt relieved to get away from that Illinois lynch mob!

Proceedings began on July 10. Mayberry's defense offered no exculpatory evidence because there was none. The jury found him guilty on July 11, after twenty minutes' deliberation. The next day, Judge Doolittle sentenced him to life in prison.

The lumbermen of Janesville had no patience with this sentence, however, and thought frontier justice was as good as the stuff you find in law books. In the morning, just after Doolittle delivered an oration to the notably stone-faced prisoner in hopes of rehabilitating his character, a threatening crowd surrounded the courthouse. After the judge spoke with them, they calmed down and dispersed, but they regrouped after lunchtime. The mob saw policemen leading Mayberry back to his cell. A crowd estimated at four thousand pushed the officers aside and carried Mayberry away like a very surprised and frightened sack of potatoes. They dragged him down dusty Court Street with a rope and then hanged him in the public square, using a tree in front of the courthouse. Said the editor of the *Janesville Standard*, using the third-person "editorial we," "For the first time in our life, the horrible spectacle of a human being hanging by the neck until he was dead met our view." One of the jury cut down the hanging tree on the day of the lynching, perhaps to prevent it from ever again being used for such a purpose.

Hangings were not supposed to happen in Wisconsin at all. The state abolished the death penalty in 1853, which, for all we know, was one reason for Mayberry's boldness. A contemporary newspaper noted, "As the death penalty by hanging has been abolished in that state, the people determined that the culprit should no longer live, and accordingly saved the Commonwealth the necessity of keeping him a prisoner for life."

Less than a month after Mayberry's hanging, on August 1, 1855, someone killed a farming couple named Meyer (or Muehr) and their teenage hired boy "under circumstances of revolting cruelty" in West Bend, Washington County. George DeBar was suspected and barely escaped a lynching. He was mobbed for real on August 7. A Chippewa Indian was hanged by a mob in Buffalo County on March 18, 1857. He had shot two white men in a fight, though not fatally. If pioneer folks wanted a hanging, then, by Jove, they had one, whether capital punishment was legal or not.

BIBLIOGRAPHY

Murderous Missouri

The Maxwell Trunk Murder

Louisville Courier-Journal. "Afraid That Maxwell Will Commit Suicide." January 28, 1888, 4.
———. "Application for a Respite." August 4, 1888, 6.
———. "Clearing Away." April 16, 1885, 1+.
———. "A Dark Crime." April 15, 1885, 5.
———. "A Deep-Dyed Villain." May 25, 1886, 1.
———. "Down They Go." August 11, 1888, 1+.
———. "For His Boy's Life." April 8, 1888, 4.
———. "The Ghost Room." January 25, 1889, 2.
———. "Guarded by a Beauty." September 8, 1888, 5.
———. "History of a Crime." April 19, 1885, 4.
———. "Identified at Last." October 25, 1885, 12.
———. "Improved by Burial." August 16, 1885, 5.
———. "Law-Breakers' Deeds." January 24, 1888, 2.
———. "The Law's Clutches." May 7, 1885, 1.
———. "Living a Lie." May 28, 1886, 4.
———. "Longer Life for the Trunk Murderer." July 8, 1887, 5.
———. "Maxwell Again Convicted." June 21, 1887, 2.
———. "Maxwell Breaking Down." May 31, 1886, 1.
———. "The Maxwell Murder Case." July 13, 1885, 5.
———. "Maxwell Pleads Not Guilty." November 15, 1885, 2.
———. "Maxwell-Preller Mystery." April 24, 1885, 6.
———. "Maxwell Sentenced." July 15, 1886, 4.
———. "Maxwell, the Alleged . . ." August 14, 1885, 1.
———. "Maxwell, the Trunk Murderer." July 5, 1885, 12.
———. "Maxwell's Arrest." June 16, 1885, 4.
———. "Maxwell's Executioner Goes Insane." June 8, 1897, 2.
———. "'Maxwell's Father Goes." March 26, 1888, 4.

———. "Maxwell's Hopeless Case." July 9, 1887, 3.

———. "Maxwell's Last Chance." June 29, 1888, 1.

———. "Maxwell's Last Hope." July 3, 1888, 4.

———. "More Light on the St. Louis Trunk Murder." June 11, 1885, 4.

———. "Murderer Maxwell Becomes a Catholic." December 28, 1887, 4.

———. "Murder or Manslaughter?" June 2, 1886, 1.

———. "A Mystery No More." May 19, 1886, 1.

———. "A New Hope for Maxwell." July 4, 1888, 5.

———. "The News." June 6, 1886, 2.

———. "News and Comment." September 24, 1886, 1.

———. "News and Comment." January 10, 1888, 1.

———. "The Penalty Is Death." June 6, 1886, 4.

———. "Ready for the Jury." June 1, 1886, 4.

———. "The St. Louis Sensation." April 17, 1885, 2.

———. "The St. Louis Sensation." May 22, 1886, 1.

———. "The St. Louis Trunk Murder." August 19, 1885, 2.

———. "The St. Louis Trunk Murderer." October 13, 1887, 2.

———. "The St. Louis Trunk Murderer Gets a Stay." February 1, 1887, 4.

———. "To-Day They Must Die." August 10, 1888, 2.

———. "To Save His Neck." May 27, 1886, 1.

———. "The Trunk Murderer." August 17, 1885, 1.

———. "The Trunk Murderer." August 23, 1885, 10.

———. "The Trunk Murderer." February 10, 1888, 1.

———. "The Trunk Murderer Arrived." August 11, 1885, 2.

New York Times. "Preller's Uneasy Ghost." January 22, 1889, 5.

Two Frenchmen Walk into a Hotel . . .

Louisville Courier. "A Magnificent Present . . ." November 10, 1851, 2.

———. "Young Montesquion [*sic*], the Insane Frenchman . . ." May 19, 1852, 3.

Louisville Journal. "Barnum Died this Morning." November 8, 1849, 3.

———. "The Brothers de Montesquious [*sic*]." October 15, 1850, 3.

———. "The Brothers Montesquieu [*sic*] Have Been Removed . . ." November 2, 1849, 3.

———. "Commitment of Gonsalve and Raymond Montesquiou [*sic*]." November 14, 1849, 3.

———. "Criminal Court." April 13, 1850, 3.

———. "Criminal Court." May 2, 1850, 2.

———. "Criminal Court." May 6, 1850, 2.

———. "Criminal Court." June 10, 1850, 3.

———. "The Defense in the Case . . ." April 1, 1850, 3.

———. "The Elder of the Montesquious [*sic*] . . ." January 28, 1850, 3.

———. "A Few Days Since . . ." October 31, 1849, 3.

———. "Gonsalve Montesque [*sic*] Has Been Indicted . . ." February 2, 1850, 3.

———. "Gonsalve Montesquiou [*sic*], Recently Pardoned . . ." October 25, 1850, 3.

———. "The Governor of Missouri Has Discharged Raymond . . ." October 31, 1850, 3.

———. "The Jury in the Montesquious [*sic*] Case . . ." April 22, 1850, 3.

———. "A Jury Was Empaneled . . ." March 27, 1850, 3.

———. "A Large Crowd of Persons . . ." November 1, 1849, 3.
———. "The Montesquiou [*sic*] Trial." April 25, 1850, 3.
———. "The Montesquious [*sic*]." May 16, 1850, 3.
———. "The Montesquious [*sic*]." July 19, 1850, 3.
———. "The Montesquious [*sic*]." August 30, 1850, 3.
———. "The Montesquious [*sic*]: Attempted Suicide of Gonsalve." June 24, 1850, 3.
———. "A New Trial Was Granted . . ." May 4, 1850, 3.
———. "No Verdict Has Yet Been Rendered . . ." April 20, 1850, 3.
———. "A Second Trial . . ." July 3, 1850, 3.
———. "The Trial of the Brothers . . ." April 8, 1850, 3.
———. "The Trial of the Brothers . . . Closed Today." April 19, 1850, 3.
———. "Trial of the Montesquious [*sic*]." June 8, 1850, 2.
———. "Trial of the Montesquious [*sic*]." June 25, 1850, 3.
———. "Trial of the Montesquious [*sic*] ." July 2, 1850, 3.
———. "The Trial of the Montesquioes [*sic*] Commenced . . ." March 26, 1850, 3.
———. "The Trial of the Montesquious [*sic*] Is Drawing to a Close . . ." April 16, 1850, 3.
———. "The Trial of the Montesquioes [*sic*] Is Slowly Progressing . . ." March 29, 1850, 3.
———. "We Think from the Statements . . ." November 5, 1849, 3.
———. "We Understand that the Count Arthur . . ." December 22, 1849, 3.
———. "The Younger Brother of the Montesquies . . ." February 4, 1850, 3.

The Murdered Parsons Family

Burns, Stanley B. *Sleeping Beauty: Memorial Photography in America*. Altadena, CA: Twelvetrees Press, 1990.
Hearn, Daniel Allen. *Legal Executions in Illinois, Indiana, Iowa, Kentucky and Missouri: A Comprehensive Registry, 1866–1965*. Jefferson, NC: McFarland, 2016.
Louisville Courier-Journal. "Bungling Execution." December 22, 1906, 1.
———. "Family of Five Killed by Fiend." October 15, 1906.
———. "Fiendish Murderer Said to Be Maniac." October 16, 1906, 1.

Michigan Mayhem

Too Clever for His Own Good

Wakefield, Lawrence. *Butcher's Dozen: 13 Famous Michigan Murders*. West Bloomfield, MI: Altwerger and Mandel, 1991.
Wells, Anna Mary. "The Trick Alibi of Irving Latimer." In *The Quality of Murder: 300 Years of True Crime*, edited by Anthony Boucher, 29–38. New York: Dutton, 1962.

The Right to a Speedy Trial

Louisville Courier-Journal. "Chloroform Killed Woman, Experts Say." February 27, 1936, 15.
———. "Estranged Wife, Tots Die, Boarder Blamed." April 7, 1933, 15.
———. "Girl's Slayer on Way to Serve Life Term." August 5, 1932, 1.

———. "Guilty Plea Planned by Girl's Slayer." January 18, 1928, 1.
———. "Hotelling in Prison Week after Murder." January 20, 1928, 1.
———. "Kidnapped Girl Found Dissected." January 13, 1928, 1+.
———. "Kidnapper Gets Life at Hard Labor." January 19, 1928, 1+.
———. "Kidnapper Search Fails." January 14, 1928, 1.
———. "Man Admits Killing Wife, Gets Life Term." February 28, 1936, I, 1.
———. "Man Gets Life Term in Slaying of Sweetheart." November 15, 1935, III, 6.
———. "Man Given Life Day after He Kills Three." April 8, 1933, 12.
———. "Mob of 10,000 Storms Jail . . ." January 17, 1928, 1+.
———. "Murderer Gets Life 8 Hours after Crime." January 11, 1935, 15.
———. "Police to Guard Search Clues." January 15, 1928, I, 1+.
———. "Recluse Confesses Killing Girl, 17." August 4, 1932, 1.
———. "Signs of Struggle Clue to Lost Girl." August 2, 1932, 2.
———. "Swamp Hunted for Girl Feared Kidnapped." August 1, 1932, 1.
———. "3 Airplanes Seek Car of Girl's Killer." January 16, 1928, 1.

Crazy Jealous

Louisville Courier-Journal. "Girl Slayer of Dean's Daughter . . ." December 16, 1936, I, 9.
———. "Girl Slayer of Friend Puzzles Psychiatrists." December 11, 1936, IV, 12.
———. "Shoots Her Dead on Impulse." December 9, 1936, I, 1.

Blood Bank, or: The Seldom-Used "I Soiled My Trousers" Defense

History of the Trial of George Vanderpool for the Murder of Herbert Field. Detroit, MI: Tunis Steam Printing Company, 1870.
Louisville Courier. "Summer Complaint." August 14, 1848, 3.
New York Times. "The Case of George Vanderpool." March 6, 1870, 1.
———. "The Testimony of Blood." Editorial. November 20, 1870, 4.
———. "The Vanderpool Murder Case." Editorial. November 23, 1870, 4.
———. "The Vanderpool Murder Trial." November 24, 1870, 6.
Wakefield, Lawrence. Butcher's Dozen: 13 Famous Michigan Murders. West Bloomfield, MI.: Altwerger and Mandel, 1991.

Mrs. Tabor's Many Contradictions

Ambs. "Maud Emma 'Maud' Tabor Virgo." Find a Grave: Memorial 107680183. April 2, 2013. https://www.findagrave.com/memorial/107680183/maud-emma-virgo.
Genealogy Trails. "Buried in a Trunk in Her Bridal Gown." Genealogy Trails: Welcome to Van Buren Co., MI., News Articles. Accessed March 4, 2020. http://genealogytrails.com/mich/vanburen/newstabor2.html.
Louisville Courier-Journal. "80-Year-Old Mother Is Quizzed . . ." April 4, 1920, I, 1.
———. "Charge of Manslaughter in Tabor Case Dismissed." May 24, 1921, 5.
———. "Left Daughter's Body Unburied . . ." December 9, 1919, 4.
———. "Mother and Son to Be Extradited as Slayers." December 12, 1919, 4.
———. "Mother, 82, Faces New Trial in Girl's Murder." November 20, 1920, 7.
———. "Mother, Held in Girl's Death, on Trial Today." December 23, 1919, 3.
———. "Mrs. Tabor, Once Rich, Penniless." March 19, 1922, I, 10.

———. "Repudiates Story that Mother Killed Sister." January 17, 1920, 2.
———. "Tabor Girl's Husband Faces Murder Charge." December 24, 1919, 10.
———. "Tabor Murder Trial Held Up." December 21, 1919, IV, 8.
———. "Telegraphic Flashes." June 22, 1920, 4.
———. "Trunk Murder Near Solution." December 3, 1919, 4.
———. "Woman, 60 [sic], Bound Over for Daughter's Death." February 1, 1920, IV, 7.
New York Times. "Mrs. Tabor Accuses Virgo." December 24, 1919, 8.
———. "Woman in 1919 Trial Ends Life in Michigan." March 8, 1931, 18.

Ill-Tempered Illinois

Brockelhurst, the Proto-Starkweather

Louisville Courier-Journal. "Arkansas Youth Gets Last-Minute Reprieve." March 4, 1938, III, 9.
———. "Brockelhurst Dies Blaming Girlfriend." March 19, 1938, I, 3.
———. "Brockelhurst Faints." August 13, 1937, II, 8.
———. "Brockelhurst Is Sent to Mental Hospital." June 11, 1937, IV, 16.
———. "Condemned Killer Chained to Floor." February 10, 1938, I, 3.
———. "'Crime Tourist' Fails at Suicide." June 22, 1937, I, 8.
———. "'Crime Tourist' to Face Trial in Arkansas." May 18, 1937, I, 9.
———. "Girl Acquitted in Murder Held for Car Theft." June 27, 1937, I, 13.
———. "Girl Gloats Over Acquittal, Is Told to Leave Town." June 26, 1937, I, 1.
———. "Hitch-Hiking Slayer Faints When Doomed." June 25, 1937, I, 1.
———. "Romance Over, Girl to Aid State . . ." June 23, 1937, I, 8.
———. "Scene of Murder Showed to Officers . . ." May 20, 1937, II, 8.
———. "Sweetheart of Killer Is Given 5-Year Term." May 20, 1939, I, 3.
———. "Write Is Denied Slayer Condemned to Chair." March 18, 1938, I, 10.
———. "Youth Wants to Know When He'll Get Chair." May 19, 1937, I, 12.

Soft-Hearted Chicago

Adler, Jeffrey S. "I Loved Joe, but I Had to Shoot Him." Journal of Criminal Law and Criminology 92, nos. 3–4 (2003): 867–97.
James, Laura. The Beauty Defense: Femmes Fatales on Trial. Kent, OH: Kent State University Press, 2020.
Lesy, Michael. Murder City: The Bloody History of Chicago in the Twenties. New York: W. W. Norton, 2007.
Louisville Courier-Journal. "Again Chivalrous Chicago Frees a Beautiful Killer." May 19, 1935, Magazine, 3.
———. "Annan Jury Is Beauty Proof." May 24, 1924, 2.
———. "Can Beauty Be Sent to Electric Chair?" August 19, 1923, Magazine, 3.
———. "Chicago Goes a Month Without Gang Murder . . ." December 4, 1933, 10.
———. "Chicago Jury Votes Death for Woman." July 17, 1936, 1+.
———. "Chicago Murders Show Average of One Daily." December 28, 1921, 1.
———. "Chicago Woman Freed of Slaying Husband." May 13, 1937, I, 5.
———. "Double Standard in Murder." April 8, 1914, 6.
———. "First Woman Sentenced to Chair in Illinois Given Commutation." February 26, 1937, I, 1+.

———. "Girl, 15, Freed Under Unwritten Law Plea." June 23, 1921, 1.
———. "Girl Found Not Guilty in Chicago Burr Case." October 14, 1919, 2.
———. "Girl Giggles as She Tells How She Killed Man." July 9, 1919, 1.
———. "Hold Chicago Woman." June 3, 1929, 1+.
———. "Inasmuch as Murder Isn't Risky." June 8, 1918, 4.
———. "Judge Tries Case of Pretty Slayer." August 31, 1932, 4.
———. "Jury of Chicago Men Astonishes the Country . . ." July 15, 1923, I, 8.
———. "Miss Plotka Acquitted in Chicago Murder Trial." June 28, 1918, 4.
———. "Mrs. Annan Is Freed by Beauty-Proof Jury." May 25, 1924, I, 1+.
———. "Mrs. Nusbaum Gets Life, Winn Death." March 7, 1926, I, 1+.
———. "Pretty Killer Is Acquitted." September 2, 1932, 20.
———. "Retrial Refused for Mrs. Nitti." July 15, 1923, IV, 1.
———. "Safer for Woman to Kill than Steal in Chicago . . ." May 5, 1918, III, 2.
———. "60-Day Stay Given to Mrs. Cassler." October 26, 1927, 1.
———. "10,000 Fight to See Beautiful Slayer." August 2, 1932, 1.
———. "Thug Dies Natural Death; Record Set." March 11, 1930, 22.
———. "20th Gangster Slain in Chicago." April 2, 1930, 1.
———. "Twenty-Seventh Woman Acquitted of Murder." May 4, 1918, 10.
———. "Twenty-Eighth Woman of 31, in Chicago, Freed of Killing." June 25, 1921, 6.
———. "Widows Killing Husbands Lose Risk Claims." November 3, 1937, I, 13.
———. "Woman Foils Hangman as Noose Yawns." October 21, 1927, 14.
———. "Woman Tells Jurors She Shot Husband." July 16, 1936, 15.
———. "Woman to Be Held on Murder Charge." April 5, 1924, 8.
———. "Woman to Die Feb. 26." December 11, 1936, IV, 11.
———. "Woman to Die on Gallows, Jury Decrees." May 20, 1927, 1+.
———. "Woman's Unwritten Law Plea Frees Her." July 28, 1921, 1.
———. "Woman's Weapons." September 19, 1900, 4.
McQueen, Keven. *Horror in the Heartland: Strange and Gothic Tales from the Midwest.* Bloomington: Indiana University Press, 2017.

Mr. Merry Finds an Unorthodox Use for Potatoes

Louisville Courier-Journal. "Another Pair Arrested." December 16, 1897, 5.
———. "Death Penalty Promised . . ." December 20, 1897, 2.
———. "Merry's Brutal Crime." December 16, 1897, 5.
———. "Murder Mystery Solved." November 29, 1897, 1.
———. "Taken Back to Illinois." December 17, 1897, 5.
———. "Thought to be Chicago Murderers." December 1, 1897, 3.
New York Times. "Mrs. Merry's Body in a Ditch." November 29, 1897, 1.
———. "X Rays for a Murderer." February 10, 1898, 3.

Chicago's Other Homicidal Sausage Baron

Louisville Courier-Journal. "Another Luetgert Case." February 26, 1899, I, 7.
———. "Becker as a Witness." July 6, 1899, 1.
———. "The Becker Case." March 3, 1899, 4.
———. "Becker Hanged." November 11, 1899, 2.
———. "Becker Must Hang." July 7, 1899, 2.

———. "Blood Stains Found." February 27, 1899, 1.

———. "Confesses Again." March 15, 1899, 1.

———. "Error in Indictment." June 30, 1899, 3.

———. "Evidence against Becker." March 1, 1899, 5.

———. "Key to the Murder." March 12, 1899, I, 2.

New York Times. "Chicago Murderer Confesses." March 2, 1899, 3.

———. "Chicago's New Luetgert." February 27, 1899, 2.

———. "Chicago's Second Luetgert." February 26, 1899, 11.

Going Clubbing

Louisville Courier-Journal. "Confessed Killer Is Linked to Three Deaths." February 3, 1932, 17.

———. "Fourth Man Is Found Victim of Club Killer." February 1, 1932, 3.

———. "Police Guards Two from Ire of Madman." February 14, 1938, I, 5.

———. "Two Insane Criminals Escape Hospital." February 13, 1938, I, 11.

Nash, Jay Robert. *World Encyclopedia of 20th Century Murder.* Lanham, MD: Rowman & Littlefield, 1992.

Try Harder, Hubert

Daily Banner [Greencastle, IN]. "Hubert Moor Found Guilty." June 4, 1934, 1.

Louisville Courier-Journal. "Defense Rests in Slaying Case Trial." June 2, 1934, 8.

———. "Dirty Dishes Led to Slaying, Claim." January 13, 1933, 1.

———. "Illinois Teacher Held for Murder of Wife." August 17, 1932, 1.

———. "Pastor, Father of Slain Teacher Wants Chair . . ." August 30, 1932, 1.

———. "Sinkful of Dishes, Messy House . . ." August 29, 1932, 1+.

A Rash Act and a Rash

Hearn, Daniel Allen. *Legal Executions in Illinois, Indiana, Iowa, Kentucky and Missouri: A Comprehensive Registry, 1866–1965.* Jefferson, NC: 2016.

Louisville Courier-Journal. "Bridegroom Slain Mysteriously . . ." July 5, 1937, I, 1.

———. "Clemency Refused to Doomed Mother." January 20, 1938, II, 8.

———. "Doomed Woman Gets Week Stay from Chair." January 21, 1938, I, 5.

———. "Pair Sentenced to Chair." November 27, 1937, I, 8.

———. "'Poison Ivy Clew' Brings Arrest . . ." July 10, 1937, I, 1+.

———. "Sister Admits Part in Man's Killing . . ." July 13, 1937, I, 1.

———. "Two Condemned to Chair in Insurance Slaying." November 6, 1937, I, 11.

———. "'Wedding Day' Slaying Solved, Police Report." July 12, 1937, I, 5.

———. "Woman, Youth Die in Chair for Killing of Her Brother." January 28, 1938, I, 1.

Naughty Nebraska

Mutual Terror of Omaha

FRANK CARTER

Louisville Courier-Journal. "Mad Rifleman Kills 2 . . ." February 19, 1926, I, 1+.

———. "Maniac Shot to Prevent His Capture." February 23, 1926, 1+.

———. "Mad Slayer Shoots Cop 4 Times." February 20, 1926, 1.

———. "Maniac Sniper Plans Break for Freedom." February 24, 1926, 1.
———. "Sniper Bandit Is Given Death." March 21, 1926, I, 9.
———. "Sniper Bandit to Die July 9." March 25, 1926, 14.
———. "'Sniper' Carter, the Omaha Assassin . . ." June 25, 1927, 6.
———. "Sniper Declares Himself Failure." March 19, 1926, 11.

JAKE BIRD
Louisville Courier-Journal. "400 Omaha Cops and Citizens on Watch . . ." November 21, 1928, 1+.
———. "Hundreds Seek Mad Axe Killer." November 22, 1928, 1.
———. "Negro Named as Axe Killer Safe from Mob." November 24, 1928, 1.
———. "Omaha Axe Man Is Found Guilty." February 3, 1929, I, 6.
———. "Omaha Cops Baffled in Hatchet Killer Hunt." November 23, 1928, 1.
———. "Victim Identifies Bird." November 28, 1928, 1.
McQueen, Keven. The Axman Came from Hell and Other Southern True Crime Stories. Gretna, LA: Pelican, 2012.
———. Forgotten Tales of Indiana. Charleston, SC: Arcadia/History Press, 2009.
———. Weird Wild West: True Tales of the Strange and Gothic. Bloomington: Indiana University Press, 2019.
New York Times. "Hatchet Slayer Terrorizes Omaha." November 20, 1928, 12.
———. "Omaha Seizes Man as the Axe Slayer." November 24, 1928, 3.
———. "Sticks to Murder Denial." November 25, 1928, 19.

With a Little Help from His Friends?

Louisville Courier-Journal. "Another Move in Rustin Case." September 13, 1908, IV, 1.
———. "Arguments Begin Tomorrow." November 13, 1910, II, 1.
———. "As Suspect, Young Woman Arrested . . ." September 5, 1908, 2.
———. "By Person Unknown . . ." September 10, 1908, 1.
———. "C.E. Davis Charged with Rustin Murder." September 11, 1908, 1.
———. "Davis Acquitted of Murdering Dr. Rustin." December 11, 1908, 3.
———. "Davis Held to Answer." September 30, 1908, 8.
———. "Depositions in Rustin Trial." November 10, 1910, 5.
———. "Depositions Taken in Rustin Case . . ." September 18, 1910, I, 11.
———. "Dramatic Story Told by Mrs. Abbie Rice . . ." December 4, 1908, 8.
———. "$40,000 Insurance." November 8, 1910, 7.
———. "Jury Wrestling with Davis Murder Case." December 10, 1908, 2.
———. "Life Insurance Sought in Four Suits Filed . . ." February 12, 1909, 7.
———. "Mrs. Grace Rustin Wins in Court of Appeals." December 11, 1912, 3.
———. "Mrs. Rice Finishes Her Story and State Rests." December 5, 1908, 1.
———. "Mrs. Rustin on Stand." December 3, 1908, 1.
———. "Mrs. Rustin Wins." November 16, 1910, 5.
———. "Rustin Insurance Case with Jury." November 15, 1910, 8.
———. "Rustin Made Suicide Pact." September 9, 1908, 1.
———. "Rustin Verdict Stands." February 26, 1911, II, 3.
———. "Saw Abbie Rice Buy a Paper . . ." December 8, 1908, 2.
———. "Two Witnesses Give Important Testimony." September 25, 1908, 2.
———. "Weird Story of Suicidal Mania." September 8, 1908, 1.

Criminal Kansas

Little Slaughterhouse on the Prairie: The Benders and the Stafflebacks

Louisville Courier-Journal. "Cells for the Stafflebacks." October 3, 1897, I, 5.
——. "The Crimes of the Stafflebacks." September 21, 1897, 5.
——. "Has Become a Maniac." September 25, 1897, 2.
——. "In Prison Cell." March 10, 1909, 1.
New York Times. "The Galena Murder Mystery." September 17, 1897, 12.

Willie's Poor Conduct

Louisville Courier-Journal. "Monstrous Crime." March 9, 1886, 5.
——. "Pardon for Willie Sells." April 10, 1907, 1.
New York Times. "A Boy Murderer Sentenced." August 27, 1886, 8.
——. "The Kansas Boy Murderer." July 31, 1886, 2.
——. "Willie Sells's Crime." July 18, 1886, 3.

Sometimes Everyone Else Is Right

Kasper, Russell. "Samuel Purple." Find a Grave. June 15, 2013. https://www
.findagrave.com/memorial/112378199/samuel-purple.
New York Times. "A Series of Tragedies." November 11, 1886, 2.
Weide, Richard. "Johannah Lauber." Find a Grave. January 10, 2016. https://
www.findagrave.com/memorial/156953322/johannah-lauber.

Minnesota Massacres

Wayward Hayward

Louisville Courier-Journal. "A Fear of Body Snatchers." December 27, 1895, 3.
——. "Given a Simple Burial." December 12, 1895, 3.
——. "Hayward Hanged." December 11, 1895, 7.
——. "Hayward's Body Cremated." December 28, 1895, 6.
——. "Hayward's Confession." December 20, 1895, 5.
——. "Miss Ging's Avenger." Advertisement. April 30, 1896, 5.
——. "Murder of Catherine Ging." December 9, 1894, 3.
——. "Will Declare Him Crazy." January 22, 1895, 5.
New York Times. "Catherine Ging's Insurance Money." December 15, 1895, 7.
——. "Harry Hayward Enraged." March 3, 1895, 1.
——. "Harry Hayward Hung at Night." December 12, 1895, 15.
——. "Harry Hayward Must Die." December 8, 1895, 1.
——. "Hayward Has Confessed." December 11, 1895, 9.
——. "Harry T. Hayward a Murderer." March 9, 1895, 1.
——. "Hayward Wants Blixt Dead." December 26, 1894, 1.
——. "Her Life Lost by Doubt." December 9, 1894, 2.
——. "Murder for Insurance Suspected." December 6, 1894, 1.
——. "Murder of Catherine Ging." December 18, 1894, 13.
——. "No Insurance in a Murder Case." January 9, 1898, 4.
——. "Part of a Great Conspiracy." December 13, 1894, 6.
Schechter, Harold. *Psycho USA: Famous American Killers You Never Heard Of.*
New York: Ballantine, 2012.

Barrel of Fun, or: The Scenter of Attention

Louisville Courier-Journal. "A Traitor." November 9, 1889, 2.
St. Paul Daily Globe. "Body in a Barrel." November 9, 1889, 1+.
———. "A Crime, in Any Case." November 10, 1889, 1.
———. "The Secret Is Out." November 12, 1889, 2.

Irresistible

Louisville Courier-Journal. "Laundryman Wrecked Home, Educator Says." April 4, 1913, 6.
———. "Prof. Olson Found Not Guilty . . ." April 9, 1913, 6.
———. "Wife Swoons on Stand . . ." April 8, 1913, 10.
New York Times. "Many Weep at Olson Trial." April 4, 1913, 10.
———. "Mrs. Olson Tells All." April 5, 1913, 1.
———. "Says Darling Threatened." April 8, 1913, 22.
St. Paul Pioneer Press. "Clue in Notation to Olson Enigma." March 10, 1913, 1.
———. "Darling Worried Over a Bad Coin." March 9, 1913, II, 18.
———. "Indict Professor in First Degree." March 11, 1913, 3.
———. "Olson Tranquilly Pleads Not Guilty." March 12, 1913, 1.
———. "Took Wife Along on Laundry Route." March 8, 1913, 12.
———. "University Man Kills and Pleads Unwritten Law." March 6, 1913, 1+.
———. "Was Clyde Darling Lured to His End?" March 7, 1913, 1+.

Iowa Exterminations

A Dying Man's Love Letter

Louisville Courier-Journal. "Elrod's Body Is Exhumed for Probe." January 26, 1927, 22.
———. "Man's Death in Hotel Unsolved." February 6, 1927, I, 7.
———. "Poison Killed Suitor, Note Shows." January 20, 1927, 1+.
———. "Probe Renewed in Poison Death." January 24, 1927, 2.

By a Dirty Coward

Tama [IA] *Herald.* "George Taylor Murdered." July 24, 1913, 1.

Bones in the Basement, or: Razing the Dead

Fremont [NB] *Tribune.* "Dead Men's Bones." August 1, 1888, 1.
Louisville Courier-Journal. "Dead Men Tell No Tales." August 1, 1888, 5.
New York Times. "Clues to Early Murders." August 3, 1888, 6.
———. "Finding Five Skeletons." July 31, 1888, 2.
St. Louis Globe-Democrat. "More Skeletons Unearthed." August 2, 1888, 6.

Indiana Imbroglios

Charles McGalliard Gets a Twofer

Muncie Evening Press. "The Dana [sic] of Death." November 1, 1911, 4.
———. "Defense Planned for Youthful Murderer." November 1, 1911, 1+.
———. "Excitement of Dance and Murder Kill." November 1, 1911, 1.

———. "Father Greets Girl Slayer . . ." November 2, 1911, 1+.

———. "McGalliard Is Guilty . . ." January 21, 1912, 1+.

———. "Mental Epilepsy Is Blamed for Tragedy." January 20, 1912, 1+.

———. "Slain Girl Is Buried . . ." November 3, 1911, 1+.

"Kill Da Umpire!"

Louisville Courier-Journal. "Alleged Slayer of Umpire Is Pardoned." June 20, 1916, 3.

———. "Baseball Umpire Shoots the Pitcher." July 16, 1902, 2.

———. "Don't Kill Umpires." August 11, 1922, 6.

———. "Double Murder at a Ball Game." June 29, 1903, 7.

———. "Heckling of Umpire Costs Youth His Life." October 15, 1929, 20.

———. "Killed the Umpire." September 5, 1889, 2.

———. "Killed Umpire." January 16, 1915, 4.

———. "Let the Umpire Live." June 24, 1907, 4.

———. "The Umpire." June 21, 1916, 6.

Dias Gets the Hang of It

Louisville Journal. "Awful Murder." October 23, 1843, 2.

———. "Execution." July 7, 1844, 2.

———. "Samuel Dias Has Been Tried . . ." November 28, 1843, 3.

———. "Samuel Dias, the Murderer . . ." December 4, 1843, 2.

———. "Samuel Dias, Who Has Veen . . ." May 20, 1844, 2.

Terre Haute Daily Tribune. "Vigo's First Hanging." December 21, 1902, 2.

Wabash [IN] Courier. "Court." November 25, 1843, 3.

———. "State vs. Samuel Dias." November 18, 1843, 3.

Homicidal Honeymoon, or: Cupid's Arrow, Jane's Ax

Louisville Journal. "Extraordinary Homicide." July 13, 1839, 2.

Sharpe, Virginia Banta. A History of Waveland, Indiana. Wabash Valley Printing Co.: Montezuma, IN, 1958.

Taylor, Stephen J. "Shades State Park: What's in a Name?" Hoosier State Chronicles: Indiana's Digital Newspaper Program. January 28, 2015. https://blog.newspapers.library.in.gov/category/indiana -historic-newspaper-digitization/american-indians-in-the-news/.

Concerning Murder, Dubious Insanity, and Patriotism

Ancestry.com. 1942. Draft Notice Card for Willard Louis Schray.

———. 1900 Federal Census Record for Willard Schray.

———. 1930 Federal Census Record for Willard Schray.

Louisville Courier-Journal. "Escapes from Insane Ward." April 18, 1917, 8.

———. "Ex-Convict Confesses He Shot, Robbed Man." January 6, 1934, 1.

———. "Fugitive Slayer of Wife Nabbed." December 5, 1923, 5.

———. "Health Officer Says Schray Is Insane." March 31, 1914, 10.

———. "Indict Schray." January 22, 1914, 6.

———. "Murder Trial Date Fixed." February 16, 1914, 10.

———. "The Paroled Convict." Editorial. January 20, 1914, 4.

———. "Satisfied Over Killing of Wife . . ." January 19, 1914, 10.

———. "Schray Insane." May 19, 1914, 12.

———. "Schray Placed in Asylum." May 22, 1914, 12.

———. "Schray's Sanity Questioned." May 7, 1914, 10.

———. "Trial Delayed." February 20, 1914, 10.

———. "Wife Murdered, Police Hold New Albany Man." January 18, 1914, I, 4.

Ohio Obliterations

Tragedy of a Tree

Louisville Courier-Journal. "Aged Killer of Tree Thief Gets Two Gifts." December 26, 1938, I, 11.

———. "Christmas Tree Killer Dies." June 22, 1939, I, 7.

———. "Jury Refuses to Indict Slayer of Yule Tree Thief." April 21, 1939, I, 13.

———. "Man Who Killed Over Yule Tree Censured." December 24, 1938, I, 1.

———. "Mr. C. and His Trees." January 9, 1939, I, 4.

———. "Slayer Shouts for Freedom." December 24, 1938, I, 1.

———. "Tree Which Led to Yule Slaying . . ." December 29, 1938, I, 1.

Ohio State Campus Poisonings

Louisville Courier-Journal. "Donahey Reopens Ohio State Case." February 21, 1925, 2.

———. "New Poison Capsule Found in Ohio Plot." February 6, 1925, 1+.

———. "Ohio Is to Probe 2 Poison Deaths." February 21, 1925, 18.

———. "Ohio Poison Plot Probers Balked." February 8, 1925, I, 4.

———. "Ohio State Poison Plot Baffles Probers . . ." February 7, 1925, 1+.

———. "One Ohio State Death from Poison Plot." February 5, 1925, 1+.

———. "Poisoning Held Deliberate Act." July 2, 1926, 1.

———. "Progress Slow in Poison Probe." February 9, 1925, 5.

———. "Student Says He Dispensed Death Pellet." February 10, 1925, 1.

———. "Student Who Aided Poison Plot Victim . . . Is Cleared." February 11, 1925, 1.

The Ohio State University Archives. "Perpetrator Eluded Police in Perplexing OSU Poisonings of 1925." The Ohio State University Libraries: From Woody's Couch. January 30, 2013. https://library.osu.edu/blogs/archives/2013/01/30/perpetrator -alluded-police-in-perplexing-osu-poisonings-of-1925/.

Buckeye Bluebeard

Louisville Courier-Journal. "Alfred A. Knapp Refused a New Trial." September 3, 1903, 1.

———. "Another Confession Believed to Be Coming." March 1, 1903, I, 5.

———. "As Insane, Alfred Knapp Is Regarded by Relatives." July 2, 1903, 1.

———. "Bluebeard Junior." February 26, 1903, 5.

———. "Body of One of Knapp's Murdered Wives . . ." March 3, 1903, 1+.

———. "Details of His Crimes Minutely Given . . ." February 28, 1903, 1.

———. "Died Game." August 19, 1904, 2.

———. "Dying of Grief." January 29, 1904, 3.

———. "Emotion Displayed by Knapp . . ." March 2, 1903, 2.

———. "Evidence Offered Against Alfred A. Knapp." July 1, 1903, 3.

———. "Evidence Taken in Knapp Trial." June 30, 1903, 1.

———. "Evidence That Hannah Knapp Was Strangled." March 6, 1903, 1.

———. "Knapp Case Goes to the Jury." July 16, 1903, 3.

———. "Knapp Indicted." March 28, 1903, 2.

———. "Knapp May Plead Guilty." January 16, 1904, 6.

———. "Knapp the Degenerate." February 28, 1903, 6.

———. "Knapp Thinks He Will Escape Conviction." July 3, 1903, 3.

———. "Knapp Trial Begins at Hamilton." June 24, 1903, 3.

———. "Knapp Trial Delayed by Lack of Jurors." June 26, 1903, 2.

———. "Knapp Will Not Be Shown Corpse . . ." March 5, 1903, 3.

———. "May Suffer from Epileptic Insanity." July 7, 1903, 6.

———. "Middletown Mob Wanted Knapp's Life." July 13, 1904, 2.

———. "No Jury in Knapp Case." June 28, 1903, III, 8.

———. "The Ohio Strangler Has Lost His Nerve." August 6, 1904, 4.

———. "Positive Identification of Hannah Goddard Knapp's Body." March 4, 1903, 7.

———. "Revolting Story of Five Murders . . ." February 27, 1903, 1+.

———. "Saved from Death Chair on His Day to Die." December 13, 1903, I, 2.

———. "Testimony in Knapp Trial." July 11, 1903, 12.

———. "Verdict Is Affirmed by the Supreme Court." June 29, 1904, 1.

———. "Verdict of Murder in First Degree." July 17, 1903, 7.

———. "Warden Barner Thinks Knapp Responsible." July 8, 1903, 7.

Paducah Daily News-Democrat. "A Superstition." September 5, 1904, 2.

Another Woman in Another Furnace

Louisville Courier-Journal. "Blood Tested in Furnace Death." November 26, 1924, 1.

———. "Doctor Doubts Furnace Suicide." November 24, 1924, 3.

———. "Flesh, Blood New Furnace Death Clues." November 25, 1924, 1+.

———. "Furnace Death Baffles Police." November 19, 1924, 1+.

———. "Furnace Probe Hangs on Report." December 2, 1924, 1.

———. "Officials Investigate the Story . . ." March 10, 1925, 5.

———. "Pastor's Wife Slain, Chemist's Report Says." November 23, 1924, I, 1+.

———. "Pastor's Wife Slain, Tests of Pigs Show." December 3, 1924, 1.

———. "Police Seek Youth in Ohio Furnace Death." November 29, 1924, 1+.

———. "Sheatsley Asks Critics' Silence." January 12, 1925, 3.

———. "Sheatsley Probe Awaits Reports." November 30, 1924, I, 1.

———. "Sheatsley Reiterates Theory Wife, in Furnace, Killed Self." November 27, 1924, 1+.

———. "Sheatsley Returns to Church Pulpit." December 22, 1924, 1.

———. "Son Changes Story of Mother's Death . . ." November 21, 1924, 1+.

———. "Suicide Furnace Death Verdict." December 5, 1924, 10.

———. "Suicide Seen by Pastor in Wife's Death." November 20, 1924, 1+.

———. "Woman Is Found Dead in Furnace." November 18, 1924, 1.

———. "Woman's Death Not Due to Fire." November 22, 1924, 1+.

New York Times. "Finds a New Clue in Furnace Death." November 24, 1924, 2.
———. "Guard Put at Home of Furnace Victim." November 27, 1924, 17.
———. "Pastor and Two Sons Are Questioned Again." November 29, 1924, 15.
———. "Refers in Pulpit to Furnace Death." January 12, 1925, 17.
———. "Sheatsley to Resume Teaching of Religion." December 2, 1924, 4.
———. "Suicide Is Verdict in Furnace Death." December 5, 1924, 3.
———. "Trace Clues in Vain in Furnace Mystery." November 30, 1924, 25.

The Things We Do for Love

Ancestry.com. Marriage Record for Lillian Costlow and William Nunn.
Louisville Courier-Journal. "Attempts Suicide." November 1, 1900, 6.
———. "Ferrell May Marry If His Life Is Spared." December 14, 1900, 2.
———. "Ferrell Must Die." October 31, 1900, 1.
———. "Ferrell Papers." March 12, 1901, 7.
———. "Ferrell Says 'Not Guilty' . . ." August 15, 1900, 2.
———. "Ferrell's Nerve Failing." October 20, 1900, 8.
———. "The Final Parting." February 22, 1901, 2.
———. "From Prison, Ferrell Writes to Girl . . ." August 16, 1900, 1.
———. "Homicidal Suitor." Editorial. October 21, 1900, II, 4.
———. "I Have Nothing to Say." March 1, 1910, 6.
———. "In His Car Messenger Is Killed . . ." August 11, 1900, 1+.
———. "Marriage and Murder." Editorial. August 14, 1900, 6.
———. "Mystery of Messenger Lane's Murder Solved." August 13, 1900, 1+.
———. "No Clue to the Murder of Messenger Lane." August 12, 1900, II, 8.
———. "The State Has Rested Its Case . . ." October 26, 1900, 1.
———. "Testimony Closed." October 28, 1900, I, 8.
———. "Trial at Marysville." August 14, 1900, 2.

Wasted in Wisconsin

Blackmailers' Bloodbath, or: The Hun Also Rises

Louisville Courier-Journal. "All Acquitted in Prager Case." June 2, 1918, I, 1.
———. "Appeals to Police." April 7, 1917, 3.
———. "Berlin, Wis., Objects to Name It Has Now." May 31, 1917, 4.
———. "Bismarck Residents Don't like Town's Name." July 16, 1918, 3.
———. "German Flag Raised, Torn Down." April 12, 1917, 2.
———. "Kaufman Likes Name 'German.'" January 15, 1919, 3.
———. "Made Disloyal Remark, Is Said; Hanged to Tree." April 5, 1918, 1.
———. "Man Said to Have Headed 'Lynching Bee' Kills Himself." January 12, 1919, V, 8.
———. "Name of Kaiser Is Too Much for Youth." August 8, 1918, 3.
———. "Talk 'United States' or Keep Still . . ." August 18, 1918, I, 1.
———. "Vassar Instructor Held for Pro-German Remarks." May 1, 1918, 4.
———. "Want Township's Name Changed." May 14, 1915, 10.
———. "Weber and Fields Have Decided . . ." Editorial. March 3, 1918, II, 4.
Norman, Michael. *Haunted Wisconsin*. Terrace Books: University of Wisconsin Press, 2011.
Waukesha [WI] *Freeman*. "Another Tragedy at Hille Farm." July 18, 1918, 1.

———. "Hille Family Always Loyal." July 25, 1918, 6.

———. "Result of the Fentz Inquest Held Last Week." August 1, 1918, 3.

Winer, Richard. *Houses of Horror.* New York: Bantam, 1983.

An Early Serial Killer . . . Perhaps

Grant County Historical Society. "A Potosi Serial Killer?" Grant County
Historical Society. January 2016. https://grantcountyhistory.org
/wp-content/uploads/2016/01/PotosiSerialKiller.pdf.

New York Times. "The Wisconsin Murderer." January 25, 1874, 6.

———. "A Wisconsin Troppman." January 18, 1874, 1.

Pittsburgh Leader. "The Bender Butchery Beaten." January 18, 1874, 1.

Badly Misunderstood William

Appleton Evening Crescent. "Death Calls Victim of Tuberculosis." October 2,
1914, 1.

Louisville Courier-Journal. "Find Three Dead with Throats Cut . . ." February 3,
1912, 1.

———. "Sudden Death Preferred to Years of Suffering." February 4, 1912, I, 1.

New York Times. "Four Slain on Farm." February 3, 1912, 20.

Two Beheads Are Better than One

Louisville Courier-Journal. "Beheads Wife and Her Lover." November 27, 1911, 1.

———. "Marchesi Will Plead the Unwritten Law." November 28, 1911, 1.

Manawatu Daily Times. "Double Tragedy." March 4, 1912, 8.

State of Wisconsin, Kenosha County. "In the Matter of the Inquisition . . ."
Court document. November 27, 1911.

Wausau Pilot. "Double Kenosha Murder." December 5, 1911, 2.

Wisconsin Legislature (Senate). *Journal of Proceedings of the Sixty-Fifth Session
of the Wisconsin Legislature.* Madison: Democrat Printing Company, State
Printer, 1941.

Mayberry Meets a Mob

Kuehn, Roland. "Sunday 75th Anniversary of Alger Murder . . ." *Janesville Daily
Gazette.* June 14, 1930, 1.

Louisville Courier. "A Case of Lynch Law . . ." March 25, 1857, 2.

———. "A Foul Murder." June 23, 1855, 1.

———. "Hung by a Mob." August 9, 1855, 5.

———. "Lynch Law." July 16, 1855, 5.

———. "Murderer." August 4, 1855, 5.

———. "Tremendous Excitement at Janesville." July 18, 1855, 1.

KEVEN MCQUEEN is author of twenty books covering American history, the supernatural, biography, historical true crime, and what he calls real-life surrealism. His books include *Horror in the Heartland: Strange and Gothic Tales from the Midwest, Creepy California: Strange and Gothic Tales from the Golden State, Weird Wild West: True Tales of the Strange and Gothic,* and *New England Nightmares: True Tales of the Strange and Gothic.* His work has been anthologized by the Jesse Stuart Foundation and Texas Christian University Press. He has guested on radio shows and podcasts including *Darkness Radio, 30 Odd Minutes, Paranormal View, Controversial TV, Most Notorious, Thorne and Cross Haunted Nights Live, Mind's Eye, Still Unsolved,* and *Fringe Radio.* Recently, his books have been mentioned in articles in the *New York Times* and on the Daily Beast/Yahoo News. McQueen is Senior Lecturer in English at Eastern Kentucky University in Richmond.